FREDERIK POHL

MODERN MASTERS OF SCIENCE FICTION

Science fiction often anticipates the consequences of scientific discoveries. The immense strides made by science since World War II have been matched step by step by writers who gave equal attention to scientific principles, human imagination, and the craft of fiction. The respect for science fiction won by Jules Verne and H. G. Wells was further increased by Isaac Asimov, Arthur C. Clarke, Robert Heinlein, Ursula K. Le Guin, Joanna Russ, and Ray Bradbury. Modern Masters of Science Fiction is devoted to books that survey the work of individual authors who continue to inspire and advance science fiction. *A list of books in the series appears at the end of this book.*

FREDERIK POHL

Michael R. Page

UNIVERSITY OF ILLINOIS PRESS

Urbana, Chicago, and Springfield

Library of Congress Cataloging-in-Publication Data
Page, Michael R., 1967-
Frederik Pohl / Michael R. Page.
        pages   cm. — (Modern masters of science fiction)
Includes bibliographical references and index.
ISBN 978-0-252-03965-2 (hardback) —
ISBN 978-0-252-08115-6 (paperback) —
ISBN 978-0-252-09774-4 (e-book)
1. Pohl, Frederik. 2. Authors, American—20th century—Biography. 3. Authors, American—
21st century—Biography. 4. Science fiction, American—History and criticism. I. Title.
PS3566.O36Z83   2015
813'.54—dc23   2015010044

subvention by
Figure Foundation

to wavelength

This book is dedicated to the memory of my father, Monte M. Page
September 26, 1935–January 20, 2015

contents

ACKNOWLEDGMENTS

I wish to thank a number of people who helped with this project in various ways. Thanks to Bill Regier at the University of Illinois Press for responding enthusiastically to my initial query, guiding me through the proposal process, and answering questions as I prepared the manuscript, and to Julie Gay for her excellent copyediting. It was Gary K. Wolfe's announcement in one of his *Locus* review columns that brought the series to my attention, so I was delighted to find out that Gary served as one of my referees. Gary's suggestions and close attention to the text were instrumental in improving the manuscript. Thanks to James Gunn, Chris McKitterick, and Kij Johnson at the University of Kansas, who invited me to read part of the work-in-progress during the 2014 Campbell Conference. Their friendship and enthusiasm helped keep my batteries charged during the writing process. I need to offer a special word of thanks to Jim, first for contacting Fred Pohl on my behalf when the project got underway, and second for bringing his incomparable knowledge of the field to the manuscript, reading it in draft, making some important suggestions, and catching some mistakes before submission. Thanks to Elspeth Healy and the librarians at the Kenneth Spencer Research Library at the University of Kansas for allowing me to browse the Donald A. Wollheim Archive and the Gunn-Pohl correspondence files; Gene Bundy of the Jack Williamson Library at Eastern New Mexico University for permission to quote some of the Pohl-Williamson correspondence I had dug up during a visit for a previous project; and the intrepid Kathy Johnson at the University of Nebraska's Love Library, who saved me several trips to the library during the summer and helped track down research materials when I needed them.

One more librarian needs a shout-out: my wife, Susan Steider of Lincoln City Libraries, who brought home many a book I had requested, sometimes the same one repeatedly, during the time spent working on this project. Thank you, my dear, for living in the world of Pohl with me for a year and a half! Thanks to my mother and father for allowing me to work while visiting them—and especially my father, who persevered with Parkinson's disease until this book reached production, passing a few days after I received the copyedited manuscript. Goodbye, Dad. Speaking of fathers, my wife's dad, Lee Steider, was in home hospice care during the summer of 2013 as I was systematically reading through Pohl's works; I read a number of them on those afternoons I helped care for Lee. I wish to thank Lee and my mother-in-law Norma for the opportunity to assist in his end-of-life journey. Lee passed away six days before the death of Frederik Pohl. And I can't forget the dog: our Lab, Mary, provided much companionship and "ambience" throughout the research and writing of this book. The consummate writing companion!

Several colleagues at the University of Nebraska helped along the way: Stephen C. Behrendt gave timely advice on a number of occasions; Robert Stock generously served as first-reader as I drafted the chapters; and Bev Rilett helped with some key revisions. Further thanks to my former English Department chair, Susan Belasco, and to our new chair, Marco Abel, for allowing me the time to finish this manuscript before embarking on my new position within the department

Most especially, I would like to thank Betty Anne Hull. Betty allowed me to interview Frederik Pohl at their home in the final weeks of his life, gave me the opportunity to be her attendant at the 2014 Campbell Conference, answered many questions, and provided additional insights about Pohl's life and works. Betty also invited me to participate in the Pohl Memorial in August 2014 at Harper College in Palatine, Illinois, where I had the chance to meet the Pohl family. For these opportunities, I am truly grateful. Thanks, Betty!

FREDERIK POHL

ALL THE LIVES HE LED

The title of Frederik Pohl's final novel, *All the Lives He Led*, published in 2011 when he was ninety-one years old, appropriately describes the life and career of its author. No other writer in the field of science fiction can match Frederik Pohl's life in science fiction. Others may lay claim to the title of "Big Three"—Asimov, Clarke, Heinlein; or the "Academic Big Three"—Delany, Dick, Le Guin; while still others may vie for the title of "father of science fiction"—Verne, Wells, Gernsback; and Brian Aldiss has even claimed the title of "mother of science fiction" for Mary Shelley.[1] But while these honorifics may hold a great deal of truth, no one led as rich and diverse a life within the field as Frederik Pohl. As youthful reader, fan, agent, editor, and writer, Pohl's life in science fiction spanned eighty-three years, from when he first got hold of a science fiction magazine at age ten in 1930, to his passing on September 2, 2013, on the same morning as the final events at the World Science Fiction Convention in San Antonio. His short tribute to the convention's guest of honor, James Gunn, his longtime friend and colleague, in the convention program was his last piece of published writing before his death.[2] No one, not even Pohl's collaborator and friend Jack Williamson, had such a long association with science fiction. And very few, if any, can claim to have had an impact on the field, in all its facets, that matches Frederik Pohl's.

Pohl's wife, Dr. Elizabeth Anne (Betty) Hull, has said of Pohl's 1978 memoir *The Way the Future Was*, "It is more a chronicle of the development of science fiction than an autobiography."[3] And this is also certainly true of Pohl's companion blog *The Way the Future Blogs*, begun in 2009 and continuing posthumously as Betty and the blog team sift through his remaining files. Even after death, Pohl continues to live through the World Wide Web—perhaps not quite in the way of machine-stored consciousness as he explored in the later books of his famous Heechee saga and in *The Last Theorem*, his late collaboration with Arthur C. Clarke, but as close as it gets, for now.

Christopher McKitterick, director of the Gunn Center for the Study of Science Fiction at the University of Kansas, has recently dubbed Pohl "Mister Science Fiction," "because no one better serves to define the field by simply listing their name than Frederik Pohl."[4] It is hard to disagree with McKitterick, as that simple appellation may, indeed, be the most fitting way to describe the multifaceted career of Frederik Pohl. As McKitterick points out, "Pohl's rationality and intellectualism stemmed from a deep emotional investment in the betterment of the human species. His devotion to the field inspires the SF community to reach higher, grow deeper, and become ever more humane."[5] Algis Budrys once called Pohl "the hidden Prometheus of SF," noting that Pohl "has done more crucial things at more places and times in the history of newsstand science fiction than any other individual."[6] Budrys's notion is compellingly provocative in light of Brian Aldiss's argument that Mary Shelley's *Frankenstein*, subtitled *The Modern Prometheus*, is the ur-text for genre origins.[7] Like Prometheus *plasticator*, Pohl molded the clay of the science fiction field into the genre it is today. Isaac Asimov, who first met Pohl in 1938 when both were still in their teens, considered Pohl "one of the most intelligent men I have ever met,"[8] high compliment coming from the polymathic great synthesizer Asimov, and it tells us something about the overall scope of Pohl's achievement.

These testimonials alone convey that Pohl is one of the central figures in the field of science fiction. One can hardly claim to *know* science fiction without in some way having to encounter Frederik Pohl. Although he is, without question, one of the ten or so most important writers in the field, he was also one of the field's most important editors, if not *the* most important editor. Further, despite the financial problems Pohl faced while an agent in the years after World War II, few can question that his work in this area helped shape the field as a commercially viable literary market, not only through his nurturing of the writers he represented (Asimov, Williamson, Wyndham, Kornbluth, Gunn, and others) but also through his direct dealings with publishers and editors to begin science fiction lines and to pay writers adequately. Pohl also played a role in the development of science fiction as a more or less respectable area of academic study, as, along with Williamson and Gunn, he was for many years one of the most visibly present writers at the Science Fiction Research Association meetings and at many other academic conferences, such as the Campbell in Lawrence, Kansas, and the Eaton at Riverside, California; and he was also a fixture at writers' workshops, for many years participating in James Gunn's at the University of Kansas. In the world of fan culture, few—again, if *any*—can claim to surpass Pohl's life in fandom, from being one of the very founders of that culture to his reflections on the genre and its culture late in life in *The Way the Future Blogs*. More so, perhaps, than Asimov, Heinlein, Clarke—or Le Guin, Dick, Delany, Gibson—Pohl is the embodiment of science fiction.

His work spans nine decades from his poem "Elegy to a Dead Planet: Luna," published by the grandfatherly T. O'Conor Sloane in *Amazing Stories* in 1937 when Pohl was seventeen, to his final book, *All the Lives He Led*, and *The Way the Future Blogs*. In between he published fifty-five novels, more than 180 short stories, twenty-four story collections, and six nonfiction books; edited thirty-nine anthologies, 168 science fiction magazine issues, and some of the landmark novels in the genre (Delany's *Dhalgren* and *Triton*, Russ's *The Female Man*); and wrote countless essays, editorials, and reviews. All of this publishing activity shaped the field of science fiction in significant ways. As Brian Aldiss observes in *Trillion Year Spree*, written when Pohl still had a quarter-century of writing ahead of him, "Pohl is one of those giant figures who have substantially shaped the genre about them, growing as the field grew, from child to man to grandfather of the field."[9]

Aldiss is right to emphasize that the growth and the development of the field of science fiction parallels the growth and development of Frederik Pohl as a human being. Many devoted science fiction readers discover SF in their early teens, experience a cooling off period in their early twenties as they explore other aspects of the social world, and then come back to it when the mundane world no longer serves. This was not the case with Pohl. Isaac Asimov once said, in a statement that has been repeated by many others, "We are now living in a science fictional world."[10] Pohl helped create that world. Early on, science fiction became the center of his life—and he spent the rest of it helping to shape the world into the vision of the future he first discovered in the science fiction magazines.

Pohl's first foray into creating a science fictional world occurred through his youthful adventures in science fiction fandom, as chapter 1 will illustrate. For the purposes of this introduction, it suffices to say that Pohl was a central figure in the creation and development of science fiction fandom, which, in turn, became the model for a variety of the fan cultures that forge the identities of individuals in this age of electronic media. Pohl's activities in the New York City fan group the Futurians in the late 1930s, whose ranks included Isaac Asimov, James Blish, Cyril Kornbluth, Donald Wollheim, and later Damon Knight and Judith Merril, went a long way in creating a science fiction world by doing a great deal to create the world of science fiction itself. As Lester Del Rey remarks, "In the long run, the Futurians made their mark on science fiction—not as a club, but through the efforts of the members. Many of them became some of the leading editors and writers in years to come."[11] Honing his editing and publishing skills on a variety of fan magazines, called fanzines, throughout his teens, Pohl's influence reaches out to a wide variety of "zine" subcultures: as noted in The World of Zines, "science fiction fandom is one of the longest-lasting subcultures in zinedom, and the one to which many other types of zines can trace their roots."[12] Now, of course, much of that written subcultural discourse has transferred to that once-science-fictional idea, the World Wide Web.

Pohl's career as editor is only surpassed by his career as writer—although for some, Pohl the editor might in fact *supersede* Pohl the writer. In the 1982 anthology *Yesterday's Tomorrows: Favorite Stories from Forty Years as a Science Fiction Editor*, Pohl reflects that he had "some sort of editorial relationship with nearly every science fiction writer alive and producing in the English language" over that forty-year period.[13] These relationships, one can conjecture, probably extended beyond writers Pohl actually published and likely included writers (Stephen King, for example) from the baby boom generation who were cutting their authorial teeth on rejection slips, some no doubt from Pohl, who was editing *Galaxy*, *If*, and *Worlds of Tomorrow* in the 1960s and book manuscripts at Ace and Bantam in the 1970s. Pohl estimated that he read around four thousand manuscripts a year while he edited his magazines. As a Bantam editor, he read in the neighborhood of 250–300 book manuscripts a year; overall he "read professionally somewhere around five hundred million words of science fiction."[14] This includes his first editorial job editing *Astonishing Stories* and *Super Science Stories* at age nineteen, magazines that published early stories by Asimov, Heinlein, and L. Sprague De Camp, and introduced new writers Ray Bradbury, Cyril Kornbluth, and James Blish. Gardner Dozois, perhaps the central science fiction editor of the last quarter-century, considers Pohl the best editor in the genre's history: "For me Fred was quite probably the best SF magazine editor who ever lived, and when I became a magazine editor myself, back in the early eighties, the editor I consciously modeled myself upon was not John W. Campbell, but Fred Pohl."[15]

Pohl also helped create the world of science fiction during his years as a literary agent in the late 1940s and early 1950s, when a large portion of the major writers in the field were his clients. Among his important achievements as an agent, Pohl negotiated the first major book contracts for genre writers—Asimov's *Pebble in the Sky* and Williamson's *The Humanoids*; facilitated the establishment of the Ballantine paperback line; launched the first original anthology series, *Star Science Fiction*; helped several writers secure editorial posts; and parlayed rate increases at the science fiction magazines—all contributing to the development of science fiction as a professional field.

Pohl's involvement with the academic study of science fiction can be traced all the way back to his days as a literary agent when he convinced Futurian comrade Robert Lowndes to publish James Gunn's master's thesis serially, as "The Philosophy of Science Fiction" and "The Plot-Forms of Science Fiction," in the short-lived *Dynamic Science Fiction*.[16] Pohl continued to be involved with the development of the field of science fiction studies, frequently attending academic conferences and participating in teaching workshops and writers' seminars. His close ties to Gunn and Williamson, both science fiction writers holding academic posts (Gunn at the University of Kansas and Williamson at Eastern New Mexico University); to Brian Aldiss, who in many ways is the central figure in British SF criticism; and to Elizabeth Anne Hull, his wife and former president of the Science Fiction Research Association, situates Pohl as an important figure within academic science fiction discourse. Surprisingly, though, Pohl's fiction has not been given the degree of critical attention it merits. Like some of his writer colleagues, he was sometimes uneasy about how academia approached the field. In the essay "The Study of Science Fiction: A Modest Proposal," which appeared in *Science Fiction Studies* in 1997, Pohl revisited the polemic broadside approach from his fandom days when he barked with Swiftian ire, "Science fiction is not entirely adequately served by the present sort of scholarly study and that Something Should Be Done About It."[17] Pohl goes on to argue that science fiction differs from other types of literature in that it engages with the sciences, has a symbiotic relationship with its readers (fans) that feeds back into the fiction, and is a "literature of ideas." Pohl asks scholars to take this into account when applying literary-critical methodology to science fiction because traditional and contemporary postmodern approaches are too narrow. For the most part, scholars have heeded Pohl's call, as an increasing amount of SF scholarship *has* become more engaged with the larger cultural and literary trajectory of science fiction, expressed in Farah Mendlesohn's confidently stated remark in *The Cambridge Companion to Science Fiction* that "science fiction is less a genre . . . than an ongoing discussion . . . an argument with the universe,"[18] a statement which signals science fiction's uniqueness.

While the activities sketched above illustrate how Pohl contributed to the shaping of the world of science fiction, it is through his own fiction that Pohl made his greatest contribution to shaping our science fictional world. In the early masterpiece *The Space Merchants*, written with Cyril Kornbluth, Pohl diagnosed a future in which hyperconsumption leads to ecological crisis. The book remains highly relevant some sixty years after its initial publication in 1952 as *Gravy Planet* in *Galaxy*. Throughout the 1950s and 1960s Pohl astutely engaged with consumerism in stories and novels such as "The Midas Plague,"

"The Tunnel under the World," and *The Age of the Pussyfoot*; with Cold War politics in "Target One," "The Knights of Arthur," *Slave Ship*, and *A Plague of Pythons*; and with confrontations with the alien other in such works as "Mars by Moonlight," "Whatever Counts," "Small Lords," and showing that the alien other may be evolved humanity in "Day Million." In the 1970s, finding a new level of maturity by drawing from the aesthetic of the New Wave, Pohl wrote what are arguably his most important novels next to *The Space Merchants*: *Man Plus*, *Gateway*, and *Jem*. Among other things, *Man Plus* and *Jem* both intensely engage with Cold War politics, while *Gateway* (and its sequels), for many Pohl's most definitive novel, is an essential work of the widescreen sense of wonder that characterizes the genre. All three, along with most of the novels Pohl wrote during the 1980s and 1990s, also demonstrate Pohl's intense exploration of the fields of science, and especially new speculative ideas coming out of physics, astronomy, and cosmology. He called his approach "chasing science." For Pohl, science was a "spectator sport" and hence the fountainhead for his imagination.

Just as important as science to Pohl's science fictional imagination is politics. Pohl consistently explored the politics of the future (often allegorically critiquing the politics of the present) in his fiction. His scrutiny of politics can be traced from what is his first mature work, "Let the Ants Try," to other Kornbluth collaborations—*Gladiator-At-Law*, *Search the Sky*, and the nongenre *Presidential Year*. His breakthrough stories of the early 1970s, "The Gold at the Starbow's End" and "In the Problem Pit," as well as the aforementioned triumphs of the later 1970s, his Reagan-era works (such as *The Cool War*, *The Years of the City*, *Black Star Rising*, *The Coming of the Quantum Cats*, *Chernobyl*), and the brilliantly somber "Fermi and Frost," intensified his political critique of the Cold War. His post–Cold War novels of the 1990s—*Mining the Oort*, *The Voices of Heaven*, and *O Pioneer!*—and, finally, his last novels—*The Last Theorem*, in collaboration with Arthur C. Clarke, and *All the Lives He Led*—examined the changing political landscape. Throughout, Pohl explored political systems and alternatives, folly and the human capacity to muck things up. When systematically read, the overall scope and trajectory of Pohl's fiction is certainly among the most intensely politically engaged within the field of science fiction, and, perhaps, in all of American literature.

These two focuses, science and politics, come together in Pohl's concern for the state of the Earth—for what human beings are doing to the planet.

Pohl was warning about global climate change long before the term came into vogue. As early as *The Space Merchants*, he cautioned his readers what the world might be like when human consumption and population overextended the planet's capacity for sustainability. His 1970 anthology *Nightmare Age* brought together a number of science fiction stories that addressed concerns about the state of the planet. In the 1979 essay "Power Play," Pohl discussed the problems ahead for a world economy run on fossil fuels: "The terrible truth is that, even so, we cannot go on with the energy madness, because we'll ruin ourselves."[19] His underrated 1989 novel *Homegoing* reminded readers that the planet will change to our detriment if we continue these current lifeways. Pohl's environmental advocacy is best seen in his 1991 collaboration with Isaac Asimov *Our Angry Earth*, a work of nonfiction that forewarns of the ecological problems facing us in the twenty-first century and offers suggestions on how these problems could be mitigated. It was Asimov's last book published in his lifetime.

Pohl's approach to these topics, and others, has often been through a satiric lens. There are certainly other science fiction satirists, but Frederik Pohl is the name that most often comes to mind when equating science fiction with satire, as famously argued by Kingsley Amis as early as 1960 in *New Maps of Hell*.[20] *The Space Merchants*, *Gladiator-At-Law*, "The Midas Plague," "The Tunnel under the World," *Jem*, "Spending the Day at the Lottery Fair," and *Black Star Rising* are masterpieces of the satiric imagination, followed closely by such works as "The Wizards of Pung's Corners," "The Children of Night," *The Age of the Pussyfoot*, *The Cool War*, *The Coming of the Quantum Cats*, *The Voices of Heaven*, *All the Lives He Led* (Pohl's final novel), and many more of his novels and stories.

Pohl often claimed that science fiction is a "very good way at looking at the future,"[21] a mode by which big questions in science, politics, ecology, and society can be thought out using different scenarios and circumstances that can work toward possible solutions. This is one of the things that makes science fiction uniquely different from other fictional modes. In the introduction to his collection *Day Million*, Pohl offers some insight into what makes science fiction unique: "'Science Fiction' is a *way* of writing stories. . . . It is a look at the human race and all its affairs from outside."[22] As he remarked in the filmed lecture "The Ideas in Science Fiction," produced by James Gunn in 1973, "What science fiction writers individually and science fiction as a kind of normative forecasting of the future in general offer us, then, is not predictions about the future so much as a sort of mail-order catalog of possible alternate futures, and from this we can compile a shopping list of the sorts of futures we would like to see and then proceed to bring them about."[23] In another essay, "SF: The Game-Playing Literature," Pohl states that science fiction "is a way of looking at the world that cannot be duplicated by any other way."[24] Finally, in the closing remarks of "The Ideas in Science Fiction," Pohl concludes that:

> One can say of at least some kinds of science fiction that they promote conceptual thinking as distinct from the crude calculation that's enough to get most of us through our daily lives, and they help us to prepare for the violent cultural shocks that the accelerating rate of change of modern society is throwing at us every day, not so much by warning us as to what will happen, but by leading us to think in terms of consequences and future developments. So, science fiction, you see, is not only about trips to Mars or giant man-eating cockroaches arising from the sea. It is about man himself, not only man as he is, but as he might be, and as he can become. Man is the thinking animal, and the tool-using animal, and the time-binding animal—and these are the things that science fiction is about.[25]

Pohl's views on what science fiction does can be seen further in some of his editorials written when he was editing *Galaxy* and *If* in the 1960s. In the February 1963 *Galaxy* editorial "Honor for Prophets," Pohl argued that "a science-fiction story is not a scratch-sheet for handicapping tomorrow's horse races—or tomorrow's nuclear arms race. It can only show what kind of world we may live in—and at that, it gives us one choice out of endless alternatives."[26] Anticipating the changes represented by the New Wave in an October 1965 editorial, Pohl wrote, "Science fiction advances in a series of quantum jumps. It may seem to you from the above timetable that we are about due for another jump. It seems so to us, too; and as a matter of fact, we think we're in one right now."[27] Yet Pohl was at the time "not particularly enthusiastic" about the New Wave, especially the polemical manifestos that were being tossed off in *New Worlds* by Michael Moorcock, who was vocally dismissive of what had come before. As Pohl told Charles Platt in a 1979 interview, "It wasn't the stories I objected to, it was the snottiness of the proponents."[28] In the March 1968 *If* editorial "What Science Fiction Is,"

Pohl points out that "there are all kinds of science fiction," but the kind that represents "*other worlds*" (not necessarily alien, but *other*), "in which some change of technology, social customs or whatever produces a change in the *environment* of man" [Pohl's italics], is something that SF uniquely does. Pohl further argues, "Every other kind of writing starts with an established environment, and the characters move inside it." For Pohl, the New Wave emphasis on style over content is not particularly inventive: "Fooling around with the *way* one writes a story seems to this reader, at least, to be inferior to inventing new things for a story to *say*. Nearly all of the New Wave concerns itself with style instead of content. Sometimes what a writer has to say affects the way he says it . . . and that seems reasonable to us. But that accounts for very little of the New Wave."[29] In an earlier editorial in July 1967, Pohl takes to task the New Wave claim that it is brazenly experimental and has "a climate of freedom of expression and liberty to experiment unmatched anywhere else in the world." Pohl counters that there's plenty of science fiction that experiments with style, content, setting, and form outside the purview of the New Wave, noting the works of Jack Vance, Cordwainer Smith, and Brian Aldiss, before he became associated with the New Wave, as examples. For Pohl, what defines a good science fiction story is "that after reading, you are glad you read it."[30] Pohl is entirely right on this count for anyone who has tried to read through the lesser pieces in Judith Merril's *England Swings SF* or Harlan Ellison's *Dangerous Visions*. At the same time, when Pohl reinvented himself in the 1970s, becoming one of the most innovative writers of the decade, he absorbed many of the lessons of the New Wave, though not its excesses. As he told Platt, "I don't think I could ever have written *Gateway* if the 'new wave' hadn't happened."[31] The battles over the New Wave are now in the distant past, yet they continue to linger on in some ways not unlike the fan wars of the 1930s.

In the final analysis, however, it must be conceded that while Frederik Pohl has written with scrupulous attention to science, with intense political engagement, with impassioned concern about the state of the Earth's habitat, and with sardonic humor and cutting satiric wit, he is also one of the foremost celebrants of the "sense of wonder," that feeling of profound awe and amazement at the wonders of the universe, that which attracted Pohl to science fiction when he first encountered it, then exemplified by the galaxy-spanning super-science space operas of E.E. "Doc" Smith and the planetary romances of Edgar Rice Burroughs. From *Gateway* onward, Pohl supplemented his serious political and scientific engagements with pure "sense of wonder" by inventing alien beings and alien societies, and in building worlds. Perhaps this turn to wonder returned Pohl to his fannish roots. If so, what better way to cap off one of the most extraordinary careers in science fiction than to embrace the fan possibilities of the World Wide Web with *The Way the Future Blogs*, for which he won a final Hugo in 2010 as "Best Fan Writer."

Although James Gunn (thankfully) is still with us at the time of this writing, with Pohl's death an era has come to an end. He was the last of the science fiction titans of the pre–World War II Golden Age. In some ways, after his death science fiction is no longer a wholly contemporary literature but has passed into the historical. Pohl's death also marks a moment in SF history that perhaps will trigger a reevaluation not only of his career but also of the broader SF phenomenon. This is an ongoing process, of course, but Pohl's death seems to be a major marker in SF history. Pohl reflected on his life in science fiction (up to that point) in the 1976 retrospective collection *The Early Pohl*: "Everything considered, the world of science fiction is not a bad place to live" (183). Frederik Pohl lived the science fiction life more fully than anyone. In the chapters that follow, this study will seek to provide an overview of all the lives he led in *our* science fictional world.

CHAPTER 1

THE WAY THE FUTURE WAS, 1930–1951

Like many of his young contemporaries in the early 1930s (and those generations to follow), when Frederik Pohl discovered science fiction at age ten in 1930, it was a revelation. At that time, science fiction as a defined category of fiction was only in its fifth year, although science fiction itself had a much longer pedigree. Hugo Gernsback launched the first science fiction magazine, *Amazing Stories*, in April 1926, initially filling it with reprints of stories and novels by H. G. Wells, Edgar Allan Poe, Jules Verne, Abraham Merritt, and others, before establishing a group of new writers from the readers of the magazine, such as E. E. "Doc" Smith, Dr. Miles J. Breuer, Jack Williamson, and Harl Vincent. These were the writers whom the young Pohl encountered in the pages of *Amazing* and its rivals, *Wonder Stories* and *Astounding Stories of Super-Science*.

The first such magazine Pohl read was the Summer 1930 issue of *Wonder Stories Quarterly*, which entranced him with its cover illustration of a scaly green monster about to heave a giant boulder at two human explorers, illustrating "The Monsters of Neptune," by Henrik Dahl Juve. From there on, Pohl was hooked.[1] A few months later he discovered another science fiction magazine, the 1927 *Amazing Stories Annual*, containing Edgar Rice Burroughs's novel *The Master Mind of Mars*. He read the Burroughs novel over and over again. This magazine, with a different title from the first and with a date a few years in the past, helped Pohl realize that there was more of this species of reading out there, and he began actively seeking it out at newsstands, used bookshops, and flea markets. He also received his first library card around this time from the Brooklyn Public Library, where he discovered books by Wells, Verne, Twain, Kipling, Poe, and other writers of the fantastic. But as his teens went on, he read widely also outside of the fantastic field, as most of his contemporaries did, encountering writers such as Dostoyevsky, Huysmans, Proust, Kant, and T. S. Eliot, for example.[2] Pohl has written of the significance of the library: "When I was old enough to own a card in the public library the world opened up totally to me. I read everything I could put my hands on, out of the limitless resources of one of the largest library systems in the world."[3] He later wrote, "The Brooklyn Public Library was, I think, the best thing that ever happened to me."[4]

Closing out that first year of SF discovery, Pohl spent the summer of 1931 at his uncle's farm in Pennsylvania, where he found a collection of pulp magazines in the attic, mostly the general fiction pulp *Argosy*, which often published science fiction among its regular fare of Westerns, court room dramas, and adventures, but also a significant run of *Weird Tales*: "I remember a hot summer in my uncle's attic, smelling of salt and curing tobacco, where I found a treasure trove, twenty back years of *Argosy* and *Weird Tales*."[5] In those *Argosy* issues Pohl read A. Merritt's *The Moon Pool*, SF novels by Ray Cummings (whom Pohl would later publish in *Astonishing Stories*), and Otis Adelbert Kline.

In his book *Age of Wonders* David Hartwell famously observed that "the real golden age of science fiction" is age twelve,[6] and this was certainly true of Pohl, who, between age ten and age twelve, managed to "read every scrap of science fiction I knew to exist."[7] As Pohl was a rapid reader, averaging a book a day for most of his life, we can well imagine that he worked his way through a tremendous amount of what constituted the genre at the time.

Pohl was already a voracious reader before he discovered science fiction and, like most kids, read countless tales of the fantastic. For instance, in an autobiographical sketch written for *Contemporary Authors*, Pohl claims that he "read every Tom Swift book in print" before age ten.[8] Because they moved around frequently, Pohl was a lonely child whose "best friends were books."[9] His reading set him apart from other children: "I perceived quite early that I was a reader, and most of the people I came in contact with were not. It made a barrier. What they wanted to talk about were things they had eaten, touched or done. What I wanted to talk about was what I had read. When it developed that what I was thinking and reading was more and more science fiction, the barrier grew."[10]

As he read through the existing science fiction magazines, Pohl was particularly influenced by the satiric science fiction of Stanton Coblentz and David H. Keller: "That was there, in those ragged pulp magazines of four or five decades ago: social satire. It made a whole generation of us cynics and dreamers: cynics, because we could see the shoddiness of the now, dreamers, because at the same time other writers were offering us Utopias and magnificent challenges."[11] Satire would become Pohl's calling card, from the early masterpiece *The Space Merchants* to his final novel *All the Lives He Led*. Pohl recalled another early pulp novel that "so enraptured" him that "the drug had been tasted and the addiction formed." That novel was Jack Williamson's *The Stone from the Green Star*, which appeared in the October and November 1931 issues of *Amazing*.[12] Pohl and Williamson would later collaborate on ten novels and travel the world together. Reflecting on the nearly seventy years of their acquaintance, Pohl wrote, "I told him at one point I wanted to be as good a writer as he was. What I didn't tell him, although it was true, was that I wanted to be as good a person as Jack was."[13]

Pohl's enthusiasm for science fiction reading was matched by an equal hunger for science fiction films—notably *Frankenstein*, *Dr. Jekyll and Mr. Hyde*, *The Invisible Man*, and *The Island of Lost Souls*—and films in general. He estimated that he watched three or four movies a week, not counting repeats.[14] Pohl recalled seeing his first science fiction film in 1930: "*Just Imagine* was the first science-fiction film I ever saw. I had barely discovered science fiction itself, and the revelation that it existed even in the movie theaters blew my mind."[15]

Frederik Pohl was born on November 26, 1919, in New York City, just thirty-seven days before the reported birthdate of his contemporary and close friend Isaac Asimov. Pohl's father was a dreamer who was always looking for the next big financial opportunity, and when Frederik was born, his father had secured a job at the Panama Canal. Baby Fred spent his first Christmas at sea, as he and his mother traveled by steamer to meet his father. During Pohl's infancy his father continued to chase the next best thing, moving to Texas, New Mexico, and California over the ensuing few years. By the time Pohl was old enough to remember where he was, they were back in Brooklyn.[16] Even in Brooklyn, the Pohls moved from apartment to apartment; Pohl suspected that it was because they couldn't pay the rent. Sometimes he would have to stay with relatives until his father could get the finances sorted out again.[17] Like many other notable science fiction figures (Robert Silverberg, Raymond Palmer, Jo Walton), Pohl suffered from childhood illness, and his mother kept him out of school until he was eight years old. Instead, encouraged by his mother, he read, developing his early appetite for reading, an aptitude to read quickly, and a sharp mind for retention. So by the time Pohl attended school, he was already ahead of the class and found the work to be insipidly boring.

His father left when Pohl was eleven, shortly after Pohl discovered SF, and his parents divorced amicably when he was thirteen. This may have played a role in Pohl's seeking out male companionship among other science fiction fans.[18] Eventually, his father would finally come upon some prosperity, running a successful manufacturing plant, though his financial fortunes would continue to go up and down. The manufacturing entrepreneur in the mainstream novel *A Town is Drowning*, written with Cyril Kornbluth, is likely drawn from Pohl's father, as are some of the science fictionalized factory scenes in stories such as *The Space Merchants* and "The Waging of the Peace."

Like many young science fiction enthusiasts, Pohl began writing his own stories and dreamed of the day when his work would appear in the magazines. He attempted his first SF story in his eighth grade English class. Needless to say, his teacher did not approve. In that same class, a fellow student introduced him to another new science fiction magazine, *Astounding Stories of Super-Science*, loaning him the June 1931 issue, which featured Arthur J. Burks's "Manape the Mighty."[19]

Pohl entered high school at Brooklyn Tech in the fall of 1932. Tech was a new school (in old buildings) created to produce young technologists and scientists—the kind of science-oriented young men and women that Hugo Gernsback was championing in his magazines. A quick study, Pohl would read the school textbooks in the first week of class and then otherwise be bored the rest of the semester. At Brooklyn Tech Pohl met another science fiction enthusiast named Harry Dockweiler, who would later change his name to Dirk Wylie. Dockweiler was the first person like himself whom Pohl had encountered, and they became best friends, spending their time discussing science fiction while roaming the city, walking for hours and stealing rides on the subway: "School could not compete. Outside it we were learning the world."[20] The world was changing, and Pohl could see it changing all around him as he explored the city. Science and technology were coming to the forefront, and this was evident in the urban environment.

★   ★   ★

Pohl's discovery of science fiction, his enthusiastic reading of everything he could get his hands on, and his friendship with another young science fiction enthusiast in Dockweiler paralleled the development of science fiction fandom and culture. In fact, Pohl was among the prominent foundational figures in fan culture. By the time Pohl was fourteen years old, science fiction fandom was about to take shape.

To boost magazine sales and promote the growing youth culture surrounding science fiction, Hugo Gernsback launched the Science Fiction League in the May 1934 issue of *Wonder Stories*. According to fan historian Sam Moskowitz, the Science Fiction League created the fan field by coalescing it, forming a community of the disparate youths across the country and in Britain who were avidly reading science fiction.[21] Pohl signed up immediately; nevertheless, his membership number was 490.[22] He joined the Brooklyn chapter, headed by a man named G. G. Clark, who was member number 1 of the SFL and had received the personal imprimatur of Gernsback himself to form the club.[23] The kids who joined, however, found the older Clark to be somewhat stiff, and they would often hold their own "meeting after the meeting" at a nearby soda fountain.[24]

As science fiction fans gathered in the clubs set up by Gernsback, they began exchanging their fanzines. The Brooklyn Science Fiction League published their proceedings in a small, mimeographed publication called the *Brooklyn Reporter*. This was the first science fiction fanzine that Pohl was involved with; though not the first fanzine, it was the first to emerge from organized fandom. These early fanzines contained stories and poems by fans and pros, reviews of each new issue of *Amazing*, *Wonder*, and *Astounding*, gossip about what was happening in the world of science fiction, and political debate among fans.[25] The fanzines were the gateway to professional writing and editing for many SF fans, including Pohl. And they were the foundations for professional SF criticism, a legacy for books such as this one; for instance, Damon Knight and James Blish published their early criticism in fanzines. In a recent article in *Asimov's Science Fiction Magazine*, film critic Roger Ebert, who had been an active science fiction fan in the 1950s, claimed, "It was in the virtual world of science fiction fandom that I started to learn to be a writer and a critic."[26] Ebert further compares the fanzines and fan culture to an early paper version of the internet: "Fanzines were web pages before there was a web. . . . Someday an academic will write a study proving that the style, tone, and much of the language of the online world developed in a direct linear fashion from science fiction fandom."[27] This virtual network of contacts and critical writing through fanzines was consistent with Pohl's experience, as he honed his writing skills by writing critical reviews and commentary and editing others' work, and made contact with science fiction fans across the country, including Robert Lowndes, a youngster from Connecticut who would eventually move to New York and become one of Pohl's closest companions.

The power dynamic of the BSFL was soon to change when Donald Wollheim and John Michel joined the group. Though Wollheim was only nineteen years old and Michel seventeen, both were published writers: Wollheim's first story had appeared in the January 1934 issue of *Wonder Stories*, and Michel shared a byline with Raymond Z. Gallun in the Summer 1932 issue of *Wonder Stories Quarterly*. The fourteen-year-old Pohl was starstruck. These guys were pros. Wollheim and Michel had come to the BSFL meeting to announce that Gernsback was not paying writers, a charge Gernsback and other pulp editors had faced before, and they were mad. This led to the first schism in fandom, as Wollheim proposed that all members of the Science Fiction League should assert their independence by seceding from affiliation with Gernsback, form their own clubs, and proclaim loudly the misdeeds of Gernsback in fan publications.[28] This kind of rough-and-tumble fan politicking appealed to Pohl, who, like Wollheim, liked to stir things up. The group soon split, with Pohl, Dockweiler, and others joining Wollheim and Michel, leaving the Gernsback loyalist Clark. With Wollheim and Michel, Pohl formed the East New York Science Fiction League and then joined the International Scientific Association, where they connected with a fan named Will Sykora.[29] As documented in several letters in the Wollheim Archive in the Spencer Library at the University of Kansas, after only a few months, Pohl, Wollheim, and Michel squabbled with Sykora over the club's finances, publications, leadership, and politics. By April 1937, following defections by the triumvirate, Sykora resigned the presidency and Wollheim briefly seized power long enough to dissolve the ISA.[30] These fan wars, which have been chronicled in Sam Moskowitz's *The Immortal Storm*, Harry Warner Jr.'s *All Our Yesterdays*, Damon Knight's *The Futurians*, and elsewhere, shaped the genre, and Pohl's presence on the front lines are central to that development.

As Pohl's career in fandom continued in the latter half of the 1930s, he demonstrated a penchant for editorial work, editing a number of publications for the fan groups he was part of, including such titles as *Mind of Man*, *Flabbergasting Stories*, and the *International Observer*. This capacity for editorial work would be important for Pohl's later career in the field, first when he became the editor of two magazines at age nineteen—*Astonishing Stories* and *Super Science Stories*—and later when he edited the first original anthology series for Ballantine Books, *Star Science Fiction*, succeeded Horace Gold as editor of *Galaxy* and *If* in the 1960s, and held the post of science fiction editor at Bantam during the 1970s.

After the collapse of the ISA, Pohl and his friends continued to shape the world of science fiction through their fan activities, and by late 1937 their group began to coalesce into what they eventually called the Futurians, which would become the most significant fan group in science fiction history. Along with Pohl, the original members included Isaac Asimov, Donald Wollheim, Cyril Kornbluth, Robert Lowndes, David Kyle, Richard Wilson, Dirk Wylie, John Michel, and other less notable names. In later years, James Blish (who had been a member of the ISA), Judith Merril, Damon Knight, Virginia Kidd, and Hannes Bok were members. Among this group are several of the most important writers and editors of the genre.[31] The first official meeting of the Futurian Science Literary Society was held on September 18, 1938. On September 15, Isaac Asimov received a postcard from Pohl inviting him to the meeting. Of that first meeting, Asimov wrote in his diary:

> I attended the first meeting of the Futurians and boy! did I have a good time. Attending likewise were such famous fans as Don A. Wollheim, John Michel, Frederik Pohl, "Doc" Lowndes. . . . We enjoyed a three-hour session of strict parliamentary discipline. . . . This was a meeting of organization in which we settled details, adopted a constitution, elected officers, and so on. Next time, we will proceed to the business of speeches, debates, and so on. . . . After the meeting we all went down to an ice-cream parlor. . . . There I had an uproarious time. . . . They all know me from my letters to *Astounding* and *Amazing* and I got along famously.[32]

Pohl and his Futurian cohorts were not only interested in science fiction, they also became involved with leftist politics. In January 1938 they organized the "Committee for the Political Advancement of Science Fiction" and began promoting "Michelism" to encourage progressive thinking among SF fans.[33] Pohl was an active member of the Young Communist League for four years and considered himself a communist from age sixteen to twenty.[34] Like many young intellectuals in the Depression years of the 1930s, Pohl was looking for answers to an economic system that had failed and a social system that was inequitable and intolerant. But he awakened to the folly of the extreme Left with the Stalin-Hitler pact of 1939, making his final break in June 1940 when France fell to Germany.[35] At that time, Pohl resigned from all activities of the Communists, although his politics remained in the broader tradition of the Left, following the trajectory of someone like George Orwell.[36] Eventually, Pohl would come to identify with the left-liberal wing of the Democratic Party. Much later, he identified himself as a Green: "As some of you are aware I'm pretty much a Green, in that I think we human beings are committing great acts of folly in the way we are destroying the world we live in. . . . I care about it very much, and I think I have been led in that direction largely because of my lifelong interest in science fiction. . . . I think it would be very nearly fair to suggest that the environmental movement in America actually began with science fiction."[37]

All told, the Futurians published 129 stories by the end of 1942, and at one point they controlled half of the magazines in the field.[38] By the 1950s, former Futurians dominated the science fiction scene. Judith Merril, who joined the group during the war years and later had a tumultuous marriage to Pohl, reflected on the Futurians in her memoir *Better to Have Loved*: "The Futurians were extraordinary people. They were a group of young writers who were set to start history, not to repeat it. They each had their own visions about the future; it was coming, and they were thinking about it better than anybody else."[39]

Pohl and the Futurians were also instrumental in setting up the cultural phenomenon of science fiction conventions. In the fall of 1936, Pohl, Wollheim, Michel, and a number of others in their group traveled to Philadelphia to meet a group of Philadelphia fans. Thus was the inauspicious beginning of science fiction conventions.[40] When the New York group returned home, they began working on the idea of hosting a national convention to bring together writers and fans from across the country; this was the genesis for the first World Science Fiction Convention held in New York City in 1939, in which Pohl's notorious involvement plays a significant part. The initial idea was Wollheim's, and he and the other Futurians worked to put it together with other New York–area fans. As planning moved forward, a rift along political lines developed between the Futurians and a group led by Sykora, who wanted to keep politics out of science fiction. Sykora was backed by an enthusiastic young fan from New Jersey, Sam Moskowitz, and James Taurasi, a fan from Queens; and the Futurians lost control of the committee. [41] The convention was to be held in conjunction with the World's Fair over the Fourth of July weekend.

A legendary incident in science fiction lore occurred when the Futurians arrived at the convention hall on Sunday, July 2, where they were met at the elevator by Moskowitz and Taurasi and barred from entering. Moskowitz describes the encounter at the elevator with tongue partly in cheek: "At this point it might be asked why the much larger Futurian group did not simply brush past Taurasi and Moskowitz since, as they later stated, they debated the ethical grounds on which they were being kept out. Aside from the wish to enter properly, readers should be reminded that both Taurasi and Moskowitz weighed close to 200 pounds, and next to science fiction Moskowitz's greatest enthusiasm was boxing."[42] While Pohl, Wollheim, Michel, and Lowndes were banned from the proceedings, Asimov, Kyle, and Kornbluth were allowed in and relayed events to Pohl and company, who had set themselves up in a café across the street. There, Pohl and the banished Futurians met with professional writers, like Jack Williamson and L. Sprague de Camp, and prominent fans who had come from as far away as California, such as Forrest J. Ackerman and Ray Bradbury. Additionally, Pohl probably crossed paths with, but didn't formally meet, another young fan in attendance, fourteen-year-old Harry Harrison, with whom he would later form World SF with Brian Aldiss and others.[43]

Pohl's science fiction activities at this time were not merely confined to fan wars, however. Since Pohl avidly roamed New York City and just as avidly pursued all things science fiction, he began to make the rounds of the editorial offices in Manhattan, peddling his stories and the stories of his friends. At the offices of *Amazing*, although he never got past the reception desk, the ancient editor T. O'Conor Sloane, with long white beard, would shuffle out of his office and accept the young enthusiast's manuscripts personally. This personal contact, however minimal, kept the aspiring writer from being discouraged, and, indeed, Sloane would publish Pohl's first professional sale, under the byline Elton Andrews, the poem "Elegy to a Dead Planet: Luna," in the October 1937 issue (Sloane wisely substituted Satellite for Planet, though Pohl preferred the original title).[44] Despite the crudity of construction, the poem does offer a compelling concept of the Moon as a living biosphere—hence Pohl's choice to call it a planet rather than a satellite—and conveys the deepness of time indicative of science fiction as informed by evolutionary theory. In this sense, it speaks to the reader's imagination in a way not unlike that introduced by Wells in *The Time Machine*.

Pohl had a deeper interaction with the editor of *Astounding Stories*, F. Orlin Tremaine. With Tremaine, Pohl would develop a similar relationship to the one Isaac Asimov had with Tremaine's successor, John W. Campbell,[45] stopping by the offices to chat about science fiction, story ideas, and how to improve his writing. Occasionally, Tremaine would even take Pohl out to lunch.[46] Pohl would develop a similar routine with Campbell, albeit without the publication success Asimov enjoyed, serving as a sounding board for Campbell's editorial ideas: "John was if anything more receptive of my visits (and John was quite as unreceptive of my stories) than Tremaine; he would admit me to his office and sit me down next to his rolltop desk and fit a cigarette into a holder and explain to me why commercial television would never succeed, or how Bell Telephone was the best-run company in the world. After a while I noticed that the subject we talked about in any given month would appear on the stands as his editorial two months later, and realized what he was doing."[47]

At this time Pohl also went into his first venture as a literary agent and got John Michel involved as well. Pohl would take stories written by other fans from outside the New York area to the editors when he made his visits. For instance, after the first World Con, Los Angelino Ray Bradbury wrote to Pohl asking him to represent his work, none of which was published at the time.[48] Another prominent example is Milton A. Rothman, a Philadelphia fan, whose story "Heavy Planet" (*Astounding*, August 1939) is a well-known example of hard SF. Pohl took Rothman's stories, rewrote them, and sold a few of them to Campbell at *Astounding*, under the byline Lee Gregor.[49] Even though Pohl was for many years an uncredited collaborator on the Gregor stories, it is now acknowledged that he had a significant hand in them, thus making his first unofficial appearance in the pages of *Astounding* in the same issue that saw Robert A. Heinlein's debut story "Life-Line." Pohl's name did not byline a story in *Astounding* until 1961, when the magazine had changed its name to *Analog*, and that in a posthumous collaboration with the late C. M. Kornbluth. Pohl did not appear solo in the magazine until after Campbell's death in 1971, with his major novella "The Gold at the Starbow's End" in March 1972 (discussed at length later), which dramatically signaled the changes in editorial policy by Campbell's successor, Ben Bova.

Pohl left school in the year the Futurians were formed. At age seventeen he briefly held a job delivering letters across the city for a firm of insurance underwriters.[50] This experience contributed to the 1955 novel *Preferred Risk* and much later to *The Years of the City*. After about a year, Pohl left the job, hoping he could get an editorial post at one of the pulp chains. He stopped in at the office of Popular Publications, a company that produced some fifty magazines in various genres, primarily known for Western, detective, and single-character magazines such as *The Spider*. Pohl had an interview with the managing editor, Rog Terrill, and by the time the meeting was over Pohl had been introduced to the publisher, Harry Steeger. Before he left, the nineteen-year-old Pohl found himself editor of two science fiction magazines, *Astonishing Stories* and *Super*

Science Stories. His salary was ten dollars a week, about half the salary of a Popular Publications secretary, but Pohl didn't care: he was too elated by the prospects of being a professional editor.[51]

Pohl's budget for each issue was under $450, and he needed about sixty thousand words of fiction for each issue, which allowed for around a half-cent-per-word payment to writers. The story, partially perpetuated by Pohl himself, is that he relied on his Futurian comrades to supply stories at a lower rate so that he could pay artists and, much to Pohl's consternation, the veteran pulpster Ray Cummings, who on Steeger's instruction was to receive acceptance on submission and a higher rate for routine, unimaginative stories.[52] Although it is true that Pohl did publish quite a number of stories by his fellow Futurians, he did not rely on them quite as heavily as did Wollheim in *Cosmic Stories* and Lowndes in *Future* and *Science Fiction Quarterly* when they broke into the professional editing field shortly thereafter. Looking at the table of contents and what is known of pseudonyms used in both magazines during Pohl's tenure as editor, it is evident that Pohl published an impressive range of veteran writers (John Russell Fearn, Raymond Z. Gallun, Frank Belknap Long, Neil R. Jones, Harl Vincent), newly emerging stars (Robert A. Heinlein, L. Sprague de Camp, Leigh Brackett, Alfred Bester, Henry Kuttner, Manly Wade Wellman), and fellow Futurians (Asimov, Kornbluth, Blish, Wollheim, Richard Wilson). Among the Futurians, Pohl himself and in collaboration (mostly with Kornbluth) published eleven stories, all under pseudonyms. Asimov had seven stories in Pohl's magazines, most of these having been rejected by Campbell at *Astounding*. These include Asimov's first robot story "Robbie," which Pohl, whose later history for changing titles is notorious, changed to "Strange Playfellow." Blish appeared three times, including his first sale, "Emergency Refueling"; Wollheim twice; and Michel, Lowndes, and Wilson each once. Another impressive legacy of Pohl's magazines is that he published the first professional sale of Ray Bradbury, "Pendulum," written in collaboration with veteran writer Henry Hasse, paying thirty dollars for the story.[53] It is clear that Pohl *did not* fill his magazines mostly with early stories by his Futurian friends. Given the variety of publication in Pohl's magazines, it is also evident that *Astonishing* and *Super Science* were preferred secondary markets after *Astounding*, and indeed many of the stories Pohl published by veteran writers and up-and-comers had probably gone to Campbell's desk first.[54]

Nevertheless, it is true that Pohl published a number of his own early stories in his magazines, a practice Steeger expected his editors to utilize to supplement their meager salaries. Aside from Pohl himself (and Ray Cummings), the writer who most frequently appeared in Pohl's magazines was seventeen-year-old Cyril Kornbluth, a surly youth who was just then exhibiting his gifts as a writer. Many of the Kornbluth stories were collaborations with Pohl. Pohl developed a method by which they worked: he came up with a story idea and wrote out an "action chart" with "takes" of around six hundred words (about the number of words on a pulp magazine page); Kornbluth would then write a first draft, which Pohl would rewrite for sale. Most generally the purchasing editor was Pohl himself, so in his capacity as agent and purchaser, Pohl, much to Kornbluth's aggravation, took a slightly higher cut of the proceeds. These came to be known as the "60/40 stories."[55] This was not unlike the writing routine that would emerge when the two would collaborate on their novels in the 1950s, though then they worked out a more even financial split. Interestingly, this process would reverse after Kornbluth's death, when Pohl took a number of Kornbluth's ideas and fragments and fleshed them out into stories later published in Critical Mass. Some of the other Futurians, as well as future historians and biographers, resented the 60/40 arrangement, feeling that Pohl was exploiting Kornbluth for Pohl's own benefit, giving him the nickname 60/40 Pohl.[56] Pohl's editorial practices also caused additional resentment, and the Futurians would sarcastically refer to him as "The Great Benefactor" as they awaited payment for their stories.[57] However, collaborating and helping one another out was part of the Futurian zeitgeist, which, in turn, influenced the overall professional practice of science fiction. No other form of storytelling, with the exception of television and film writing, has seen as many collaborative endeavors as science fiction. As George Slusser has noted in his book on Gregory Benford in this series, "Collaborative work, in fact, is a hallmark of science fiction in general."[58]

Meanwhile, most of the other Futurians (with the exception of Kornbluth, who was still in high school) arranged to rent an apartment in Brooklyn, where they could live communally, write, and pursue their fannish activities. They christened the apartment the Ivory Tower.[59] Pohl didn't live at the Tower, though he had initiated the first experiment in Futurian communal living the previous fall when he and his fiancée Doris Baumgardt rented a house in

Brooklyn, dubbed the Futurian House. In the Wollheim Archive, a scribbled note from Doris dated July 25, 1939, indicates Wollheim paid rent up front: "Received from Donald A. Wollheim—$40.00 for rent—against payment in Futurian House."[60] Pohl and Doris never actually lived in the Futurian House, as their wedding was postponed until August 1940, and they would instead take an apartment in Knickerbocker Village in Lower East Side Manhattan, across from Richard Wilson and his wife.[61] Nevertheless, Pohl would spend a great deal of time at the Tower. Yet Pohl's ascendancy to professional editing and his marriage were signs that his camaraderie with the group was beginning to splinter, and his rivalry with Wollheim for leadership of the Futurians was simmering.[62] Wollheim was particularly perturbed that the women introduced "a pernicious bourgeois influence" into the group.[63] Damon Knight said that by the time he arrived in New York City from Oregon in the summer of 1941, factions had developed centering around Wollheim and Pohl; those who were part of Wollheim's circle were still essentially Bohemians, while Pohl's faction had "gone establishment"—they were married, employed, and relatively prosperous. According to Knight, the only one in Pohl's group who still regularly showed up at the Tower was Pohl himself: "I'm not sure if he did this because he liked our company, or because he enjoyed walking into the lion's den."[64] At one point that summer, Pohl, who was evidently feuding with Lowndes and Kornbluth, tendered a letter to Wollheim wherein he considered resigning from the Futurians.[65] Things got so heated that by the fall Pohl was in fact expelled.[66] In turn, in a letter dated October 16, 1941, Pohl threatened to sue Wollheim for libel for remarks he made about Pohl's departure from Popular Publications in a fanzine called *Futuria*.[67] This rivalry would carry on for the rest of their careers until Wollheim's passing in 1990, although it would soften at times as the two met professionally over the years. But Wollheim's acrimony toward Pohl still surfaces in his remarks in his short study of the field, *The Universe Makers* (1971), where he offhandedly says Pohl was "more than usually egotistical" in those days and had become "a disillusioned idealist, a latter-day cynic."[68]

On Pohl's end, he honored the memory of his rival in a brilliant late work of skiffy called "The Golden Years of *Astounding*" (1997), which posits an alternate past in which John W. Campbell was fired after only a few months as editor of *Astounding* for smoking in the potentially disastrous environs of the paper presses, and Wollheim is hired in his place. In Wollheim's alternate *Astounding*, Pohl has him "discover" Tennessee Williams, instead of Heinlein, in the Golden Age of 1938 to 1941; pull Bradbury out of the slush pile; publish Burroughs's later Mars novels, Stapledon's extraordinary uplifted-dog novel *Sirius*, and Lovecraft's *The Dream-Quest of Unknown Kadath*; and convince Tolkien to transform his Middle Earth epic into a planetary romance titled *The Lord of Saturn's Rings*. The fired Campbell goes on to write stories for *Amazing* about "his famous 'Three Laws of Robotics'" and a story that sounds like a variation of Asimov's "Nightfall," both referring to the fact that Campbell fed these ideas to Asimov and others; and, then, Pohl has fun imagining Campbell's "controversial later works," involving ideas Campbell actually championed in his 1950s *Astounding* editorials—psionics, the Hieronymous Machine, the Dean Drive, and so on—conflated with ideas Ray Palmer promoted in his magazines—Deros, saucer people—as if Campbell became Palmer's resident crank instead of Richard Shaver.

Pohl's tenure at Popular Publications came to an end in May 1941 when he demanded a raise. Years later, Pohl could not recall if he quit or was fired, but either way he found himself without a job in the summer of 1941 and free to pursue writing full time.[69] He continued to write stories on his own and in collaboration with fellow Futurians, developing interests in music and chess in between, which would feed into later novels.[70] Ironically, Pohl returned to Popular seven months later in early 1942 to work as an assistant to Alden H. Norton (who, in addition to editing Pohl's former SF magazines, was editing the sports, mystery, horror, Western, and air-war titles) and was paid almost double the salary he'd had previously.[71] Under Norton, Pohl worked on a variety of pulps, acquiring stories, copyediting, and writing editorial blurbs, filler material, and editorials for such magazines as *Strange Detective Mysteries* and *G-8 and His Battle Aces*.[72] Working on these other pulps under an experienced editor like Norton taught Pohl a lot about the workings of the publishing industry that would serve him well in the future. In addition to writing science fiction stories during this time, Pohl wrote a number of stories and poems for the various Popular magazines, many of which still remain unidentified. However, as Pohl notes on his blog, one of his "sappier 25-cents-a-line effusions" was mistakenly published under his own name in one of the love pulps by an unwitting editor.[73]

　　★　　★　　★

Pohl's fiction from this earlier period is mostly workmanlike. None of the stories reaches the level of his later work. Unlike Kornbluth, who has at least one exceptional story ("The Words of Guru") from this period, or Asimov, who produced a number of outright classics before the war, most of Pohl's early stories come across as routine adventures, indistinguishable from most of the forgotten stories from the era. In fact, had Pohl not gone on to later fame, all of these stories would likely have fallen into complete obscurity. Most of Pohl's early solo stories were published under the pseudonym James MacCreigh and have appeared in the collection *The Early Pohl*, with a few more scattered in other Pohl collections, while most of his early collaborations with Kornbluth appear in the volume *Before the Universe*. *The Early Pohl* is a particularly useful volume because it includes much interstitial biographical material and commentary as well, which in many ways is more important than the stories themselves. Despite having shortcomings, a few of these early stories stand out and are worth considering, if only to show how Pohl was developing as a writer.

"The Dweller in the Ice" (*Super Science*, January 1941) was Pohl's first solo story; he had published three collaborations with Kornbluth prior to its appearance. The story is set in Antarctica, a location Pohl and Kornbluth would later use at the first major turning point in *The Space Merchants*, when Mitch Courtenay is ambushed. Kye Whalen, a mining engineer, joined by his wife Beatta, has been sent to oversee operations for International Milling Machines Inc., who need "semi-precious and precious stones for drill-points" (11). A wandering comet has passed through the solar system before crashing into the sun, and International Milling's astronomers have observed "an unusual display of meteorites strike the Earth's Southern Hemisphere" (11). At the worksite, more than fifty accidents have occurred in a month, and Whalen recognizes that it is not the equipment at fault but the men, who have become careless and torpid. Soon, Whalen himself returns home in the same listless state, and Beatta is determined to find out what is going on. With Christine Abrudsen, the recreations director, she goes to the worksite and descends the shaft to investigate a borer that had gone off course; both women get lost down the shaft. Whalen deduces where they have gone and follows, assuming that they have fallen into the frigid waters beneath the ice. When Whalen sees Beatta's light ahead and finds her, Beatta believes Christine is dead, and they find themselves in an underground cavern: "At first he could see nothing. Then he realized that there was a vast cavern before them, hundreds of feet high and wide" (20). There, they see an immense shape, almost "like some sort of a statue, or an animal" (20) and see Christine ascending the cable toward them. Christine had, indeed, died, but the being in the ice brought her back: "Kye, *I have been dead*. That monstrous, terrible, frightening thing out there—it killed me and brought me to life again!" (21). In an interesting twist, Pohl counters the Antarctic menace tales of H. P. Lovecraft (*At the Mountains of Madness*) and John W. Campbell ("Who Goes There?"), which are among the masterpieces of the 1930s and stories Pohl certainly would have read when they appeared in *Astounding*, by revealing a natural benevolence to the superior being trapped in the ice from the cometary impact. Christine explains:

> It came from the comet. It lived there, Kye, and when the comet broke up in Earth's gravitational field, it was on a section that was drawn to the Earth. It is an incredible creature. It fell, Kye, fell all the way to the surface of the Earth. And it's still alive—though it is dying. It told me that. It read my mind, and it spoke to me. And it made me a promise, too. A promise—that it would kill itself! Because it's a highly rational creature, and it found in my mind that it was interfering with us (22).

Although the female characters are reasonably well drawn, the story is marred by the conventional sexism of the era: the reason men were affected by the creature was that it was exuding the emotion of longing for home: "That's a basic feeling of every human being. But—women are not as subject to it as men. A woman is trained to cling to a man; a man, to support his country . . ." (22). Interestingly, Pohl cuts off Kye's speech at this point, as the creature dies, making the reader wonder if the young writer was keenly aware of the bombast of his character. Overall, the story has an interesting concept and a compelling-enough narrative pace, but it doesn't stand out; nonetheless it is competent enough for a first solo story.

"It's a Young World" (*Astonishing*, April 1941) is an adventure story using first-person narration, a narrative voice that became Pohl's signature style in such works as *The Space Merchants*, *Gateway*, *The Voices of Heaven*, and his final novel, *All the Lives He Led*. Here it allows Pohl to limit the viewpoint, so as more is revealed to the hero, the reader experiences the hero's growing awareness of his world. The adventure narrative echoes Charles R. Tanner's *Tumithak of the Corridors* stories, the last of which was published in the November 1941 issue of *Super Science Stories* and was probably one of the last stories Pohl bought for the magazine. In *The Early Pohl*, Pohl writes that when he began seeing the fan mail coming into his magazines, he realized that "being a Writer was not enough"; what he wanted to become was a writer whom the readers responded to enthusiastically. So he was determined to write better stories. "It's a Young World" was the first product of this resolve.[74] The story involves a young warrior named Keefe and a girl named Clory who must flee their "Tribe" after committing a blasphemous act: slaying his blood brother, Lurlan, who has been declared an "Enemy" and who was about to be ritually burned at the stake. They encounter a pilot whose garb is unfamiliar to them, and then they come across beings with advanced technologies, eventually finding another couple like themselves in a ship. Keefe inadvertently starts the ship, which cruises back to its base of origin in a subterranean city. There they encounter an advanced society, and the truth is revealed. In this case, Keefe turns out to be head of the council; humankind is now immortal, but the mind must be renewed every century or so; consequently, people must be "reborn" psychologically, by reverting to a state of primitivism. The story follows the pattern of "conceptual breakthrough," where, in the pattern of a quest, an intellectual outsider questions the apparent certainties of his world—among the best examples are Clarke's *Against the Fall of Night*, Blish's "Surface Tension," and Heinlein's "Universe"—where the insular world of the viewpoint character is revealed to be part of a larger reality.[75] Like "The Dweller in the Ice," the story is conceptually interesting and is told competently enough. Yet it does not quite rise to the level of another classic "conceptual breakthrough" story written by one of Pohl's Futurian comrades, which appeared in *Astounding* only a few months later, Asimov's "Nightfall."

Finally, "Earth, Farewell!" (*Astonishing*, February 1943) involves an alien invasion that has put an end to war. It also uses the first-person narrator, and in this case the narrator is a "true believer," believing in the benevolence of the aliens, even when it is revealed to him that their intentions are far from benevolent. There are seventy-seven aliens on Earth, administering different sectors, who wish to learn as much about humans and human culture and history as they can. Therefore, "Four and the Four" are selected periodically to be sent to the alien planet: four young men who are transformed into supermen and four young women who serve as "libraries," carrying the vast knowledge of humanity. The narrator, Ralph Symes, is selected as one of the Four. When they arrive on the alien planet, the men take the women into a vast chamber, where they gasp in horror when they see previous initiates denuded on slabs, kept alive by intravenous tubes. Led by Collard, one of the four, the men revolt, shatter the communications tower, and discover that the aliens are, in fact, organic robots. A similar theme of alien control is found in a number of Pohl's later works, such as "Mars by Moonlight" (1958) and "We Purchased People" (1974), where superior alien races have come to Earth and imposed their will upon humankind. "Earth, Farewell!" however, most resonates with *Wolfbane* (1959), Pohl's last collaborative novel with Kornbluth, in which machine invaders overtake Earth. Another interesting element in the story is the use of a crown that controls the characters' behaviors. This use of mind control resurfaces in various ways in, again, "Mars by Moonlight," *A Plague of Pythons* (1965), and in somewhat different ways in *Wolfbane*, *Drunkard's Walk* (1960), and *The Starchild Trilogy* (1964–9). In an interesting twist, the story is framed as Symes's confession in the manner of Poe's "Cask of Amontillado," as Collard contemplates what to do with him. In the end, Symes remains an unawakened "true believer," failing to acknowledge that the robots are a menace to humanity. Like the two other stories discussed here, this story is conceptually interesting; however, the writing does not take it to the level that Pohl would reach in later works. These are the works of a young writer learning his craft and honing his skills. The stories are competent and interesting but do not have the narrative ease and conceptual sophistication that Pohl would display in his stories of the 1950s.

Of the early collaborative stories written with Kornbluth, Pohl selected "Trouble in Time" (*Astonishing*, December 1940) and "Mars-Tube" (*Astonishing*, September 1941) for the collection *Our Best*. But "Best Friend" (*Super Science*, May 1941), which was included in the earlier collection *The Wonder Effect*, is a more effective story than these routine adventure narratives. "Best Friend" is a delightful man-and-dog story set one hundred thousand years in the future where, through genetic engineering, dogs have been uplifted to an intelligence equivalent to contemporary humanity, while humans have become increasingly remote, living in isolated and automated dwellings and leaving the activities of the world to the dogs. The story anticipates Clifford Simak's *City* stories by a few years and Cordwainer Smith's "Underpeople" stories, most of which Pohl published in *Galaxy* and *If* in the 1960s. The story is shorter than most of the other early stories and is more concisely told. The authors set the scene nicely in the first few pages, exhibiting a growing command of storytelling. The tightness of the story is seen in the first paragraph, when the reader is given the first clue that this is an SFnal world: Moray, the viewpoint character, lights "a meat-flavored cigarette." Next, Moray is listening to "Yahnn Bastien Bock" on the radio, easily recognized as Bach, of course, but through a distorted lens, and then Moray reflects that he "never could get used to the Masters' music." The word Master, capitalized, further cues the reader that this is in fact a dog flying a plane, smoking a cigarette, and listening to music. Later, things are explained: over a period of one hundred thousand years dogs have been genetically engineered and are now the equivalent of twentieth-century humanity, while a languid humankind has retreated into their automated dwellings, no longer meeting with one another, recalling E. M. Forster's "The Machine Stops" and any number of stories from the 1930s (for example, Laurence Manning's *The Man Who Awoke* series and David Keller's "The Revolt of the Pedestrians"). The dog-people remain loyal to "Masters" who call them when they want them. Pohl and Kornbluth convincingly maintain familiar dog behavior patterns—loyalty, desire for human praise—that the reader recognizes, and, like Simak in his masterful "Desertion," create convincing sentiment that allows the reader to feel deeply for Moray's dilemma. Called before his master on his thirteenth birthday, Moray shows little enthusiasm for the gift his master presents him—"biographies of the lives of North American presidents"—resulting in a cold dismissal: "As he stepped into the plane once more he blinked rapidly. In the hundred thousand years of evolution dogs had learned to weep" (87–88). For several weeks, Moray's master does not call him, and Moray is heartbroken. Finally, he receives the master's call: he is to research an ancient explosive technique in order to stabilize the continental plates of North America, which are on the verge of a catastrophic slippage. Moray successfully recreates the process and returns to the good graces of his master: "He felt a light, soft touch on his arm. It was the Master—the first time in all Moray's life when the Master had touched him to draw attention, Moray suddenly knew, and rejoiced—he had found his Master again! . . . His heart was light enough to bear a world!" (95). This is certainly not the cynicism and wry wit we generally associate with the work of Pohl or Kornbluth, but nonetheless it illustrates the inherent optimism that Pohl, at least, always maintained for the possibilities of the future. Curiously, Pohl said that this particular story was "written to fill a hole in one of the magazines." Yet he also said that it was sparked by a throwaway line in Wylie and Balmer's *After Worlds Collide* "about a vanished alien race whose pets had been as intelligent as modern human beings," suggesting its genesis was more thoughtful than merely filler.[76] Pohl wanted to explore the idea from the pet's point of view. The result is a particularly fine story, perhaps the best of Pohl's early work.

★   ★   ★

As Pohl was working for Norton at Popular, the United States was gearing up the war machine in response to the Japanese attack on Pearl Harbor and the German bombardment of Britain. Various members of the science fiction community were enlisting. Futurians Dirk Wylie, David Kyle, and Jack Gillespie had all signed on. Isaac Asimov joined Robert Heinlein and Sprague de Camp at the Philadelphia Navy Yard working on aircraft materials development.[77] Like most young men of the era, Pohl felt it his duty to offer his services to the cause, and undoubtedly his work on *G-8* and other Popular war pulps, with their stories of wartime heroism, reminded him that his country awaited. Initially, he joined a civil defense group called the City Patrol Corps, which was supposed to patrol the docks against "spies and saboteurs."[78] By the end of 1942, Pohl was ready to enlist. However, voluntary enlistments had been suspended; he had to be drafted. Pohl spent the next few months trying to get reclassified. Meanwhile, his father's business schemes had finally paid off: he was getting rich manufacturing aircraft parts and wanted Fred to join him in business. Fred declined, feeling that after all those years when he spoke out against fascism, both in science fiction fandom and in the Young Communist League, it was time that he put all that talk into action. He had also gotten involved with an assistant editor at Popular, Dorothy LesTina, who went by the name Tina—she would become his second wife—and she joined the WACs when she heard of his plans to enlist. Finally, in the spring of 1943, Pohl was sworn into the army.[79]

Pohl went through basic training at Camp Upton on Long Island and then at Miami Beach for two months, where he was assigned to the Air Corps.[80] He then went for technical training as a weather observer at Chanute Field, Illinois. There he met up with Jack Williamson, who had already been forecasting at training fields around the country for a year and had come to Chanute for advanced training.[81] Next, he was sent to Enid, Oklahoma, to observe at the pilot training field. While in Enid, Pohl wrote "Highwayman of the Void," a bug-eyed-monster story set on Pluto, which appeared in *Planet Stories* in 1944. His time in Oklahoma would inform the later mainstream political novel, *Presidential Year*, written with Kornbluth, where a key scene involving a political rally takes place in Enid. Pohl's final posting before leaving for the European theater was at Buckley Field, Colorado, after he had volunteered for Arctic service. Although Pohl never did serve at either of the poles, this connection with the icecaps is interesting for how often it shows up in his work, from the previously discussed "The Dweller in the Ice," to *The Space Merchants* and the bitter little story "The Snowmen" (1959). Pohl took his Remington #5 portable typewriter along with him wherever he was stationed and continued to write stories. The last story he wrote before his deployment was "Double-Cross," which appeared in the Winter 1944 issue of *Planet Stories*.[82]

When Pohl shipped out, he was sent to Naples, Italy, as a weather observer for the 456th Bomb Group.[83] Farther up the coast, another Brooklyn boy was flying missions for the 340th: Joseph Heller, who would transform his experiences into the surreal classic satire *Catch-22*.[84] Heller's was not the only seminal novel to have its genesis in the Italian theater. While in Italy and missing his beloved New York City, Pohl began a contemporary novel about the advertising business, titled *For Some We Loved*, out of which some of the ideas for *The Space Merchants* would emerge.[85] As a weather observer, Pohl had a lot of free time and spent much of it exploring nearby Italian towns and beaches, especially the environs around Mount Vesuvius, where he was stationed. These surroundings show up frequently in Pohl's work. For instance, in *Preferred Risk*, his collaborative satire with Lester Del Rey, all of the action of the novel takes place in and around Naples and Vesuvius. Similarly, Pohl utilizes the Italian setting in *The Cool War* (1981), a novel of just-around-the-corner political intrigue, and in his last novel, *All the Lives He Led* (2011), where a parallel is drawn between ancient Pompeii and a near-future cataclysmic explosion at Yellowstone that destroys most of the United States. Vesuvius influenced Pohl's work in other ways: in addition to appearing in those novels set in Italy, volcanoes feature frequently in his work, such as Mt. Kilauea in *Terror* (1986). Pohl remarked on his fascination with volcanoes in *Chasing Science* (2000): "I've had a personal weakness for volcanoes ever since the tail end of World War II, when I happened to live on one for some months. It wasn't any old volcano, either. It was Mount Vesuvius, perhaps the most famous volcano in the world" (100). Later, Pohl's Italian experience contributed to his first nonfiction book, *Tiberius*, an often wry study of the Roman Emperor Tiberius, published under the pseudonym Ernst Mason in 1960. To this day Pohl remains the primary contributor on Tiberius for the *Encyclopedia Britannica*.[86] While Pohl was stationed on the volcano, his mother died of cancer. He had hoped to get an emergency furlough through the Red Cross but never found the liaison in his office because the man was out playing golf. By the time he tracked the fellow down, it was too late.[87]

Pohl stopped making weather observations and was assigned to be the public relations man for his squadron. In this capacity Pohl edited the squadron newspaper, which he converted into the more familiar form of a magazine, creating "one of the nicest fanzines you ever saw."[88] Public relations would feature in a number of Pohl's future activities and in his fiction. His editorial work for the army is the genesis of Mitch Courtenay in the advertising firm of Shocken and Associates in *The Space Merchants* and of Gunnarsen, the P.R. man from "The Children of Night" (1964). It was also Pohl's training ground for his postwar career as a literary agent. He managed to talk his superiors into having him write the squadron history and was transferred to Eremo on the slopes of Vesuvius, where he also wrote the first draft of the novella "Donovan Had a Dream," published after the war in *Thrilling Wonder Stories*.

"Donovan Had a Dream" is a planetary frontier adventure set on Venus. Venus is controlled by the Hags, a quasi-religious order "composed of women who thought that the men had made a mess of the world," banished from Earth for "using men in biological experiments" (170). The Donovans are a rebel group who for 150 years have opposed the Hag dictatorship in hopes of restoring freedom to Venus. Pohl never quite develops the implied political dimension of the story, as it quickly breaks down into a mere action story, with Valentine, the hero and a member of the Donovans, combating the Hags' robots and raiding the Hag palace, just as the women prepare to flee Venus for Ganymede as the Earth space fleet arrives to oust their regime. The plot wraps up much too quickly (and conveniently) as the Hag ship blows up, putting an end to the order. The perhaps unintentional sexism inherent in the appellation "Hag" can be grating to a modern reader, but since Pohl wrote the first draft on Vesuvius during the war, he may have been meditating on the rise and fall of a fascist regime rather than on creating an allegory of the Battle of the Sexes. Nonetheless, despite some crude plotting and stilted exposition, the story is fast-paced and evinces further honing of Pohl's writing craft. Yet in terms of ideas, it never quite rises above the level of Pohl's earlier stories.

While stationed in Italy, Pohl kept up a postal love affair with Tina, who was stationed in Germany. As the war wound down, the two got together in Paris and were married on August 3, 1945, three days before the atomic bomb was dropped on Hiroshima.[89] Science fiction had become all too real.

By the time Pohl returned to the States, the Futurians had imploded. In September 1945 Wollheim filed suit against seven other members for libel.[90] Pohl was discharged from the army on November 26, 1945, and spent the first few months at his father's thousand-acre farm next to Camp Upton on Long Island; his father had made a lot of money during the war.[91] While awaiting Dorothy's discharge and for the next year after, he spent his time writing detective stories for *Detective Story Magazine*—"Murder's Million" (August 1947) and "Murder Strikes Three" (September 1947); science fiction for *Thrilling Wonder*—"A Hitch in Time" (June 1947) and "Donovan Had a Dream" (October 1947); and a story titled "Stolen Tires" for the *Toronto Star Weekly*.

However, Pohl wanted to get back to the novel he had started during the war. Since the novel was intended to be about the world of Madison Avenue advertising, he conceded to himself that he did not *actually* know all that much about advertising beyond what he had gleaned while working for Popular. So he set out to learn more by taking a job as an advertising copywriter in the spring of 1946. Pohl primarily wrote advertising copy for book clubs and magazines, first at the Thwing and Altman agency and then at *Popular Science*, where he wrote subscription ads and special book offers.[92] He also anonymously edited a number of anthologies of *Popular Science* and *Outdoor Life* articles, continuing these projects for a number of years after his tenure at the company.[93] Pohl has said of these experiences, "Advertising writing should be under constant surveillance by the narcs; it is addictive, and it rots the mind. When you spend your days persuading Consumers to Consume articles they would never in their lives dream of wanting if you didn't tickle them into it, you develop fantasies of power. . . . If you do not end your day with a certain contempt for your fellow human beings, then you are just not paying attention to what it is that you do."[94]

While Pohl was at lunch with his boss George Spoerer at *Popular Science*, Spoerer suggested the idea for a story, which Pohl turned into "Let the Ants Try." Though it would still be a few years before Pohl's full maturity as a writer, "Let the Ants Try" marks the beginning of the stories and novels that made his reputation as one of the leading writers in the field. Clearly, it is one of Pohl's personal favorites: he included it in the first anthology he edited, *Beyond the End of Time*, in his first story collection, *Alternating Currents*, again in *In the Problem Pit and Other Stories* and in *Platinum Pohl*—and it was one of the four stories Pohl selected for his contributions to the *The SFWA Grandmasters* anthologies.

"Let the Ants Try" is a time-travel story in the manner of Ray Bradbury's "A Sound of Thunder." Responding to the growing anxieties about nuclear armament, the story begins in the aftermath of atomic war—"the Three-Hour War"—in 1960. One of the few human survivors, Salva Gordy, a physicist, tries to survive among the ruins of Detroit. John de Terry has been sent by what remains of the government to find out if Gordy had completed the secret weapon he had been commissioned to make. Gordy has, in fact, invented a weapon of sorts: a temporal coordinate displacer, a time machine. Gordy observes to de Terry: "Humanity has had its chance, John. The atomic bomb wasn't enough; we had to turn everything into a weapon. . . . And our weapons have blown up in our faces" (37). Using the temporal coordinate displacer, Gordy and de Terry take mutated ants back forty million years to see if they can evolve better than humankind. After depositing eight ant queens in the ground, they return to the present to find that the ants have evolved into sentient beings and, in turn, humankind never evolved. De Terry is cruelly killed by the ants and Gordy lives as a prisoner until the ants bring him to his machine, which they have dismantled, wanting him to rebuild it. Gordy repairs the machine and after a brief skirmish is able to propel himself back through time to the moment when he and de Terry deposited the ants, in hopes that he can avert the action and prevent the ant civilization from rising. Alas, when Gordy emerges into the clearing, he finds another, much larger time machine next to his own, and he realizes that the ants have come back in time to prevent him from warning his other self. Critic Colin Manlove has observed that the "manipulation of the past does not produce escape from a miserable present . . . the ruthless ants are no more satisfactory an outcome of evolution's labours than were human beings."[95] On the surface, the story reads as a typical time-paradox story mixed with monstrous menace. But there is a deeper political commentary here on the approaching folly of nuclear armament and war, which marks Pohl's maturity into an astute political commentator in his fiction. Although not the bald, witty, satiric irony of the "comic inferno" stories of the 1950s, "Let the Ants Try" is a bitter indictment of the atomic age. Joining stories like Theodore Sturgeon's "Thunder and Roses," Judith Merril's "That Only a Mother," Poul Anderson and F. N. Waldrop's "Tomorrow's Children," and H. Beam Piper's "Time and Time Again," "Let the Ants Try" is one of the important stories from the late 1940s that confronted the possible consequences of atomic warfare.

Pohl wrote very little fiction in the three years following the publication of "Let the Ants Try," seeing publication of only two short fantasy stories, "The Little Man in the Subway" and "Legal Rites," in 1950, written in collaboration with Asimov in the prewar Futurian days, and two novellas, "The Genius Beasts" (aka "Figurehead") and "Red Moon of Danger," in 1951, both of which had been completed a few years prior to "Let the Ants Try."

★ ★ ★

In the summer of 1947 Pohl's marriage to Tina came to an end when she went to see her mother in California and filed for divorce. By this time, Pohl had lost touch with most of his Futurian comrades. However, feeling at loose ends again, he wanted to get reconnected with science fiction, so he attended the World Science Fiction Convention in Philadelphia over Labor Day weekend. There he got acquainted with Judith Merril, who had become a Futurian in the year or so before the group dissolved and who was now an editor at the fledgling Bantam Books. They had met before, but at the time they had both been married; now that both were single, a mutual attraction grew. Exceeding Kuttner and Moore and Brackett and Hamilton, they were to become science fiction's top power couple for the next five years as the genre emerged from the pulp ghetto to become a leading pulse of American (and global) culture.

Pohl and Merril were married in 1949, and they became the center of the science fiction community in New York City. They were mutually attracted to one another, though Merril was, at times, equally attracted and repelled by Pohl's powerful personality, which, among the dominant personalities and intellects of the science fiction community, was the strongest of them all. In *Better to Have Loved*, she writes, "Fred was indeed clever. He was knowledge-able. He was powerful. He showed me I could be a great success as a writer and an editor. And he knew how to make people do what he wanted. That didn't work to a great extent with me, but it made him the central man in any crowd. While we were together, from 1946 to 1951, Fred and I were a total centre in the SF community."[96] Although Merril here misstates the dates—they were together from 1947 to 1951—the relationship was passionate, tumultuous, intellectually invigorating, and professionally productive. The couple had one child, a daughter, Ann, who was born on September 25, 1950.[97] Ann's own daughter, Emily, would assist her grandmother in preparing her memoirs and in eventually getting them published; Emily Pohl-Weary is now a successful writer for young adults in her own right.

Not only was Pohl invigorated by the sexual energy between him and Merril, he was inspired by the intellectual energy of the science fiction community at the convention and wanted to get back into the game. Upon returning to New York, he and Lester Del Rey came up with the idea of having a monthly gathering of science fiction professionals, what amounted to a more mature, professionally oriented version of the prewar fan organizations. This was the genesis of the Hydra Club, which became the meeting place of the science fiction world in New York City throughout the 1950s. Named the Hydra Club because nine people attended the original meeting, Pohl, Del Rey, and Merril were the leading figures; after Pohl and Merril were married, the early club meetings and parties were often held in their Manhattan apartment. Merril's reflections on the Hydra Club reveal how it contributed to the commercial development of the genre, in which Pohl played an instrumental role: "The Hydra Club became the big meeting place for SF writers. Isaac Asimov would attend. German-born scientist and science writer Willy Ley was there. The meetings became the big marketplace for writers and publishers, and editors from the various publishing houses would be there. It co-existed with the development of science fiction as a commercial genre. Fred and I were able to bring all of this together."[98] Del Rey comments that it "was basically a fan club for professionals and their close friends. It had an elaborate constitution, designed to prevent the feuds that had beset the other New York clubs. . . . [I]t was the effective center of much of the professional activity of science fiction."[99]

Around the same time, Pohl got involved in the literary agency business. Coincidentally, another survivor from the heady days of the 1930s fan wars, Scott Feldman, had also set himself up in downtown Manhattan as a literary agent, under the name Scott Meredith, and as such he would become one of the most powerful, innovative, and quirky literary agents in publishing, as brilliantly documented in Barry Malzberg's essay "Tripping with the Alchemist."[100] After the war, Pohl's longtime chum Dirk Wylie went into business as a literary agent, with Pohl as a silent partner, representing a small group of science fiction writers. Like Kornbluth, Wylie had fought at the Battle of the Bulge; he had suffered a severe back injury when jumping off a truck, so as Wylie began experiencing debilitating back problems and was in and out of the hospital, his wife Rosalind, assisted by Pohl, kept the agency going. In the early months of 1948 Wylie's condition worsened, and he developed tuberculosis of the spine, leading to his death in August. Pohl was devastated by the death of his oldest friend, but he and Rosalind decided to keep the agency going under the Dirk Wylie name, and Pohl quit his job at *Popular Science* to devote himself to the business.[101]

As an agent, Pohl was instrumental in transforming the science fiction field. Among his first clients was his old friend Isaac Asimov. Asimov had emerged as one of the stars of the field as his Robot and Foundation stories were appearing in Campbell's *Astounding* throughout the 1940s. Pohl's former boss at *Popular Science* told Pohl that he had heard that Doubleday was going to start a science fiction line. Pohl then had a meeting with Doubleday editor Walter Bradbury where he told him all about the field of science fiction and its potential. The first book Pohl sold to Bradbury was Asimov's *Pebble in the Sky*, a book-length manuscript that had failed to sell to the magazines. This was to be the beginning of a long and profitable relationship between Asimov and Doubleday.[102] Asimov later said of the deal, "In 1950, Pohl was instrumental in the highest degree in getting my first novel published. In short, Fred, more than anyone else but John W. Campbell, Jr., made my career possible."[103] Just before the book's release in January 1950, the normally teetotaling Asimov recalled getting giddily drunk at "the most crowded and successful Hydra Club meeting I ever attended," after which, "Fred Pohl had to drive us home and see that we managed to get safely through the Blugerman [Asimov's parents-in-law] door."[104] This was not the first book Pohl had sold to a major publisher; he had already sold Jack Williamson's *The Humanoids* for hardcover publication to Simon and Schuster.[105]

Indeed, Williamson thought Pohl was a good agent and an innovator: "He has always known science fiction better than nearly anybody; he's an inventive creator of new opportunities in fiction or out of it; he can be a most persuasive salesman. His clients, for a few exciting years, were writing most of the best science fiction."[106] One of Pohl's innovations as an agent, which would ultimately lead him into financial difficulties, was his method of financing writers so that they could do their best work. Pohl worked out a system whereby he would pay writers in advance so that they wouldn't have to fret about working to the markets and too often producing hackneyed work. He reasoned that by giving writers advance payment, it would allow them more creative freedom to produce better work, which would ultimately sell to the better magazines, such as *Astounding* or *Galaxy*. Another important change that Pohl instigated was a rise in word-rate from two to three cents a word among the higher-paying markets, what he called the squeeze. On Pohl's recommendation Damon Knight secured his first editorial post with Hillman Periodicals editing a new magazine called *Worlds Beyond*. Knight came by to ask Pohl how he could get first look at some of the stories going to Gold and Campbell. Pohl told him to "pay more than they do," and Knight went back to his boss and got a budget that would facilitate a higher word rate. Pohl then went to Gold and Campbell and played them against each other by saying whoever had the higher word-rate would get first look at his clients' manuscripts. Since about half the material in both magazines was coming from Pohl's clients, both Campbell and Gold subsequently raised their rates from two cents to three. Pohl claimed that "it happened when it did because I squeezed."[107]

Other significant novels Pohl sold were Merril's *Shadow on the Hearth* and John Wyndham's *The Day of the Triffids* to Doubleday, after it first appeared as a serial in the mass circulation slick magazine *Collier's*. After *Shadow on the Hearth* was published in 1950, Merril began working on a novel based on a fragment of Pohl's. This would turn into the novel *Mars Child* (published in book form as *Outpost Mars*), which Merril co-wrote with Cyril Kornbluth, who was then living in Chicago. The ever-confident Pohl sold the novel to Gold at *Galaxy* before it was completed and Gold started publishing it serially almost immediately in May 1951.[108] In desperation, and despite having an infant child to care for, Merril journeyed to Chicago to work with Kornbluth to finish up the novel on time for the final serial installment. While staying with the Kornbluths, Merril engaged in an affair with Pohl's client Fritz Leiber, a dapper gentleman several years older than Merril, who had made a name for himself by writing both science fiction and fantasy, notably *Conjure Wife* and the Fafhrd and the Grey Mouser stories, for Campbell's *Astounding* and *Unknown*. This was a sure sign that the Pohl-Merril marriage was beginning to unravel; Pohl himself was having affairs in the city. But it particularly shocked the prudish Kornbluth, who would side with Pohl when things turned bitter, though Merril believed he never said anything about it to Pohl.[109] Nonetheless, the Kornbluth-Merril collaboration would produce one more novel, *Gunner Cade*, published in *Astounding*, and a short story, "Sea Change," which Pohl sold to Bob Lowndes for *Dynamic Science Fiction*.

As *Mars Child* began its run in *Galaxy* in the spring of 1951, Pohl and Merril bought a house in Red Bank, New Jersey, even though their marriage was on the rocks. Over the summer the Kornbluths came for an extended visit; Merril and Kornbluth worked on *Gunner Cade*, and a few months later Pohl and Kornbluth would begin work on *Gravy Planet* (*The Space Merchants*). The final segment of *Gunner Cade* ran in the May 1952 issue of *Astounding*, and the same year's June issue of *Galaxy* would see the first segment of *Gravy Planet*. It was an active period for the Pohl-Kornbluth-Merril nexus. Even so, that fall Pohl and Merril filed for divorce.[110] After they split, Pohl moved into an apartment in the city, while Merril kept the house. In a June 10, 1952, letter to

James Gunn, Pohl told him that he and Merril had separated in October: "She gets custody of the house, I get custody of Kornbluth."[111] Eventually, Merril left the house in Pohl's hands, and he would continue to live in Red Bank for thirty years, until relocating to the Chicago area in the 1980s.

Pohl's work with James Blish was also significant. Pohl was Blish's agent in the early 1950s when Blish wrote his masterworks "Surface Tension," "A Case of Conscience," and the Okie stories. In addition to representing these significant works, Pohl was sometimes called in as a "project editor" at Ballantine Books to work with manuscripts that needed more personal attention—one such manuscript was the novel version of *A Case of Conscience*.[112] Blish's biographer, David Ketterer, notes that in an exchange of letters between Blish and Pohl, Blish's "respect for Pohl's opinions" and "the impact of Pohl's suggestions on the final novel" are made evidently clear, ending with a letter where Pohl remarked, "I expect great things of this book."[113] Such arrangements were not unusual. Blish himself was called in by Scott Meredith to rewrite the ending of Arthur C. Clarke's "Guardian Angel," although without Clarke's knowledge, which sold and was subsequently published in the April 1950 issue of *Famous Fantastic Mysteries*. Clarke liked Blish's ending and kept it when he expanded the story into his masterful novel *Childhood's End*.[114] Once again, collaboration, even such behind-the-scenes collaboration as these examples, is a hallmark of science fiction.

In another instance where Pohl can claim some responsibility for igniting a major science fiction career is the case of Harry Harrison. In 1951 Harrison, who had up until then aspired to working as an illustrator, needed a literary agent after selling his first story "Rock Diver" to Knight's *Worlds Beyond*. He took the story to Pohl, who read it and then bought it for an anthology he was editing, and then became Harrison's agent. Harrison gave up artwork and started his long and illustrious writing career.[115]

In addition to Asimov, Merril, Kornbluth, Blish, Knight, Harrison, Williamson, Leiber, and Wyndham, Pohl's client list included Clifford D. Simak, Hal Clement, Robert Sheckley, Frank M. Robinson, William Tenn, H. Beam Piper, Algis Budrys, and James Gunn. Pohl's relationship with his writers can be seen in some of the letter exchanges he had with clients, in particular Williamson and Gunn. In a letter to Williamson dated May 9, 1952, regarding possible publication of Williamson's 1930 collaborative novel with Miles

J. Breuer, *The Birth of a New Republic*, Pohl advises Williamson to "drop the whole project" because Breuer's estate lawyer "is adamant in refusing to go below one-third of the profits," even though Williamson will have to revise the antiquated novel for publication. At the same time, Pohl speculates that "the single attractive element in any sort of publishing deal involving 'Birth of a New Republic' is that it is the sort of elementary idea that might—as a hundred thousand to one long-shot—attract someone in Hollywood. But it is much too much of a long-shot to warrant any investment of your time, or to justify taking much less than your time is worth."[116] Williamson heeded Pohl's advice, and *The Birth of a New Republic* was not reprinted until some years later, when Breuer's lawyer was out of the mix.

Of further interest is an exchange between Pohl and James Gunn in the early months of 1952. In an undated letter Gunn sternly writes to Pohl, remarking that he hasn't heard from Pohl's assistant Larry Shaw for several months and wants to know what's going on with his stories: "The last letter (after a long silence) I had from Larry Shaw was in September. Since then I have received no report on the status of my stories in your hands, no acknowledgment of receipt of a story I sent you several months ago, no statement of my income from your agency for 1951 for tax purposes, and no answer to a letter of inquiry sent over a month ago. In addition, Larry wrote on a Christmas card something to this effect: 'Lots to tell you. Will write soon.' That is a hell of a note to leave hanging in the air."[117] On March 3 Pohl writes back formally that Shaw has left the agency, and he skillfully appeases Gunn's chagrin. The next day he sends Gunn another short letter disclosing the financial information he requested. When Gunn writes back on March 8, Mr. Pohl is now Fred; and in Pohl's return letter, Mr. Gunn is now Jimmie.[118] Hence the spark that ignited a lifelong friendship. Although he had been Gunn's agent for a number of years, Gunn and Pohl first met at the 1952 World Con in Chicago. Gunn was working as an editor for Western Printing Company in Racine, Wisconsin. When he met Pohl, Williamson, and others at the Con, Gunn was inspired to quit and pursue freelance writing full time. As Gunn reflects in his unpublished memoir:

> I remember standing in a corridor talking to Fred; he said he had sold four stories for me: "Survival Policy" to John Campbell at *Astounding*, "The Misogynist" to

Horace Gold at *Galaxy*, "The Boy with Five Fingers" to *Thrilling Wonder Stories*, and "Breaking Point" to Lester Del Rey at *Space Science Fiction*. I took the train back to Racine, filled with renewed enthusiasm about a writing career and a deeper sense that I wanted to work harder and write better to earn the right to belong to this wonderful group, who were dedicated not just to literary pursuits but to its vision of a better world. . . . And I decided, on the feeble evidence of Fred's announcement, that I would quit my job and return to full-time writing.[119]

That first meeting between Pohl and Gunn would be the beginning of a fruitful professional friendship, capped by a long association with Gunn's summer teaching institute and writing workshop at the University of Kansas. As if anticipating their sixty-year friendship, Pohl wrote to Gunn on November 7, 1952, regarding a second encounter in New York that fall: "Enjoyed meeting you again and talking with you at greater length. I think our association can be mutually enjoyable and profitable."[120]

Pohl's agency was a financial sinkhole. By the time he folded it in the summer of 1953, he was thirty thousand dollars in debt and left a number of his clients hanging. On July 21 he wrote to Gunn that he was closing the agency:

Dear Jimmie:

> With a great deal of reluctance, I am going to have to retire from the literary agency profession, effective as soon as I can wind up all the loose ends. It has been an interesting seven-year experiment; I am proud of what has been accomplished in that time, but a man has to make up his mind what he intends to devote his life to, and I don't intend to devote mine to this. The writers I have been handling, yourself included, are, for my money, just about the best group of writers assembled anywhere on the face of the earth. . . . If you like, I will continue to work with your material for a while yet; but, on the other hand, if you wish to make other arrangements for your new material, please feel free to do so with or without notification to me. . . . It has been a pleasure working with you, Jimmie. I expect you to go far.[121]

It took him many years to clear the ledgers. But through it all, Frederik Pohl's years as a literary agent elevated the field of science fiction in terms of both literary art and as a financially viable commodity in the literary marketplace.

At this time, Pohl also got involved in editing for the booming anthology market. After the war, in 1946, R. J. Healy and J. F. McComas published a major anthology of stories, mostly from *Astounding*, called *Adventures in Time and Space* for Random House, and Groff Conklin put together the first of many anthologies for Crown, *The Best of Science Fiction*. These were followed by the first "Best of the Year" anthology in 1949 for Frederik Fell, edited by E. F. Bleiler and T. E. Dikty. Doubleday wanted to get into the game, and they asked Robert Heinlein to edit an anthology, *Tomorrow, the Stars*, published in 1952. Heinlein was happy to put his name on the project and write an introduction, but he didn't want to select the stories. Since Merril had already edited an anthology for Bantam, and since Pohl was representing a good portion of the writers in the field, they were enlisted to "ghost" the anthology for Heinlein.[122] Heinlein acknowledges their contribution in the introduction.[123] The success of *Tomorrow, the Stars* led Pohl to edit two anthologies for Doubleday's paperback imprint Permabooks, *Beyond the End of Time* and *Shadow of Tomorrow*, later followed by *Assignment in Tomorrow* in hardcover.

⋆ ⋆ ⋆

As his marriage with Merril was coming apart, Pohl had not been writing much for several years and wanted to get back to it. He started tinkering around with an SF novel about advertising (which he called *Fall Campaign*) that salvaged some of the ideas from his wartime advertising novel, transforming them into an SFnal setting. By 1951 Pohl had about twenty thousand words in rough draft. He sent it to Gold who, wanted to buy it and run it right after Alfred Bester's *The Demolished Man* concluded. By then Pohl and Merril had moved into the big house in Red Bank, New Jersey. The Kornbluths were staying with them at the time. One night, Pohl showed the manuscript to Kornbluth, who began working on it where Pohl left off. The Pohl-Kornbluth collaboration was reignited. The novel was published in the June, July, and August issues of *Galaxy* in 1952 as *Gravy Planet*. And thus began Pohl's *Galaxy* years, the subject of the next chapter.

CHAPTER 2

THE GALAXY YEARS, 1952–1969

The early 1950s were marred by the Cold War paranoia of McCarthyism, when intellectuals around the country were investigated, indicted, and otherwise harassed. Curiously, the science fiction community, by and large, was not brought before the McCarthyite witch hunters, even though they had been writing stories about atomic war, political oppression, and future power-politics and global political realignment for years. For instance, read in light of the era in which they were written, it is surprising that the Pohl and Kornbluth novels *The Space Merchants* and *Gladiator-At-Law* (let alone any number of novels by other SF writers) did not attract the forces of political oppression, particularly given Pohl's former dabbling in communist political circles. Pohl believes that while free speech was under attack in other arenas, science fiction was able to maintain a level of subversiveness simply because the mundane reader was unable to penetrate the reading protocols of science fiction. In "Ragged Claws," Pohl conjectured that "there was one surviving area of free speech in the country: the science fiction magazines."[1] And the magazine that was publishing the most edgy and subversive SF was *Galaxy*.

Pohl had been selling his clients' stories to Horace Gold, editor at *Galaxy*, since the magazine's launch in October 1950. *Galaxy* had an immediate impact on the SF marketplace and instantly established itself as the leading competitor to Campbell's *Astounding*. Like *Astounding*, *Galaxy* ran on a monthly publication schedule and featured two or three serialized novels a year. Through early 1952 the magazine had featured such serials as Simak's *Time Quarry* (*Time and Again*), Asimov's *Tyrann* (*The Stars, Like Dust*), Kornbluth and Merril's *Mars Child* (*Outpost Mars*), Heinlein's *The Puppet Masters*, and Bester's *The Demolished Man*. The next serial following this illustrious group was Pohl and Kornbluth's *Gravy Planet* (*The Space Merchants*), which in many ways would come to define the magazine. Pohl would go on to contribute a total of eight serials and thirty-seven stories to *Galaxy* over the next two decades, becoming the writer most representative of the magazine's vision, and eventually he succeeded Gold and became its editor.

Gravy Planet took the SF world by storm. Here was a slick, cynical, dystopian world where corporate greed and dubious business practices had blunted the minds of citizens, mass-consumption had eaten up the planet, and overpopulation was leading humanity to the brink of cataclysm. Appearing immediately after Bester's *The Demolished Man*, these novels were redefining the genre *and* the future. In the editorial preceding the first installment, Gold prepared the audience for what they were about to read, claiming that, like its predecessor, *Gravy Planet* "should also be a landmark in science fiction," waxing enthusiastically by calling it as "brilliant as a blaze in a fireworks factory, suspenseful as crossing Niagara Falls on a tight wire." Gold remarks that *Gravy Planet* is a quintessential "what if" story: "What would happen if any given situation is carried to the utmost extremes we are capable of imagining?"[2] Retitled *The Space Merchants*, a revised version that leaves out the last chapter from the serial, it was published in book form by the fledgling Ballantine Books, simultaneously in hardcover and paperback.

But before *The Space Merchants* launched in April 1953, Pohl was to initiate Ballantine's science fiction line with another book. Ian and Betty Ballantine had been the founding editors of Bantam Books but decided to branch out and start their own paperback line. Pohl was a key figure in the establishment of Ballantine Books, as he supplied them with manuscripts from many of his clients and most prominently from Pohl himself. To start Ballantine's science fiction line, Pohl began the *Star Science Fiction* series, the first original anthology series in the genre. The first *Star* anthology saw print in February of 1953. Pohl paid double the rate the magazines were paying, and because he was the agent for many of the leading writers, he was able to select their best work.[3] The volume included stories by William Morrison, Kornbluth, Del Rey, Leiber, Simak, Wyndham, William Tenn, Gold, Merril, Bradbury, Sheckley, Kuttner and Moore, and Murray Leinster; the most important story in the volume is undoubtedly Arthur C. Clarke's "The Nine Billion Names of God." *Galaxy* reviewer Groff Conklin recognized *Star* as a breakthrough in SF publishing, congratulating the publisher for "selecting an editor who knows good science fiction."[4] In *Imagination*, reviewer Mark Reinsberg said the "remarkably good anthology" was "a tribute to [Pohl's] gathering as well as editorial abilities."[5] *Star* was to become the model for all subsequent anthology series, such as Damon Knight's *Orbit*, Terry Carr's *Universe*, and Robert Silverberg's *New Dimensions*. Silverberg claims, "[*Star*] served me for many years as a model of the kind of science fiction I wanted to write and the kind of anthology I wanted to edit."[6] By the end of the year Ballantine had published an impressive array of science fiction novels and story collections, including Clarke's *Childhood's End* and *Expedition to Earth*, Bradbury's *Fahrenheit 451*, Sturgeon's *More than Human*, Wyndham's *Out of the Deeps*, Ward Moore's *Bring the Jubilee*, and, of course, *The Space Merchants*.

The Space Merchants is a satire on advertising and consumer culture as it was emerging in the 1950s (lately on display in the popular television series *Mad Men*). It resonates with a number of studies in the social sciences from the decade, particularly Vance Packard's *The Hidden Persuaders* and *The Status Seekers*, William Whyte's *The Organization Man*, Erich Fromm's *The Sane Society*, and David Reisman's *The Lonely Crowd*. The novel is set in a just-around-the-corner future, some of which has now come to pass. The world is dominated by corporate advertising. The task of Fowler Schocken Associates that is set in motion at the beginning of the novel is to sell people on migration to Venus. The world is overpopulated, and there are deep class divisions among consumers and laborers and the "Star class" elites. Government is controlled by corporations to the extent that members of Congress represent corporations, not states, with the more powerful corporations having more votes accordingly. The president is merely a figurehead; the presidency is, in fact, an inherited office.

The novel is told through the first-person narration of Mitch Courtenay, one of the leading executives within Fowler Schocken Associates. He is ambitious, sharp, sly, and wholly believes in the system, demonstrated when he tries to garner Fowler's approval after Fowler's speech in the conference room: "I leaned forward with Expression One—eagerness, intelligence, competence—all over my face" (5). By using the first-person narrator, Pohl and Kornbluth limit the viewpoint but nonetheless are able to convey the backdrop of the world through Courtenay's remarks and observations. As a "true believer," like the narrator of "Earth, Farewell!" Courtenay perceives his world through a distorted and naïve lens. Thus, the reader immediately feels as if he or she understands Courtenay's world better than he does, so that as Courtenay's perceptions are gradually enlightened to the reality of his world, the reader has already connected with what is wrong and is therefore able to identify with Mitch's awakening.

Pohl and Kornbluth masterfully establish the science fiction setting in the first few pages of the novel, when Courtenay prepares for the workday. The world is going to hell; resources are depleted and the natural environment is virtually destroyed. The reality of the situation is revealed immediately, allowing the reader to pick up similar clues as the novel moves forward, expanding the image of a world on the edge of apocalypse. Consider the first sentence of the second paragraph: "I rubbed depilatory soap over my face and rinsed it with the trickle from the freshwater tap" (1). In his classic critical essay, "Science Fiction and 'Literature'; or, The Conscience of the King," Samuel R. Delany points to this opening sentence as indicative of the science fiction sentence, which asks us to imagine "what in the world of the tale would have to be different from our world for such a sentence to be uttered."[7] The trickle of fresh water quickly "stopped and didn't start again." To use freshwater is "wasteful, of course, but I pay the water taxes, and saltwater always leaves my face itchy" (1). This establishes that there is a severe water crisis, when even a luxury apartment has limited access to fresh water. In Delany's terms, "As the sentences build up, we build up a world in specific dialogue, in a specific tension, with our present concept of reality."[8] Further, Mitch watches the "morning newscast above the shaving mirror" (1), indicating that there is video all over the place, mostly devoted to advertising, but it also is the first clue that Mitch's living space is tiny. There is simply no room in his "luxury" apartment for the differentiations of space between bathroom, living room, bedroom, and so on.

More world-building occurs when Courtenay goes to work. When he enters the Fowler Shocken office's ten-by-twelve-foot conference room, he comments that "every piece of furniture is constructed from top to bottom of authentic, expertized, genuine tree-grown wood" (3). This emphasis on authenticity indicates that wood is a rare, luxurious commodity, which further implies severe environmental degradation. Fowler Schocken has "authentic" furnishings because they are rare and he can afford it. As Fowler calls the meeting to order, he remarks, "I don't think there's a person in this room who has less than a two-room apartment," more directly emphasizing that space is at a high premium, that even the elites have very small apartments. Next Fowler boasts, "I haven't tasted any protein but new meat for years, and when I go out for a spin I pedal a Cadillac" (3). This clues the reader in that food is synthetic and that there are varying gradations of quality—"new meat" is not meat, but it is presumably the best on the market; fuel is scarce, at least for ground vehicles. We get a hint of what the non-elite consumers are eating later in the conversation: "'[F]or the school lunch program[,] soyaburgers and regenerated steak'—there wasn't a man around the table who didn't shudder at the thought of soyaburgers and regenerated steak" (4)—one suspects that regenerated steak is composed of Star-class waste. Further, the degree to which consumer manipulation (and addiction) starts early is indicated by the fact that there is a "Kiddiebutt cigarette ration" included with the meals. Similarly, "Coffiest," a coffee product that is laced with an addictive alkaloid, is pushed onto consumers, who will subsequently be addicted for life.

Thus, in the first few pages through Courtenay's narration and Fowler's discourse, Pohl and Kornbluth are able to establish, without relying on an omniscient narrative infodump, that overpopulation and overcrowding are the norm, that the biosphere is vastly diminished, that human consumption has nearly eaten up the planet, that advertisements run constantly through invasive media, that consumer products are deliberately made addictive, and that *all this is taken for granted*: Courtenay blithely accepts this as it is, having no awareness that *it was ever different* or *that it could be different.* It is a brilliant sequence of science fiction stage setting and would have enormous influence on the development of the storytelling methods of the genre. Referring to Fowler's speech to the executives, James Gunn considers it exemplary as a science fiction touchstone, which he defines as "the element of discontinuity that makes the work science fiction. Science-fiction touchstones should bring the reader up short, cause a re-evaluation of older ideas or an adjustment to new conditions, make the reader think."[9] Touchstones pile upon touchstones throughout the narrative of *The Space Merchants.*

A key theme in the novel is hyperconsumption, which has led to the entire subcontinent of India being turned into Indiastries, "a single manufacturing complex" (4). Advertising is ubiquitous and invasive: the next step will be to project ads directly onto the retina of the eye. Courtenay eerily observes, "The highest form of our art is to convince the customer without letting him know he's being convinced" (70). Spying is rampant, and companies must set up defenses to keep others out. There is literal corporate warfare, but it has to follow set rules of battle. Pohl and Kornbluth also suggest a degradation of language and art: poets are hired as jingle writers and the Metropolitan Museum of Art proudly exhibits a brazier display as the pinnacle of product advertising. Further, the memorial Mall in Washington has become a place where one makes solemn pilgrimage to see the "martyrs" of advertising, and the Lincoln Memorial has a corporate sponsor emblazoned on its once hallowed marble.

As one of the top men at Fowler Schocken, Courtenay is put in charge of the Venus account, teaming up with Jack O'Shea, a dwarf who is the only human to successfully complete a mission to the planet. O'Shea explains that Venus is uninhabitable, just "sand and smoke" (22), but Courtenay is not interested in the practicality of Venus migration, only in the game of salesmanship. An attempt is made on Courtenay's life after their meeting and then again at his apartment. Suspecting his rival in the firm, Matt Runstead, Courtenay travels to San Diego to check on the market test in the Cal-Mex testing zone, the home of 100 million people, where earthquakes are now almost a daily occurrence due to H-Bomb tests that fractured the San Andreas Fault. When he finds the test has been sabotaged, he tracks Runstead to the

Antarctica resort where Star-class executives vacation, following him far out onto the glacier. There, Runstead clubs him over the head, leaving him to die on the ice, ending the first section of the novel.

Courtenay wakes up in a transport ship to find that he has been shanghaied and is heading to Costa Rica to be impressed into the Chlorella food factory, where a vast lump of flesh called Chicken Little is cultured, sliced, and processed to provide the meager "real" meat supply for the world's wealthiest elites. His identification tattoo has been altered to twenty-one digits, masking his real eight-digit Social Security number. Now a faceless consumer, Courtenay is unable to make contact with the people who know him in New York; he sees his own obituary and realizes he's been railroaded. In the slave labor conditions of the Chlorella plant, Courtenay's job is to skim the algae tanks for nutrients to be pumped into Chicken Little. The work is grueling, and he soon realizes that if he doesn't find a way out soon, he never will; he will thus fall permanently into a life of hopeless anonymity, endless consumption, and wage slavery. Courtenay begins, then, to use his advertising skills to work the system in order to find his way out. Working his way to the top of the proletarian hierarchy, where he befriends Chicken Little's "Master Slicer," Herrera, he is initiated into a secret Consie (radical conservationists) cell whose base of operations is under the mass of Chicken Little's throbbing flesh. The irony that the secret organization fighting against the environmental degradation hides under hyperconsumerism's greatest symbol, Chicken Little, is just one of the many wry ironies built into the framework of the novel.

At first, Courtenay's intentions are merely to use the Consies to get himself back to New York and Fowler Schocken, where he can then expose them and use the situation as a springboard to the higher reaches of the firm. But as he experiences what life is like for the consumer class, his obtuse assumptions about his world begin to break, made especially vivid when he faces the cycle of addiction that his firm has perpetuated:

> I'd been paid again, and my debt had increased by eight dollars. I'd tormented myself by wondering where the money went, but I knew. . . . The Crunchies kicked off withdrawal symptoms that could be quelled only by another two squirts of Popsie from the fountain. And Popsie kicked off withdrawal symptoms that could only be quelled by smoking Starr Cigarettes, which made you hungry

for Crunchies. . . . If I didn't get out soon I never would. I could feel my initiative, the thing that made me *me*, dying, cell by cell, within me. The minute dosages of alkaloid were sapping my will, but most of all it was a hopeless, trapped feeling that things were this way, that they always would be this way, that it wasn't too bad, that you could always go into trance or get really lit on Popsie (110–11).

Still, the veil has not completely lifted from Courtenay's eyes at this point: he still believes in the perpetuity and efficacy of the system. The reader, however, clearly sees that the topsy-turvy values of hyperconsumption must change for humanity to survive.

Once back in New York, Courtenay journeys to the executive suites of the Fowler Schocken building, finally making contact with his secretary, Hester. Fowler has gone to the Moon, having taken on the Venus account himself. Courtenay follows, and in a dramatic scene in the enclosed Moon habitat, he is escorted to Fowler by the company's armed Pinkertons. Courtenay lays out the story to Fowler, but Fowler refuses to believe him. At this moment, Courtenay attains his own enlightenment and understands the problems facing his world:

> Poor old Fowler. Who could blame him? His own dream-world was under attack by every word I had to say. My story was blasphemy against the god of Sales. He couldn't believe it, and he couldn't believe that I—the real I—believed it. How could Mitchell Courtenay, copysmith, be sitting there and telling him such frightful things as:
> The interests of producers and consumers are not identical.
> Most of the world is unhappy.
> Workmen don't automatically find the job they do best.
> Entrepreneurs don't play a hard, fair game by the rules.
> The Consies are sane, intelligent, and well-organized. (190–91)

Things move quickly from there: all return to Earth; Fowler is murdered, as Courtenay feared; and a power struggle ensues between the executives in the firm. In a sequence of events that recalls Keefe's rise to the seat of power in "It's a Young World," Courtenay follows a trail of dummy corporations that Fowler had set up and is able to secure enough shares to ascend to the leadership of Fowler Schocken Associates. From there he is reunited with his contract-wife Kathy, a leader in the Consie underground, and he covertly works with the Consies to prepare for a Consie migration to Venus, finally appearing before Congress in Washington, where it becomes evident that the only option left for the Consies is to flee Earth, leaving the planet to its own demise. In the *Galaxy* serial, Gold insisted on a concluding chapter showing the expedition living on Venus. This chapter was cut for the book version, which ends with Courtenay, Kathy, and the Consie radicals reaching free fall in space as they escape Earth's gravity well.

In addition to its indictment of a corporate social order, the novel is notable for its environmental perspective. *The Space Merchants* anticipates the contemporary crisis of global climate change and shows how the problem can be denied even though the evidence is strikingly apparent. In the degraded future of *The Space Merchants* people accept the status quo, erasing history and never considering the future. In this way, the novel sounds an alarm to take action, to resist drifting into complacency. Some critics consider this merely background, secondary to the primary theme of advertising satire, but it is a central theme throughout, for the world is on the brink of collapse, though still more or less barely functioning in chaos. Eric Otto observes that the ethos of consumer capitalism and environmental degradation go hand in hand: "The exhausted ecology represented in *The Space Merchants* is the result of the reckless consumption encouraged by advertising's ubiquitous fictional and concealing narratives."[10] The outside air of Manhattan is so polluted that people routinely don "antisoot plugs." Plants and animals are in short supply, evident when Kathy chides Courtenay for wanting to buy her a real flower: "Oh, Mitch, you needn't be extravagant. We aren't courting and I already know you have more money than God" (54). At dinner, Courtenay is incensed at the quality of the faux meat: "I don't pretend to be an epicure who can't stand anything but new protein. I definitely am, however, a guy who gets sore when he pays new-protein prices and gets regenerated-protein merchandise" (33). Fossil fuels are virtually depleted: not only does Fowler Schocken own a "pedi-Cadillac," but Courtenay flags down a "two-man pedicab" (35), brilliantly depicted in the original cover illustration in *Galaxy* by Emsh. And to make matters worse, topsoil depletion is leading to cataclysm, but Courtenay takes the standard do-nothing position when bombasting about a hypothetical debate with a Consie: "It always winds up with him telling me the world's going to hell in a handbasket and people have got to be made to realize it—and me telling him we've always got along somehow and we'll keep going somehow" (65). In Washington, the "famous cherry blossoms" are still "beautiful," even though the trees no longer exist: "With my newfound Conservationist sentiments, I found them objectionably ostentatious. 'A dozen would have been plenty,' I objected. 'Scattering them around in vase after vase this way is a plain waste of the taxpayer's money'" (225). As if to reinforce the point for readers, as Mitch and Kathy prepare for the trip to Venus, Pohl and Kornbluth have Kathy remark: "Wait till we take over Venus. Did you ever think of what it's going to be like to have a whole *planet* to grow things in? Acres and acres of flowers—trees—everything?" (226). It is surprising that Pohl and Kornbluth were able to imagine such an environmentally degraded future at the time, since the more common outlook in science fiction, and even in a significant portion of mainstream discourse, was that human beings weren't likely to survive long enough to gobble up all of the planet's resources. Instead, nuclear holocaust was presumed imminent, as in Bradbury's *Fahrenheit 451* or Wilson Tucker's *The Long Loud Silence*, a scenario that Pohl himself would explore in some of his short works as the decade progressed.

The cause of this environmental catastrophe is not only hyperconsumption but also the overextension of the environmental niche by human overpopulation. There are simply too many people on Earth, as O'Shea remonstrates: "Too damn many people, Mitch. Too damn much crowding. I'm with you every inch of the way. We *need* Venus, Mitch, we need the space . . ." (30). People are cooped up. The high premium put on living space is evident throughout the novel. When Mitch goes to Kathy's apartment, there is no room for furniture, even though she is a successful professional. The typical family routinely folds up the daytime furniture to get out the beds at night. Most, however, find themselves sleeping in stairwells in the corporate skyscrapers, paying a hefty premium to do so. The implication is that most people are essentially homeless. This overpopulation theme is worked out to its fullest form in Harry Harrison's *Make Room! Make Room!* filmed as *Soylent Green*, but overpopulation is a recurring theme throughout Pohl's work, still emerging as a central focus in such late works as *Land's End*, *The World at the End of Time*, and *The Voices of Heaven*.

At the same time, Pohl and Kornbluth do not really resolve the problem that they set in motion. Mitch Courtenay and the Consies flee Earth at the end of the novel, leaving it to its own environmental catastrophe. Roger Luckhurst reminds us, however, when writing in the context of the novel, "Satire is driven by the desire to interrogate the Establishment, not to formulate alternatives."[11] To solve the problems of Earth, the book posits that humanity must first get off planet, expand the human nest within the solar system. The novel ends with the dream of space, the common SFnal belief of the time that space travel might be the means by which humanity resolves many of its earthly problems, the message that the way to fix Earth is to expand into space. Perhaps that is the solution Pohl and Kornbluth had to offer.

Reviewers found *The Space Merchants* scintillating, although many found fault with the title change. *Galaxy*'s reviewer Groff Conklin compared it favorably to Huxley's *Brave New World*, found it better than Vonnegut's *Player Piano* and "vastly superior" to Orwell's "dull and overrated" *1984*. Conklin lauds the changed ending from the original serial, arguing that "what we now have is a well-nigh perfect attack on the stupid, the cynical, the mercenary, the power-crazy tendencies of the Salesmen's Civilization," concluding that *The Space Merchants*, in the broad sense of all literature, is "a permanent addition to the good books of our era" and "*not* 'just another science fiction book.'"[12] In an astute review in *Dynamic Science Fiction* Katherine MacLean remarked that on first reading in its serial form, she took the story "to be merely an entertaining hunt-and-chase thriller, with the background of advertising horrors for laughs, a satire on the way things are now." But on second reading in book form, and having reflected on "the gruesomeness of the advertising we have grown numb to," MacLean shuddered to think "it begins to look more like a trend than a joke." Like Conklin, MacLean also favored the revised book version as "smoother and more entertaining," but confessed she couldn't "read more than a few pages at a time before the background gives me the whillies."[13]

Above, I have sketched only some of the details from this rich, engrossing, thought-provoking novel. *The Space Merchants* is now considered one of the essential books of the field. Writing three decades ago, David Pringle remarked that "the book has succeeded in becoming more relevant to the decades that followed,"[14] and that remains true today. It certainly remains the best of the Pohl-Kornbluth collaborations—sharp, witty, edgy, and politically relevant. And because of the environmental theme and its diagnosis of consumer culture, the book still holds up pretty well. Students with only a dim view about what life was like in the early stages of consumer capitalism, when the novel was written, find the story particularly engaging and relevant to the future they are facing.

It would be almost another two years before Pohl returned to the pages of *Galaxy*, as he spent much of 1953 closing up the agency, ending his marriage with Merril, and starting a new one with Carol Ulf. When Pohl and Merril had initially split, he rented an apartment in Greenwich Village, and Ulf had moved in with him. The break with Merril had become messy, as they got embroiled in a custody battle over Ann, instigated by Merril's first husband, who was seeking custody of his own daughter by declaring Merril an unfit mother. Finally, a shared custody agreement was reached, but then Merril ceded custody to Pohl, feeling that her own life was too unstable at the time. Eventually, Ann went back to live with Merril once she had settled down in Milford, Pennsylvania, and over the years Pohl and Merril were to become friends again, brought together, in part, by having mutual grandchildren, but also because of their shared interest in developing the field of science fiction.[15] Pohl's only story published during 1953 was a collaboration with Merril with the intriguing title "A Big Man with the Girls," about a tiny alien spaceship that lands on a woman's lawn, and this still appeared under the James Mac-Creigh pseudonym. Meanwhile, Pohl prepared a second volume in the *Star* series, which included Jerome Bixby's "It's a *Good* Life," later adapted into a classic *Twilight Zone* episode.

The beginning of 1954 saw the publication of "The Ghost Maker" in *Beyond* in January, Gold's short-lived fantasy companion to *Galaxy*, and the second Pohl-Kornbluth novel, *Search the Sky*, as a Ballantine original in February, before two major works appeared in *Galaxy* later that spring: "The Midas Plague" and *Gladiator-At-Law*. Pohl would finish this first really productive year with his first of ten collaborative novels with Jack Williamson, *Undersea Quest*, for the juvenile market. In the meantime, Fred and Carol proceeded to start a family: Frederik Pohl III was born in November 1954.[16] Tragically, the infant developed an illness and died only a month later, leaving them devastated. When their next child was born in January 1956, they named him Frederik Pohl IV. Pohl would later collaborate with his son on a book about science fiction cinema, *Science Fiction: Studies in Film*.

"The Midas Plague," Pohl's single story in *Galaxy* in 1954 and the first solo work that would appear under his own name, was, like *The Space Merchants*, a different order of magnitude than Pohl's prior stories, and it came to be one of the defining works of his career, later being selected as one of the "Hall of Fame" novellas by the Science Fiction Writers of America. Like *The Space Merchants*, "The Midas Plague" is a satire on hyperconsumption. Here, Pohl presents a topsy-turvy world where instead of the austere, near-cataclysmic world of scarcity seen in *The Space Merchants*, the problem is abundance and endless cycles of production. In the world of "The Midas Plague," to be poor is to live in opulent luxury and have the legal obligation to consume goods at an alarming rate in order to keep up with manufacturing quotas. Whereas to be rich is to have the luxury not to consume and live in inauspicious circumstances.

The story presents the life of Morey Fry, a poor man who is set to marry a rich girl, turning about the classic poor girl/rich boy theme brilliantly. Being poor, Morey has to consume at a high level, and his wife from a wealthy background, having little experience with excessive consumption, is unable to keep up. Morey's ridiculous consumption obligations are highlighted when he attends his weekly group psychotherapy session, where instead of a group of patients sharing their problems with a therapist, Morey has group therapy with a parcel of therapists: "four Freudians, two Reichians, two Jungians, a Gestalter, a shock therapist and the elderly and rather quiet Sullivanite" (10). Initially, Morey tries to cheat the system by taking up the slack, but to consume at such a rate is exhausting. In an effort to dispose of some of their extra ration coupons, Morey gets in contact with the fringe underworld of disenfranchised consumers, where he learns that the cycle of consumption is a direct result of over production facilitated by robots, or, rather, by quite literal means of mechanical production: "'Robots!' she hissed. 'Supposed to work for us, aren't they? Hah! We're their slaves, slaves for every moment of every miserable day of our lives. Slaves! Wouldn't you like to join us and be free, Morey?'" (27). Like the Consies in *The Space Merchants*, the idea of an underground movement seeking to change the world and anticipating a better future is consistent with the overall attitude of the Futurians and the science fiction community.

In a fit of drunken desperation, Morey sets his robots the task of consuming his goods, the gravest crime imaginable. In the end, Morey's crime revolutionizes society, and he becomes a hero by resolving the problem of consumption: "Mr. Fry, the National Ration Board is delighted to know of your contribution toward improving our distribution problem. Pending further study, a tentative program has been adopted for setting up consuming-robot units all over the country based on your scheme. Penalties? Mr. Fry, you're a *hero!*" (55). At first glance, this exaggeration seems absurd, and one might feel that Pohl cheated in the resolution of the problem he set up. Why have the robots consume? Why not change the consumption paradigm altogether? But this is, after all, satire—the initial premise is meant to be absurd. What Pohl cleverly allows the reader to realize is that human beings seldom act rationally or make sensible life choices.

Like Jack Williamson's *The Humanoids*, "The Midas Plague" takes the assumptions of Asimov's robot stories and turns them upside down. But whereas Williamson's humanoids make human action impossible, killing humanity with kindness, Pohl focuses more on the resultant social system of a robot economy of abundance. As noted earlier, Pohl was tightly connected with both writers. Together, the three variations on the robot theme give readers a range of thought experiments to facilitate thinking on the question of machine intelligence and the possible social consequences such a technological breakthrough could bring about. This illustrates Pohl's point that SF is "the game-playing literature." SF writers use what Pohl calls the "science-fiction method": "The sf method is parallelistic, universal, and antideterministic. If we throw dice and see a six come up, the layman sees only a six; the writer using the sf method sees that a six *has* come up, but that any of five other possibilities *might have* come up."[17]

The second Pohl-Kornbluth collaboration appeared in the pages of *Galaxy* precisely two years after *Gravy Planet* in the June 1954 issue. *Gladiator-At-Law* has a similar pattern to its predecessor, with Wall Street venture capitalists filling the role of the Madison Avenue advertisers. A classic in its own right, it nonetheless fails to rise all the way to the level of *The Space Merchants*. This is perhaps because the story is told in the third-person and does not have the insider-who-wises-up, tightly focused, first-person voice that was so effective in the prior novel—although the third-person narration does allow for a greater range of narrative exploration.

The major themes Pohl and Kornbluth focus on in *Gladiator-At-Law* include the law, housing, venture capital and corporate shareholding, poverty, and, again, overpopulation. As in *The Space Merchants*, the government has become repressive: there are hints throughout that people are living under a corporate dictatorship. The main conceit is that a cheap form of mass-produced dome-housing, "G.M.L. Homes," has been created, but speculative venture capitalists, who reap profits while the majority of people slip into abject poverty, have overinflated the housing market, rendering the homes unaffordable. The initial democratizing purpose behind the homes has been corrupted by these greedy capitalists, who have used the homes to create a contract-labor system under which labor has no recourse but to fall in line or else be cast out among the disenfranchised in the slums. Anticipating the housing crisis in contemporary America and the growing wealth gap, in this sense *Gladiator-At-Law*'s message is in some ways more powerful than what we encounter in *The Space Merchants*, though *Gladiator*'s narrative is not quite as potent. Like the previous works, *Gladiator-At-Law* is also a satire on American consumerism. But here Pohl and Kornbluth look at how big business suppresses innovation, manipulates markets, and fosters complacency among citizens, turning them into "customers" rather than patrons or free democratic citizenry.

Lawyer Charles Mundin is retained by Norma Lavin, the daughter of the inventor of the homes. Mundin is a public defender of sorts, not having a great deal of success in his practice because of a hierarchical social structure that benefits the unqualified children of the wealthy elite at the expense of everyone else. The social order privileges inheritance, nepotism, and personal favors rather than merit and hard work. As in "The Midas Plague," computers and robotization have contributed to the disenfranchisement of human labor and civic obligation. The Lavins are being squeezed out of the company by Moffatt, a corporate raider who took over the enterprise and quashed the democratizing vision of its founders, who nevertheless still hold 25 percent of the shares. Norma Lavin wants to uphold the original vision of her father. To keep the founders at bay, Norma's brother has been illegally "conditioned" by the other side: he's the only one who knows where the shares are, but due to the conditioning he can't remember where. Norma's explication of how Moffatt took over the company is an intense depiction of how corporate America has developed, with unscrupulous venture capitalists making fortunes by doing nothing more than manipulating stocks, products, and markets. Although not as crisply told as its predecessor, *Gladiator-At-Law* is still quite effective in critiquing the links between rapacious venture capitalism and the decay and destruction of civil society.

In New York, the disenfranchised poor live in the slum "Belly Rave," which is located in the districts that were the suburbs of the 1950s. Pohl and Kornbluth recognized the pattern of urban development and decay, where the suburbs would eventually decline into zones of poverty and the inner city would be gentrified for elites, a trend many metropolitan cities have been going through in the past few decades. The description of how Belle Reve decayed into the slum Belly Rave reads like something out of Upton Sinclair's *The Jungle*: the corruption of the real estate salespeople, the poor quality of construction, the inescapable payments, the environmental problems, the decline of hopes and dreams into despair.

Another important theme that emerges from the poverty of Belly Rave is violent youth gangs in the slums. The rise of these gangs is an important element in the novel, and one which was highly topical at the time. Psychiatrist Frederick Wertham had released his notorious report on the dangers of comic books, *Seduction of the Innocent*, that year, linking comics with juvenile delinquency. Hal Ellson, a recreational therapist at Bellevue Hospital in New York, who worked primarily with troubled youngsters, was penning timely novels about delinquent inner city kids and youth gangs, such as *Duke* (1949) and *Tomboy* (1950). His 1952 novel *The Golden Spike* was the second book published by Ballantine Books, following Cameron Hawley's novel of corporate management, *Executive Suite*, which also has resonances with the Pohl-Kornbluth novels. Indeed, inspired by Ellson's work, particularly *Tomboy*, youthful SF writer Harlan Ellison went so far as to join a street gang around the time the book version of *Gladiator-At-Law* came out.[18] In his book on science fiction film, Pohl notes that Anthony Burgess's later *A Clockwork Orange* responds to the same sort of social phenomenon examined in *Gladiator-At-Law*, albeit set in London and registering a much more intense scale of violence.[19] In *Gladiator*, very small children are drafted into street gangs, known as the Wabbits and the Goddams, first introduced when a news broadcast reports that war has broken out between the two gangs in Belly Rave and "one eight-year-old was killed instantly" (33). These gangs of roving little kids are feared throughout the city.

Violence is made even more vivid in the novel through the depiction of literal gladiatorial combat as a popular spectator sport. Opportunity for the mass of citizens is so limited that in order to survive, people can sell themselves for gladiatorial combat during "Field Day," with proceeds going to their families, especially if they are killed—a likely outcome, anticipating such stories as Robert Sheckley's *The Tenth Victim*, Stephen King's *The Running Man*, and Suzanne Collins's *The Hunger Games*. There are three things going on here that have led to the rise of the Field Day as an accepted part of social ritual: overpopulation, a chasm-like gap between rich and poor, and media spectacle. Here Pohl and Kornbluth anticipate the observations of Guy DeBord in his famous argument *Society of the Spectacle*, where "commodity fetishism" comes to override all else and "all life presents itself as an immense accumulation of spectacles."[20] Indeed, the Field Day is an extreme, though natural, extrapolation from the rising spectacle of sport in American society.

The Field Day plot introduces a second major character, Norvell Bligh, who has the qualities of those down-and-out characters often seen in the works of Philip K. Dick, which may indicate a Pohl-Kornbluth influence on the younger Dick. Bligh is an "emotional engineer" for the Field Days, events which provide "escape" to the masses—"it siphons off their aggressions so that they can devote their time to—uh—to comparatively harmless activities" (41), meaning it keeps people complacent and deluded as the venture capitalists seize control of enormous amounts of capital and power at the people's expense, nullifying the values of the democratic ideal. Bligh gets double-crossed by an assistant who wants his "contract" job, forcing him, his wife, and his daughter to lose all and move to Belly Rave. In Belly Rave Bligh eventually meets up with Norma Lavin and Mundin. Bligh's trajectory into the faceless mass follows the pattern of Mitch Courtenay in *The Space Merchants*, except here, Bligh is not the central viewpoint character but is instead a supporting character whose trajectory adds another dimension to the main storyline involving Mundin's attempt to restore the Lavins' legacy.

In order to get the Lavins a hearing before the stockholders, Mundin sets out to buy one share of G.M.L. at the New York Stock Exchange, which will allow him to attend the stockholder's meeting. The stock exchange is portrayed to be almost like a casino: instead of traders buying and selling shares, Mundin literally throws dice to determine whether the money he put down will secure a share. In the meantime, Norma Lavin has been kidnapped to keep her out of the meeting. While Mundin looks for her in Belly Rave, the two plots come together, and he encounters Norvie Bligh. Bligh has made friends with the Wabbits, led by a sharp, streetwise little girl named Lana, and he enlists them to help find Norma. On the morning of the meeting, Lana and her gang are able to track Norma's whereabouts to the same building as the meeting. At the meeting, Mundin manipulates the proceedings, enlists some sympathetic stockholders to the Lavin camp, and frees Norma from captivity. Eventually, Don Lavin's conditioning is reversed, and they find out where the Lavin stock has been kept, allowing them to plan a takeover by enlisting more allies and securing majority stock. They do this by sabotaging a G.M.L. home in a museum, causing a panic that devalues the stock and allowing them to buy it up at the exchange.

Downtown Manhattan is mostly abandoned, though many of the elite secretly live there. As the novel winds down, Mundin meets with Green and Charlesworth, two ancient investors who live in the Empire State Building and secretly control the market. Green and Charlesworth are so old they live in tanks, floating in baths of nutrient fluid. In a sense they are vampires, sucking the capital of the nation into vast, meaningless personal holdings to satisfy their insatiable lust for power, a scenario that has become all too familiar in recent years. Mundin succeeds in breaking their hold on G.M.L., and their vampiric capitalist paradigm is exposed.

But Green and Charlesworth are not done with the Lavins. A subliminal message compels Don Lavin to sign up for Field Day. All the main characters descend upon the Field Day grounds to prevent a fatal accident. In the end, Bligh saves Don through a heroic decision to sacrifice himself, but instead the Master of Ceremonies at the games is pushed into a tank of piranhas, and Bligh is rescued. Soon following, the takeover succeeds and G.M.L. homes are made affordable, as they were intended, thus defeating the greed of the investment banking culture and allowing the legitimate values of American democracy to prevail.

When the novel began serialization, Gold devoted his editorial to it. He points out that the novel works on many levels besides plot: it features a logically constructed society; characters are "the inevitable products of that society"; and most imminently, "the society itself is equally inevitable *if certain factors come about*. As I've said before, we're not concerned with whether they *will*, only with whether they *may*."[21] This is an important statement about the purpose of science fiction. As Pohl would later reiterate in his lecture for James Gunn's *The Literature of Science Fiction* film series, science fiction does not set out to predict the future, but rather to create *possible* futures.[22] Gold is making much the same point here, and he goes on to consider the novel's breakthrough as being about a "dramatic advance in architecture" and the social consequences such development would entail.

Reviewers rated the novel on the same plane as its predecessor. In *Galaxy*, Conklin observed that "today's suburbs have become unspeakable slums; the economy is divided (as in *The Space Merchants*) between huge monopolies; and the 'bread and circuses' of the Romans are back in newer, shinier and crueler form as means of popular entertainment."[23] It seems that Pohl and Kornbluth got quite a bit right.

Earlier in the year, Pohl and Kornbluth produced the novel *Search the Sky* for Ballantine, published simultaneously in hardcover and paperback in February. Quite different in setting than the two *Galaxy* serials, the novel is set in a Galactic future in which humankind has spread throughout the stars, in the process losing contact with the planet of origin, Earth. The planets are not well connected and things are starting to fall apart on a galactic scale. In that sense, *Search the Sky* has a great deal of affinity with Asimov's *Foundation*, particularly anticipating Asimov's later additions to the series, *Foundation's Edge* and *Foundation and Earth*, where Asimov follows a similar pattern of jumping from planet to planet in search of the origin. But because *Search the Sky* itself is clearly indebted to Asimov's original *Foundation* stories, this is a clear example of the feedback loop in science fiction, where one story draws from another and later influences the originator of the concept in later work. Further, the work is important as Pohl's first foray in a novel into intergalactic space, returning in a mature way to the tales of interplanetary adventure he wrote prior to the war. The narrative is closely linked to Pohl's much later

Stopping at Slowyear and *The Voices of Heaven*, which also posit colonial worlds separated from each other by the slow process of interplanetary travel. A key feature of the novel is the FTL drive and the discussion about how it works and its importance.

Ross, an employee of the Haarland Corporation on Halsey's Planet, a society based on corporate models similar to what we see in *The Space Merchants*, is sent out to other planets to see what is going wrong. In the manner of Gulliver, Ross encounters a number of different types of societies, giving Pohl and Kornbluth an opportunity to satirize various social situations, eventually arriving on Earth, now stuff of myth, as humanity has turned its back on the planet because they had destroyed it through war. Circumstances on two of the planets Ross visits satirize contemporary social roles quite effectively. The first privileges the elderly in an uproarious send-up of relations between young and old. Reminiscent of the Struldbrugs in *Gulliver's Travels*, the doddering aged run the planet and the young believe that is the way things should be, even though they are virtually enslaved to the often senile whims of the elderly. There, Ross picks up a female companion, Helena, who travels with him through the rest of the novel. In a Battle of the Sexes scenario more pungent and aware than the clumsy handling in "Donovan Had a Dream," the second planet is dominated by women. The satire here effectively makes fun of the domestic assumptions in 1950s America. Although some contemporary feminist readers might find the satire a bit heavy-handed, there are some amusing set pieces critiquing sexual politics and chauvinism—in, for example, an episode where coarse women laborers play pinch-butt with the men whose vulnerability and distress are apparent, and other such role reversals. Another instance occurs when Ross tries to talk with a businesswoman who more or less ignores him, reflecting on men not thinking women are important or have anything to say. Religion, or in the broad sense any ideology, is satirized on the next planet, which Ross at first believes is Earth. This world is dominated by the Jones clan. There is a lack of genetic diversity, as everyone has red hair and looks the same, and those who don't look like the majority try to fake it. They follow a creed called Jonesism and practice the tenets of "The Book of Jones," the absurd, egotistical belief system put in place by their founder during ideological wars in the colony's past. In a museum in a city called "Earth," Ross uncovers the controversy that led to Jonesism, and this has parallels with "The Book of the Machines" in Samuel Butler's *Erewhon*, where ideology and strife devolve into absurdity. He also discovers the true location of Earth itself.

Upon reaching Earth, Ross is thrust into a world much like the one depicted in *The Space Merchants*. Earth is dominated by commercials and advertising, and people are blithering idiots. Taking things further than "The Midas Plague" and echoing Kornbluth's bitter "The Marching Morons," people are reduced to fools because the machines do everything for them. Ross encounters "nursemaids," the people who are at once running things and kept running by the needs of the chuckleheads, and in the last few pages things are explained: as on the other planets, genetic diversity has ruptured and the planet has fallen into stagnation. In the end, the FTL ships will open up human diversity and facilitate genetic divergence, and this will forestall the stagnation that has set in. Humans will again thrive rather than die off.

Fantastic Universe's reviewer, Robert Frazier, noted that the novel "crackles with the same action, drama and wit that characterized the authors' classic *Space Merchants* [by 1954 already a "classic"]. It contains the same underlying concern with human beings, whether they are on future Madison Avenues or in the outer galaxies."[24] In *Galaxy*, Conklin was more circumspect, noting that while the novel did not rise to the level of *The Space Merchants*, it nevertheless "is a colorful and pointed melodrama of the decay of Man's interstellar empire."[25] *Search the Sky* is the most Swiftian of the Pohl-Kornbluth collaborations, confirming Donald Hassler's assertion that the Pohl-Kornbluth collaborations were "Swiftian in sardonic attitudes and even in some specific images."[26]

Pohl continued to edit the *Star* series in 1954, producing a third volume that saw publication at the beginning of the next year; like the two preceding volumes, it had several stories that now have classic status: Asimov's "It's Such a Beautiful Day," Bradbury's "The Strawberry Window," Clarke's "The Deep Range," and Philip K. Dick's "Foster, You're Dead." Later in the year, Pohl put together a complementary volume of novellas, *Star Short Novels*, consisting of Jessamyn West's "Little Men," Del Rey's "For I Am a Jealous People," and Sturgeon's "To Here and the Easel." Although the contributions by West and Del Rey are among the best stories published that year, the series never took off, and Pohl closed it after just the one volume.

Pohl also began another collaborative relationship in 1954 with veteran writer Jack Williamson, which would become one of his richest. Pohl and Williamson would collaborate on ten novels over the years and would otherwise develop a deep friendship. *The Undersea Trilogy*, consisting of *Undersea Quest*, *Undersea Fleet*, and *Undersea City*, were written for the burgeoning SF juvenile market, where Heinlein, Andre Norton, and others were having success.

The central character in the series is Jim Eden, a young man entering into the Sub-Sea Academy at the beginning of the first novel. Eden is modeled on the teenage heroes of Heinlein's juveniles, but here Williamson and Pohl change the setting to Earth's oceans rather than outer space. The primary action takes place in domed cities under the sea, conceptually similar to the G.M.L. homes in *Gladiator-At-Law* but on a far grander scale. Like *Gladiator*, an unscrupulous businessman, Hallam Sperry, has pushed out the creator of the cities: Eden's father, now deceased. The first novel follows Eden's training at the Sub-Sea Academy, fitting the pattern of the novel of education seen in Heinlein's *Space Cadet*, and ends with Eden's estate legacy being restored and Sperry's exploitative capitalist ambitions thwarted. At one point, Eden docks at a naval base at Naples, bringing him to an area familiar to Pohl from his military service. *Undersea Fleet* involves "first contact" with an undersea species of humans, Atlanteans. As the novel begins, Jim is back at the academy, and what is perhaps most interesting in the story are these early chapters of world-building in which Pohl and Williamson effectively describe Eden's day-to-day training and the functionality of the undersea domes. *Undersea City* concerns itself with earthquakes, tsunamis, and other tectonic upheavals along the Pacific Rim. Notable in this novel are the ideas about earthquakes in the ocean, tidal effects, and the impact on weather, drawing from both authors' training as weather forecasters during the war.

Reviewing the third book in *Fantastic Universe*, Hans Stefan Santesson observed that although the books are aimed at younger readers, they *"can be read by all ages without appreciable loss of dignity!"*[27] Conklin was less satisfied with the series, feeling they somewhat endorsed the "petrifying processes that military academies put children through," which is central to the plot of the novels.[28] These novels anticipate Pohl's (and Williamson's) later enthusiasm for world travel. In their later years, Pohl and Williamson would often travel together, taking trips to China and elsewhere.[29]

Pohl's next story in *Galaxy* would begin a flood, as he devoted himself to full-time writing. "The Tunnel under the World" appeared in the January 1955 issue, and next to "The Midas Plague" it is Pohl's quintessential representative story from the decade. The story involves Guy Burckhardt, a man who lives in the perfect, neighborly little town of Tylerton. Following a bad dream of a catastrophic explosion, Burckhardt soon recognizes that the pattern of his daily routine is off-center when his cigar vendor is absent and "the *usual* commercials" have been replaced by unfamiliar brands that break the pattern: "It wasn't just that things were wrong with the pattern of Burckhardt's life; it was that the *wrong* things were wrong" (117). After moving a trunk in the basement to change a light bulb, Burckhardt discovers that under a thin layer of cement, the foundation of his house is made of metal, faked as it were: "It was as if someone had shored up the house with a frame of metal and then laboriously concealed the evidence" (123). More disconcerting is the incomplete boat hull that Burckhardt has a memory of completing: "For reasons beyond his comprehension, someone had taken his boat and his cellar away, maybe his whole house, and replaced them with a clever mock-up of the real thing" (123). When Burckhardt tries to investigate, he lapses into unconsciousness. When he awakens, he finds the daily paper has the same date, June 15, as the day before, his wife Mary repeating she had a nightmare, and the faulty light switch working properly. The daily routine repeats itself until Burckhardt is contacted by a man named Swanson, who also remembers the day before. After Burckhardt has revealed that he remembers, he and Swanson flee to the tunnel of the title, where Swanson explains that for him it has been June 15 for several weeks. Thinking they will find answers at the end of the tunnel, Burckhardt and Swanson follow it to an office, where Burckhardt finds evidence that Tylerton is a "test area" for advertising campaigns. The big reveal comes when Burckhardt finds out that he and everyone in Tylerton are not even human anymore, merely automatons imprinted with the memories of the citizens of Tylerton, all of whom were killed in an industrial accident yet maintained to test products for the marketplace. A final bizarre revelation at the story's conclusion brings Philip K. Dick's typical plotting to mind. Not believing escape is impossible, Burckhardt follows the corridors only to find that Tylerton and its people have been reconstructed at a smaller scale: his robot world sits upon a tabletop. An indictment of the insidious invasiveness of modern advertising, the story, perhaps, reaches another level of bitter and pungent irony beyond its predecessors. It is also a story of Cold War paranoia. Initially, Swanson and Burckhardt suspect "Martians" or "Russians." But in Pohl's vocabulary, advertising and the cycle of consumption are far more menacing. Burckhardt's predicament forces readers to ask the question "What is real?" and further "Who am I?" Indeed, a reader familiar with Dick's work might mistake it for one of his stories if the Pohl byline were not attached to it.

Pohl appeared in every issue of *Galaxy* in 1955, with the exception of October (there was no December issue), following "The Tunnel under the World" with "Pythias," "The Candle Lighter," "Target One," "The Middle of Nowhere," "Grandy Devil," and "The Mapmakers," the last two running simultaneously with the serial *Preferred Risk*. The story behind *Preferred Risk* is an interesting one: In early 1953, Gold had announced a first-novel contest connected with Simon and Schuster for $6,500, a substantial sum when most science fiction novels were selling for around $2,000. Finding none of the entries satisfying, when Pohl brought Gold a novelette satirizing the insurance industry he'd written with Lester Del Rey, Gold asked him to turn it into a novel to be published under a pseudonym as the contest winner. It was published under the name Edson McCann.

Preferred Risk is modeled almost directly on *The Space Merchants*. Reader reaction took the novel to task for copying its predecessor. Reviewers were equally suspicious, feeling as if the novel was a mediocre copy. Damon Knight, who likely saw through the charade, was particularly indignant in his review in Lowndes's *Original Science Fiction Stories*, calling it "the vastly disappointing winner of the *Galaxy*–Simon and Schuster contest," deriding that it "slavishly copies *Galaxy*'s 'Gravy Planet' ('The Space Merchants'), which has already been copied once by the original proprietors as *Galaxy*'s 'Gladiator-at-Law.'" Nevertheless, Knight concedes that "the extrapolation holds up brilliantly in some places" and "the plot development is logical and ingenious, but uninspired."[30] The satire is definitely more heavy-handed than that in *The Space Merchants*, almost as if Pohl and Del Rey knew they needed to push the satire over the top to satisfy the deception of the contest. One must also wonder to what extent Gold, who was notorious for editorial rewrites, manipulated the manuscript to give it that air of slight amateurism in order to set it apart from its predecessor. In *Fantastic Universe*, Santesson protested that the novel was only "masquerading as a science fiction novel," although he praised the novel's conclusion as "fast-moving reading."[31] Curiously, Santesson compares the novel to Bester's *The Demolished Man* for the element of suspense, not making the more obvious connection to *The Space Merchants*, which might also suggest Santesson, a Hydra Club regular, knew of the ruse. *Preferred Risk* saw hardcover publication later in 1955 but was not to appear in paperback until 1962, both editions under the Edson McCann byline. Having recently replaced Conklin as *Galaxy*'s reviewer, Floyd C. Gale praised the "handsome" Simon and Schuster hardcover, noting its similarity to "the Pohl-Kornbluth novels . . . in which some present aspect of society has burgeoned into a Frankenstein monster."[32] Not until a Ballantine edition in 1980 were Pohl and Del Rey's names attached to it, though the secret had long been out.

Despite being derivative of *The Space Merchants*, the novel is nonetheless interesting in its own right for several reasons, one of which is the Italian setting. Here Pohl drew upon his experiences during the war to produce the backdrop of the novel. In retrospect, and given its target, *Preferred Risk* is still effective satire and also makes some pointed cautionary assessments about a world under the shadow of the atomic bomb.

After nuclear war has damaged cities around the world, a corporate insurance hegemony emerges. You can get insurance for everything, including nuclear war insurance. The hegemony of the "Company" has led to social stagnation. Because of the implied hypercaution of a society built on insurance practices, humanity failed to go to the stars and did not pursue longevity, both seen as too risky. In a way, *Preferred Risk* is much more pessimistic than the Pohl-Kornbluth novels in its engagement with the major 1950s theme of nuclear annihilation and the anxieties connected with it. The irony that this society lives in thrall and terror of the bomb while refusing to pursue the risks of large-scale emancipatory projects, like space flight, illustrates the inconsistency of human reason during the Cold War.

Like *The Space Merchants*, *Preferred Risk* is told in first person. The viewpoint character is Thomas Willis, an adjustor for the Company. Like Courtenay, he is a true believer in Company policy, but much more starry-eyed and naïve, distinguishing him from his sharp, savvy predecessor. Willis is also somewhat suspect in the Company ranks, having, in a fit of grief after his wife died, said some things against the Company that got him in a little trouble and have led to his posting to Naples as a test to reaffirm his loyalty.

Willis arrives in Naples at a moment of crisis. A man the Company is trying to catch is in the railway terminal and is attempting to do himself harm—at the expense of the Company, of course. Willis is witness as the man jumps the track and is run over. The seeming suicide is Luigi Zorchi, whose body is capable of rejuvenation, and he has thus filed numerous insurance claims. As the story proceeds, Zorchi is revealed to be a member of an underground movement (in the manner of the Consies) trying to break the Company hegemony.

In truth, the Company is a hidden dictatorship. It controls and manipulates the global population and maintains cryonic vaults around the world—"there are enough vaults for the entire human race" (49)—for casualties from atomic bomb attacks and other small- and large-scale accidents. The idea is that they can put people in cold storage with the promise that in the future there will be treatments available for radiation sickness. However, the true purpose is to put away political prisoners and anyone else who protests the policies of the Company. The naïve Willis observes early on, "I had to admit the vaults looked a lot like morgues" (36). Cryonics would resurface frequently throughout Pohl's work, particularly in the late 1960s novel *The Age of the Pussyfoot*, inspired by the work of cryonist Robert Ettinger.

After Zorchi's latest success in making a claim, Defoe, the chief claims adjustor, arrives in Naples to investigate. Defoe is Willis's mentor and hero, and Willis believes Defoe is perfectly honest. However, in truth, Defoe has usurped the Company leadership and placed the CEO in cold storage in the Naples area. As the narrative goes on, Willis begins to see the truth, that he has been a dupe of Defoe's takeover. Willis connects with Slovetski of the underground movement and learns of their intentions to let loose a catastrophic cobalt-bomb aimed at the Company home office in New York. The fallout would spread across the world, killing all. Willis is faced with a moral dilemma and calls Defoe to inform him of the planned attack, which affords Defoe time to send his men to wipe out the insurgents who are hiding in the ruins of Pompeii. But before the Company security forces can secure the situation, the bomb is launched, detonating over the Atlantic, leaving them only a few hours to get everyone in the vaults before the fallout spreads around the world. In fifty years the human race will be able to come out of the vaults and start again. The novel ends as Willis prepares to go into cold storage with the hope that they can do things right when they awaken. Of course, this doesn't account for the damage that will be done to the rest of the ecosystem from the bomb; Pohl presented a better awareness of the ecological impact in *The Space Merchants*. This might also have been a conscious attempt to have a deliberately flawed novel for the purposes of the contest.

In an afterword titled "The Art and Agony of Collaboration," written for the 1980 Ballantine paperback edition, Pohl remarks that collaborating with Del Rey was more difficult than with Kornbluth. Pohl is an intuitive writer, "figuring out what will happen as I go along," he said, whereas Del Rey had to have everything plotted out scene by scene before he could even begin[33] (perhaps explaining the severe writer's block he suffered in later years). For Pohl and Del Rey, their contrasting approaches to writing made for a difficult collaboration. However, it did not have an adverse effect on their friendship: the Del Reys bought a house down from the Pohls in Red Bank and were their neighbors for the next seventeen years. Later, when Pohl married Elizabeth Anne Hull in 1984, Del Rey was his best man.

Pohl continued his collaborative relationship with Kornbluth in 1955, too. They expanded their repertoire by working on a novel for the mainstream, although Kornbluth had already published a few mainstream novels that Pohl, acting as his agent, had sold to Lion Books. *A Town is Drowning* was published by Ballantine in late 1955. The idea for the novel came after Hurricane Diane had taken off part of the roof of Pohl's house in Red Bank, and Pohl and Kornbluth worked quickly to get the novel to press while the aftermath of the storm was still fresh.[34] The story involves a young manufacturer, Mickey Groff, likely somewhat modeled on Pohl's father, who is scouting a location in a small northeastern town for his new factory when he is caught in the storm. There is a science fiction element in the story in that Groff's factory is going to make Cold War munitions, and so the government wants the factory outside the city, in case the city is hit by an atomic bomb attack. This Cold War mentality connects with much of the work of both Pohl and Kornbluth at the time, bringing to mind Kornbluth's solo novel *Not This August* and Pohl's later story "The Wizards of Pung's Corners." As the tempest floods the town, Groff and a handful of other displaced persons try to make it to safety, along the way exposing their own petty ambitions and selfish hearts. Though the novel is mostly 1950s-era social melodrama, the cataclysmic nature of the storm gives it a degree of affinity with the catastrophic tone in most of Pohl and Kornbluth's science fiction.

Pohl's work in the mainstream continued in 1956, as he published no fewer than four non-SF novels that year. *Sorority House*, as by Jordan Park, was written with Kornbluth to fulfill his Lion contract. *The God of Channel 1* provides an interesting glimpse into the rise of television and its effect on American culture and the cult of personality that television creates. Published under the byline Donald Stacy, the novel more playfully covers territory seen on the screen the following year in Elia Kazan's *A Face in the Crowd*. The novel was a hidden collaboration between Pohl and an anonymous network executive whom Pohl never met. The exec had sent Ballantine a loose manuscript giving an "insider" perspective about the inner workings of the television medium. Pohl turned it into a novel about a few days in the career of Danny Dahl, a vastly popular talk show host, through the viewpoint lens of his production manager Molly Hill. The novel has interesting connections with the SF Pohl was writing during the decade, as it also deals with issues of consumerism and technology and how technology changes culture. In tune with the corporate wars of *The Space Merchants*, Pohl exposes how TV networks wage competitive battle by trying to sabotage each other's shows, stealing writers, and manipulating audiences. *Turn the Tigers Loose* is a novel about bomber pilots in the Korean War that Pohl ghosted for Colonel Walt Lasly, whose name appears as the author. For the novel, Pohl was no doubt able to draw on his past experiences working on *G-8 and His Battle Aces* and his weather forecasting during the war, but the novel is a far better piece than the pulpy action stories in *G-8*. Although more or less forgotten, *Turn the Tigers Loose* compares favorably with James Michener's *The Bridges at Toko-Ri*, another novel about air raids in the Korean War. Interestingly, Ballantine offered Pohl the contract to write the novelization for *Forbidden Planet*, but Pohl turned him down. After seeing the film, though, Pohl wished he would have agreed.[35] Instead, he wound up doing the novelization for the John Cassavetes and Sidney Poitier film *Edge of the City* the following year.

Finally, Pohl and Kornbluth collaborated on *Presidential Year*, a mainstream political novel about a presidential campaign published to coincide with the election of 1956. *Presidential Year* is a novel about political campaigning and the American political scene. Readers from a later generation might find it startling to discover that the lies, deception, phoniness, and corruption—so familiar in our current political landscape—were present in much the same way when Pohl and Kornbluth wrote their novel. The novel follows the political education of Raymond Houck, a professor of constitutional law who is hired as a consultant for the campaign of Mahlon Stoddert. The novel contains a number of insights about American politics, particularly in the ways it portrays how politicians and political parties make compromises and jettison their principles through the campaign process. Pohl and Kornbluth also insightfully anticipate how television would become a factor in American politics, the simmering political battle over civil rights, and the growing populist concern with the corporatization of America, a theme *Presidential Year* shares with the science fiction novels. Film rights were sold for *Presidential Year*, but a film was never made.[36]

Political themes were central to Pohl's other novel of 1956, *Slave Ship*, which appeared serially in *Galaxy* in March, April, and May. Not only was this Pohl's first solo SF novel, but it was the first wherein Cold War politics came to the forefront, anticipating later novels and stories from the 1970s and 1980s, when the Cold War loomed large in Pohl's imagination. *Galaxy* reviewer Floyd C. Gale noted that Pohl "draws an authentically convincing picture of a wartime navy and his story's theme is a think-tank tickler."[37] The geopolitics have shifted from the contemporary Cold War alignment with the West, now identified as the United Nations rather than as disparate nations, facing an Asian-Pacific empire called the Caodai, centered around a new religion. The Soviet regime has fallen through limited nuclear war. Lieutenant Logan Miller pilots an experimental submarine crewed by psychic uplifted animals—three dogs, two chimps, and a seal—sent to infiltrate Caodai headquarters on a remote Pacific island. This allows Pohl to examine Cold War politics from a distance and to speculate on the prospects of future political entanglements and military engagements. In this sense, like the concurrent novels of Graham Greene, Pohl here anticipates some of the geopolitical wranglings of the Vietnam War (and now those in the Middle East). Despite these intriguing possibilities, *Slave Ship* is less effective than the earlier collaborations and his short fiction. Nonetheless, along with the bioengineering of the uplifted animals, a further intriguing aspect of the novel is the introduction of computers as facilitating data gathering, and, as a consequence, spying. But rather than working out the implications of advanced computers and bioengineered animals, Pohl falls back into a plot focused on ESP, taking away some of the otherwise seeming realism of the narrative. The novel included a revealing afterword that states some of Pohl's ideas about the function of science fiction, ideas that would later be more fully developed when Pohl engaged with academic writing in the early 1970s. He argues that the science fiction writer "take[s] what is already known and, by extrapolating from it, draw[s] as plausibly detailed a portrait as he can manage of what tomorrow's scientists may learn . . . and of what the human race in its day-to-day life may make of it all" (145). He spends the rest of the afterword discussing animal communication, whereas, in retrospect, the novel is perhaps more interesting for its extrapolation on geopolitics than for what it has to say about interspecies communication.

Although Pohl published a number of stories in 1956 in other science fiction magazines—"The Census Takers" (*FSF*, February), "What to Do Until the Analyst Comes" (*Imagination*, February), "The Engineer" (*Infinity*, February), "Wapshot's Demon" (*Original Science Fiction Stories*, July), "The Day of the Boomer Dukes" (*Future*, August), "The Celebrated No-Hit Inning" (*Fantastic Universe*, September)—with the exception of *Slave Ship*, he published only one other story in *Galaxy*, "The Man Who Ate the World," in the November issue, the masterful follow-up to "The Midas Plague." The story is about a poor boy named Sonny Trumble, who has everything in the Midas world and must consume to bursting, leaving him feeling empty and alone. After Morey Fry solves the distribution-consumption problem, Trumble grows into an obese, psychologically damaged man, a pathological, compulsive consumer, isolating himself on an island with his companion robots, Davey Crockett, Long John Silver, Mr. Chips, and Tarzan, who play out various scenarios to keep him entertained. To power his army of automatons and other machines, Sonny is drawing off enormous amounts of electricity, which threatens the stability of the grid. But more important, Trumble's psychological imbalance could threaten the social stability of the world. Roger Garrick, a psychologist, has been called in, and with the help of a statistician named Kathy Pender he is able to get to the root of Trumble's compulsion, ending his obsessive consumption. The story provides a nice counterpoint to the world presented in "The Midas Plague," showing the aftermath when an extreme situation is overcome. The compassion at the end of the story registers a new tone in Pohl's work, more in keeping with the stories of Theodore Sturgeon than with Pohl's usual wry cynicism. At the same time, the underlying acceptance of a managerial society to uphold "stability" is rather disturbing. Pohl's point seems to be that an inevitable consequence of a society built around advanced technologies is social engineering and management, and that a benevolent management is preferable to the cult of power interrogated, for instance, in Orwell's *1984*, or the calculated chaos implicit in *The Space Merchants* and *Gladiator-At-Law*.

Another important story from 1956 that diagnoses problems of consumption, advertising, and the distortion of values and meaning is "Happy Birthday, Dear Jesus," which first appeared as the lead story in Pohl's first story collection *Alternating Currents*. As the title baldly indicates, the story is about the commercialization of Christmas. Covering some of the same themes as *The Space Merchants* and "The Midas Plague," "Happy Birthday, Dear Jesus" is essentially a love story, as the protagonist George Martin, a manager in a department store, tries to win the favor of his new gift wrapper, the anomalous Miss Lilymary Hargreave, who is from a family that values the true meaning of Christmas, which in the future consumer world of the story has been forgotten. At first, unable to comprehend that Christmas is not strictly about carefree excess and hollow advertising jingles, Martin is awakened to life's alternatives, in the end leaving with Lilymary on a mission trip to Borneo. The story is most notable for Pohl's incisive critique of merchandising, branding, and other retail practices. When the story originally appeared, Martin's ramping up of the store's Christmas preparations in August might have seemed overly exaggerated, though today it seems merely par for the course. Reviewing *Alternating Currents* in *Fantastic Universe*, Santesson said that "Pohl explores a mildly disturbing future" in the stories and that they "do not promise us much peace or greater understanding in that sometimes uncomfortably near future," noting that the "blandly ironic glint found in the eyes of Pohl-plus-Kornbluth is absent" [38]—though one wonders how he missed that in "The Tunnel under the World."

A number of the themes that Pohl would examine throughout his fiction appear in many of the other stories from this fertile period in the mid- to late 1950s: critiques of corporate and bureaucratic organizational techniques

("Rafferty's Reasons"), commercial exploitation and consumer manipulation ("With Redfern on Capella II," "What to Do until the Analyst Comes," "The Richest Man in Levittown"), overpopulation ("The Census Takers," "A Life and a Half"), nuclear war ("Target One," "The Day of the Boomer Dukes," "The Knights of Arthur," "The Wizards of Pung's Corners"), social class and segregation ("My Lady Greensleeves"), and alien invasion ("Mars by Moonlight," "The Abominable Earthman"). These themes would appear in various guises throughout Pohl's later fiction, although he would often use interplanetary settings as the backdrop from which such themes could be explored.

Pohl and Kornbluth published their final collaborative novel, *Wolfbane*, as a two-part serial in *Galaxy* in late 1957. They finished the slightly expanded book version in the early months of 1958. By that time the relationship had cooled significantly and, indeed, once *Wolfbane* was finished, the two men were hardly speaking to each other. Kornbluth was looking to take an assistant editorial position at the *Magazine of Fantasy and Science Fiction*, with the likelihood he would succeed Tony Boucher in the editorial chair. Tragically, after a wet, late-season snow on March 21, Kornbluth scooped out the drive for his wife Mary before rushing to catch the train into the city, where he was to meet with the publisher—and he dropped dead on the platform.

Wolfbane is something quite different than the previous Pohl-Kornbluth collaborations. Not a satire on the practices of consumer manipulation, instead it is a story of alien invasion, and a quite effective one. A wandering planet has ensnared Earth and its moon and taken both out of the solar system, converting the Moon into a mini-sun that must be recharged every five years. From the wanderer comes a creature, actually a vast machine shaped like a pyramid, of enormous power; it positions itself atop Mt. Everest. From its perch, the pyramid monitors all human activity, periodically sending out electromagnetic pulses—what people come to refer to as "eyes"—that harvest humans when they are ripe for "componentness." There are a total of eight pyramids, called Omniverters by their creators, on the wandering planet. The Omniverters use humans as biological components to synthesize the chemicals needed to keep them functioning and to maintain the machine complex on their planet. Similar to the Borg in *Star Trek*, the Omniverters have been going from system to system for millennia (one "component" from another planet they destroyed has been serving them for 125,000 years), having originally been the creations of a sentient species, whom the Omniverters destroyed when their creators realized their machines had gone terribly wrong. At first, the Omniverters had been a great boon to their creators, "the flower of the mechanical genius of our race" (121). But when the Omniverters turned on their creators, all feeding-stations were shut down, and the machines were stopped and dismantled—all except the eight "Specials," sent out as interstellar probes. When the eight returned, they enslaved their masters: "They then proceeded to wipe out the people with beams of electrons, hot-plasmoids and direct pressure. When this was done they built their own feeding stations in plenty of time, and then built devices to serve the feeding stations, and devices to serve those devices until the final irony was achieved of men wired together to serve machines" (122). All of this is revealed late in the novel.

When the story begins humans have been under the yoke of the pyramid for two hundred years. The first part of the novel shows the conformity and complacency most people easily accept, once the power of the pyramid asserts itself. This illustrates an important theme during the Cold War and the McCarthy era. Thus, though the basic premise of the novel is more fantastical than *The Space Merchants*, *Gladiator-At-Law*, and many of both authors' stories, the underlying political theme in the first part of the novel is perhaps more immediate to the times. Here Pohl and Kornbluth move from extrapolation to allegory. In addition to this political element, the novel also extends Pohl's exploration of the relationship between humans and the machines they create, although the machines of *Wolfbane* are far more sinister than those in "The Midas Plague."

The first part of the novel is set in Wheeling, West Virginia. People refer to each other as "Citizens" and live in a highly regimented way, having lost most of their personalities, by following the rituals established to cope with the pyramid's constant surveillance, including a meditative practice called "connectivity," which in turn facilitates the pyramid's harvesting program. Food is scarce, and everyone lives in fear of the pyramid's "eyes" that appear seemingly at random and nab Citizens, yet they are numb to it when it happens. Occasionally, the pressure to conform—and survive—is too much, and someone goes on a rampaging killing spree. Once subdued and tried, the criminal is set for "donation," where his spinal fluid is drained and then ritually drunk by the

Citizens. Because of the fluctuating conditions due to the waxing and waning of the Moon's energy, only 100 million humans remain on the Earth.

Within this conformist society people who display traits of individuality and initiative are called Wolves and are shunned because the complacent ones fear that the Wolves may draw the wrath of the pyramid. One such Wolf is Glenn Tropile. He at first rather mildly defies the strict rules and conventions of society, but then he is caught stealing a loaf of bread while another Citizen runs amok. Fleeing with his wife, who soon retreats back to Wheeling, Tropile is picked up by an underground community of Wolves, who are planning an assault on the pyramid at Everest. Once again, Pohl and Kornbluth posit a secret underground working against the system. However, here the underground is only a fleeting episode in Tropile's trajectory: soon, an "eye" appears, seizing him, and he promptly vanishes. For the first time, however, the Wolves are able to record this phenomenon—and for the first time there is a Wolf in the machine.

In the second part of the novel (recalling Pohl's early story "Earth, Farewell!") Tropile has been transported to the pyramid planet and turned into a biological component, kept in a state of lucid dreaming in a tank of nutrient fluid and "wired into circuit" so that he can fulfill the specific function of synthesizing Protoporphin IX, the chemical that the pyramids can metabolize. The "vein" of Earth having been "worked," the pyramids must "move more rapidly to a more rewarding planet." Thus requiring more complex operations, the Omniverters link several human "components" in groupings of eight. The Wolf Tropile is put into such a configuration, attains some degree of awareness, and begins to infiltrate the system. This idea of "connectivity," seen here and in the rituals of the Citizens, probably develops from Kornbluth's mystical experiences with the "Five" at the Milford Writers' Conference in 1956. Kornbluth, Blish, Knight, and Algis Budrys were brought into intense emotional contact through the catalyzing mediumship of Jane Roberts, then an aspiring SF writer, later known for channeling an entity called Seth.[39] Although the initial idea of connectivity probably derives from Kornbluth's experiences, the imagination of the science of how it works seems to be more indicative of Pohl's vision. One can surmise that the strongly rational and pragmatic Pohl needed to create a scientific rationale for Kornbluth's quasi-mystical concept.

With his wolf-like traits of self-determination and wiliness, Tropile's thoughts begin to penetrate the others' complacency, and together they form a unity and achieve a state of higher consciousness that allows them to alter the decisions of the pyramid on Earth. Tropile and his group begin translating acquaintances and weaponry from various parts of the Earth up to the pyramid planet, where they act as "mice," damaging the processes of the machines as they try to survive. Tropile's hive makes contact and explains how they will provide food and water for the naked "mice"; the hive, called the "Snowflake," begins to spread a network of cables and receptors throughout the planet, learning about its origins and what the Snowflake must do to subvert the pyramids. Through this process, the hive discovers that much of the pyramids' activity involves experiments on "an elephantine, blue-green body with chitinous armor and seven tentacles" (99). This dead creature is the last of the pyramids' original makers. The experiments have revealed nothing, but the pyramids continue, repetitively: "By and by it became clear that the experiments were being repeated. Perhaps the word was Ritual" (99). This idea—that machine creations set in motion by sentient creatures might persist in meaningless action after their creators are gone and their original purpose is complete—is also behind Fred Saberhagen's *Berserker* series, which Pohl nurtured in the pages of *If* during his editorial stint in the 1960s. In his own work, Pohl would later tackle the concept from another angle in *Black Star Rising*—though in that case the dynamic is not with machines but with pets.

From here on, the bizarre imagery and circumstances are intensely realized as Tropile's Snowflake rewires the planet:

> Through the lowest levels of the undermined planet crawled a caterpillar-tread device, heaving the cable behind it. It extended a Teflon snout into chambers of corrosive atmosphere and skirted them; it shunned the red-lit storage and access spaces for the lower, darker tubes bored through bedrock, not yet crammed with pipes and wires, not yet visited incessantly by scuttling repair-machines. Its outriders, tapped into the cable, rolled inertly along, waiting with machine patience for their tasks. One squad of them was an excavation group—derricks, angledozers, mining machines that undercut, blasted and wiped up debris with scything paws onto an endless belt that shunted it away from the field of operation (102–3).

Tropile's hive cuts off the food and water supply from their "mice," forcing them to have to roam throughout the machine complex in search of nutrients and hydration; this, in turn, wreaks havoc, causing the pyramids to mount a defense. As the battle lines are drawn, the Snowflake is contacted by the "dead" alien, and Tropile disconnects from his hive to lead the humans to the weaponry he spirited away from Earth. Once the feeding stations and subsidiary repair machines are destroyed, the pyramids retreat into their bays and become inert: "gliding silently and slowly on their cushions of electrostatic force. They fitted themselves into the black, cliff-high booths and waited . . . They would wait thus until the end of time for food to adsorb so they could go about their business of making more food to adsorb so they could . . ." (133).

The final chapter shifts back to Earth. Tropile has been reintegrated but is shocked to find that people have reverted back to business as usual. Haendl, the leader of the Wolves, wants to restock the arsenal of atomic weapons; Germyn, the leading Citizen, has gone back to his old ways and wants Tropile to clear the "terrible blemish" against him and conform, having seemingly completely forgotten the events on the binary planet. Tropile turns to his wife, Gala, but she knows what he has in mind: "'You want to go back,' she said without stress. 'You want to get back into your tub of soup again, and float like a baby. You don't want to *have* babies; you want to be one'" (139). In the end, Tropile turns away, hoping to return to the binary and be wired back into the circuit. But he will not go alone. In typical Pohl fashion, Gala joins him: "'Wait. Wait, Glenn! I want to go with you!' And he turned and waited; but only for a moment; and then he went on. But not—for ever and always again—not alone. There was one more. There would be others! The ring of fire would grow" (140). With this, Pohl and Kornbluth usher in that element of evolutionary frontier optimism indicative of the science fiction genre. Out of the ruins of cataclysm and the stagnation of conformity can arise something new, something different, a new stage in human evolution. In the final analysis, it is difficult to compare *Wolfbane* with the three prior Pohl-Kornbluth SF collaborations, as it is, again, something quite different. But perhaps it can be said that while *The Space Merchants*, *Gladiator-At-Law*, and *Search the Sky* are each brilliantly executed satires on the pernicious nature of human enterprise, *Wolfbane* belongs in different company as a triumph of the science fictional imagination, vividly bringing to life a situation and setting on the precipice of wonder.

★ ★ ★

Although *Galaxy* suffered from the collapse of the science fiction magazine market, dropping to bi-monthly in 1959, Pohl returned to its pages with a vengeance in 1958 and 1959, publishing fifteen stories under his own name and the pseudonyms Paul Flehr and Charles Satterfield. At the same time, Horace Gold was suffering from psychological trauma from his war experiences that was further exacerbated by a car accident, and he was no longer able to fulfill the demands of the magazine. When things got particularly rough for Gold, he would call upon Pohl to help put together the issue. It reached the point where Pohl was ghost editing entire issues, and by late 1960 Pohl was listed as managing editor, though he had essentially fully assumed the editor's post. In December 1961 Pohl officially succeeded Gold as *Galaxy*'s editor, though his name did not appear as editor until the January 1962 issue. By this time *Galaxy*'s publisher had purchased *Worlds of If* from Daniel Quinn. *If* was one of the many magazines that sprang up during the boom of 1952–53, when nearly forty science fiction magazines flooded the market. Although paying less than the top markets, *If* maintained a reputation as a quality magazine during the 1950s, and it was one of the handful of magazines that survived the collapse in 1958 when the American News Corporation's distribution network was dissolved. When *Galaxy* acquired *If* in 1959, Pohl wrote book reviews and other features for the magazine.

Notable stories from these years include "Mars by Moonlight" (*Galaxy*, June 1958), an intriguing story of alien invasion that could have made for a fine *Twilight Zone* or *Outer Limits* episode, and "Whatever Counts" (*Galaxy*, July 1959), a particularly strong novella of first contact, human and alien psychology, and human potentiality, where Pohl brilliantly blends problem solving and characterization with a richly rendered alien landscape. Recalling Murray Leinster's classic "First Contact," "Whatever Counts" posits that the intentions and motivations of an alien species may be similar to our own: "Maybe with our cooperation they'll learn enough so that they can find a way to get along with the human race! After all, we're as much freaks to them as they to us—they didn't expect to find creatures with the power of star flight any more than we did!" (103). "The Wizards of Pung's Corners" (*Galaxy*, October 1958) and its sequel, "The Waging of the Peace" (*Galaxy*, August 1959), are important stories that mesh Pohl's themes of consumerism and nuclear war. In the former Pohl returns to the theme of advertising; in this case, following an atomic war, a stranger arrives in Pung's Corners to revitalize the isolated town through advertising, but the citizens of Pung's Corners are too wise to allow this to happen. In the sequel, Pung's Corners' leading citizen Tighe writes "The Bill of Wrongs"—"The first wrong that we must abolish is the forced sale of goods . . . the second wrong we must abolish is advertising . . . the third wrong we must abolish is the commercial" (69). This leads to war with the automated factories, which keep cranking out consumer goods. In what is perhaps Pohl's darkest, most bitter ending, the machines develop a way to produce goods without raw materials, trapping humanity in an un-breakable cycle of meaningless consumption. In "The Day the Icicle Works Closed" (*Galaxy*, February 1960), Pohl uses an interplanetary setting to explore questions of the commercial exploitation of the space frontier and the relation-ship between ownership and labor. The story involves a mining operation on Altair Nine for a much-needed medicinal product. The fact is the medicine can be synthesized on Earth and therefore the colony and its repressive labor system is a fraud. Another interesting story element that resurfaces in Pohl's later work is the notion that bodies can be rented, that consciousness can be transplanted temporarily into another person, an early manifestation of "purchased people," which is fleshed out in his later collaborations with Jack Williamson and in the 1974 story "We Purchased People."

Following Kornbluth's death, after a four-year hiatus Pohl edited three more volumes of *Star Science Fiction* in 1958 and 1959, after abortively launch-ing *Star* magazine, which only saw one issue in January 1958. *Star 4* was a particularly strong collection, featuring James Gunn's novella "The Immortals" and the final stories from Kornbluth ("The Advent of Channel Twelve") and Henry Kuttner ("A Cross of Centuries"); Kuttner had also died unexpectedly at age forty-four earlier in the year. In the introduction, Pohl warned against the imminent population crisis, probably reflecting on the implications in Gunn's novella, citing it as a more dangerous problem than the bomb. Pohl led off the volume with the Kuttner and Kornbluth stories, briefly eulogizing each writer before their stories begin. Of Kornbluth, he wrote, "Cyril's very special talent was to expose the wry and seamy side of man's progress."[40] The deaths of Kornbluth and Kuttner and the shrinkage of the SF magazine marketplace seemed to signal the winds of change in the science fiction field. The writers of the Golden Age had reached maturity, and with maturity comes death and transition. The last two *Star Science Fiction* volumes, both appearing in 1959, are notably weaker, reflecting the uncertain state of the field that year. Few prominent names appear, although some rising stars are present—Silverberg, Dickson, Cordwainer Smith. By the end of the decade *Star* had burned out.

In the years following Kornbluth's death, Pohl completed several fragments Kornbluth had left in various stages of completion and sold them to a variety of magazines. Of particular interest is "The World of Myrion Flowers," which appeared in *Fantasy and Science Fiction* in 1961. Bordering on the edge of the mainstream, the story relies on the science fictional device of a thought reader to address issues of race, injustice, and hatred, in dialogue with the growing civil rights movement of the era, summed up in the story's final sentence: "It was maddening and dizzying, and the man who wore the helmet would be harmed in any world; but only in the world of Myrion Flowers would he be hated to death" (52). Another posthumous collaboration of note is "The Quaker Cannon," the only story to bear Pohl's name purchased by John W. Campbell for his magazine, which he had recently redubbed *Analog*. "The Quaker Cannon" is a Cold War story told in the stark, realistic mode Pohl utilized in a few of his stories of the 1950s, but which is, perhaps, more reminiscent of Kornbluth's novel *Not This August*. Pohl would master this narrative tone in his Nebula Award–winning 1976 novel *Man Plus*. In *Critical Mass*, the head note says that Kornbluth's fragment was about three thousand words; Pohl filled it out to a twelve-thousand-word story. Set in the early 1980s, the story extrapolates a global realignment where the allies are at war with the "yutes," or neo-Utilitarians (presumably an alliance between Soviet Russia and China) and where young men are conscripted at age fifteen. After being repatriated to North America, Lieutenant John Kramer stands in disgrace following his captivity in the Blank Tanks (isolation chambers), where he was broken and made to broadcast announcements declaring his conversion to yute philosophy and denouncing the allies. Kramer is recruited into Operation Ripsaw as aide-de-camp to General Grote, a master military strategist.

As Ripsaw is about to begin, Kramer is let in on a secret: the military has been feeding the yutes false information about a planned attack led by a General Clough; this "Quaker cannon" will distract the enemy from the real attack, the Ripsaw. But Kramer has been duped: because they know he will crack in the Blank Tanks, they arrange his capture so he can reveal Ripsaw, the real Quaker cannon. This bittersweet story captures the loyalty, the betrayal, and the human cost of wartime strategy.

Pohl put together several of the Kornbluth collaborations in *The Wonder Effect* in 1962 for Ballantine, later re-collecting and expanding them for the Bantam collections *Critical Mass*, which contains the posthumous collaborations, and *Before the Universe*, consisting of the prewar collaborations of the Futurian years. Still later, Pohl collected the best of the lot in *Our Best* for Baen Books, which also includes a number of reflective essays.

As the 1960s began, science fiction was given a boost of credibility in the eyes of the literary establishment when celebrated British novelist Kingsley Amis released his considerations of the field in the critical study *New Maps of Hell* (originally presented as a series of lectures at Princeton the previous year), which caused a stir among the science fiction community, as this interloper presumed to comment astutely on their field. Nonetheless, until the rise of the academic study of SF in the early 1970s, *New Maps of Hell* was the most influential critical study of the field for many years. At the center of Amis's remarks stood Pohl, whom Amis glowingly praised as "the most consistently able writer science fiction, in the modern sense, has yet produced." In a lengthy analysis of Pohl's work, Amis positioned Pohl as focusing on "contemporary urban society and its chain of production and consumption," labeling him "a novelist of economic man." According to Amis, Pohl's "method is selective exaggeration of observable features of our society."[41] Although this definition rather limits the full scope of Pohl's work in the 1950s—for instance, *Wolfbane* and "Whatever Counts" don't easily fit into this category—Amis does here start the critical conversation that looks into the extrapolative nature of Pohl's satire. Amis introduced the term "Comic Inferno" to describe humorous, satirical science fiction set in dystopian environments, offering *The Space Merchants*, "The Midas Plague," and "The Tunnel under the World" as prime examples. Amis's endorsement cemented Pohl's reputation, one he would carry forward not only in his own writing but in the influence he held in the field throughout the 1960s as editor of *Galaxy* and *If*.

Before Gold stepped down at *Galaxy*, Pohl published one more serial in its pages in 1960, *Drunkard's Walk*. Although the initial premise of the novel involving a university professor in a future where universities are like conclaves and course content is delivered through electronic media is quite compelling, the story devolves into one about selfish telepathic immortals who are manipulating the historical trajectory of human society. This notion of mind control surfaces throughout Pohl's work of the 1950s and 1960s, and, taken as a whole, is indicative of the political paranoia of the Cold War, resonating with trends in mainstream fiction, such as portrayed in Richard Condon's *The Manchurian Candidate*. More intriguing is the novel's anticipation, in some ways, of the global digital culture that we are now accustomed to.

The protagonist is a mathematics professor named Cornut, developed from Pohl's then-current fascination with mathematics. Recently, professors have been committing suicide in large numbers, and as the novel opens, Cornut tries to jump out a window. The conceit is that the professors are being forced to do so by a secret society of immortals who have ESP, because people like Cornut have telepathic abilities in latent form. The immortals are a "new" kind of humanity, and they desire to work behind the scenes, holding power and controlling the lives of ordinary citizens. Cornut and others like him are a threat to their power. There are obvious echoes here of the Star class in *The Space Merchants*, Green and Charlesworth of *Gladiator-At-Law*, and the Company of *Preferred Risk*. Once exposed, the immortals decide to rid themselves of the "shorties" and unleash a catastrophic smallpox virus (contracted from the aboriginals of an isolated Pacific island) in the cities, leading to worldwide chaos and catastrophe. Cornut realizes that when he's drunk, the immortals cannot penetrate his mind, and thus an army of drunken shorties swarm the immortal stronghold and wipe them out. In the end, the immortal gene is found to be dominant, accessible to everyone; in typical Pohl fashion, this revelation will change everything, allowing humankind to reach its full potential.

Despite the generally unsatisfying plot, there are a number of compelling ideas in the novel. Universities are like guarded fortresses, literal ivory towers, separated from much of the troubles of an overpopulated outside world. Courses are broadcast across the country—anticipating current trends in which master teachers outsource their lectures via electronic hookup. Well-known science fiction scholar Eric Rabkin is doing something quite similar to-day. As a consequence, the gifted lecturer becomes almost like an entertainer: "A good teacher is a good makeup man" (193). Current trends of deaccessioning in university libraries are anticipated brilliantly: the university library consists of tapes and microfilm and has become a vast computer complex. Once again, Pohl engages with the theme of overpopulation and hierarchical society: the population has reached twelve billion, and many people live on vast rafts in the oceans, called "texases" because they are modeled on oil rig platforms. Alternative relationships are posited by the thirty-day marriage, similar to Mitch and Kathy's short-term contract marriage in *The Space Merchants*. The idea of contract marriages is a recurring theme in Pohl's work (and that of a number of his contemporaries), perhaps reflecting his own pattern of marriage and the larger science fiction community's attempts to rethink sexual and social arrangements. These ideas keep the novel interesting for the modern reader, but the emphasis on immortality and telepathy is now much harder to swallow.

* * *

When Pohl ascended to editor at *Galaxy* and *If*, he brought a new energy that turned them back into the most exciting magazines in the field. And Pohl loved every minute of it: "Next to making a major motion picture, I think editing a science fiction magazine is about the most fun a person can have, and still get paid for it."[42] When he took over, both magazines were on a bi-monthly schedule, and Pohl wanted to get *Galaxy*, at least, back to monthly. Instead of letting Pohl make one of the magazines a monthly, in 1963 the publisher allowed him to start a third magazine, *Worlds of Tomorrow*. Like *Galaxy* and *If*, *Worlds of Tomorrow* published a number of notable stories and serials during its run, including Robert Silverberg's "To See the Invisible Man," Philip K. Dick's *All We Marsmen* (*Martian Time-Slip*) and *Project Plowshare* (*The Zap Gun*), Brian Aldiss's *The Dark Light-Years*, and Samuel R. Delany's "The Star Pit."

Pohl built all three magazines into the best in the field, publishing a good portion of the major work of the decade. He published several controversial

Heinlein novels in the pages of *If*, including *Podkayne of Mars*, *The Moon is a Harsh Mistress*, and the notorious *Farnham's Freehold*; Philip Jose Farmer's original *Riverworld* stories; the zany stories of R. A. Lafferty; most of the Instrumentality of Mankind stories by Cordwainer Smith; and some of the best work of Harlan Ellison, Jack Vance, Robert Silverberg, Fritz Leiber, Roger Zelazny, and others. Pohl bought Harry Harrison's wacky military satire *The Starsloggers* (*Bill, the Galactic Hero*) for *Galaxy* in 1963, a novel Harrison didn't send to his regular market *Analog* because he knew Campbell wouldn't like it.[43] When James Gunn returned to writing fiction in the late 1960s, Pohl published the first story that would make up his important novel *The Listeners*.[44]

Harlan Ellison has stated that his classic story "I Have No Mouth and I Must Scream" was written as a direct result of Pohl having bought "'Repent Harlequin,' Said the Ticktockman" in 1965.[45] Pohl was an editor who could stand toe to toe with the volatile Ellison, which gave Ellison the freedom to write the kind of stories he wanted to write: "Fred Pohl, for all the aggravation he's caused me through the years—we won't mention all the aggravation I've caused him through the years—was one of the few editors who gave me my head and let me write what I wanted to write in those days before the phrase 'New Wave' started emerging in people's mouths." Ellison further praises Pohl as the best editor in the business: "But for all his cantankerous, albeit friendly, canards he remains one of the truest judges of writing ability the field of imaginative literature has ever produced."[46] Another writer who was selling important political science fiction to Pohl was the underrated Mack Reynolds (who was also selling prolifically to Campbell at *Analog*). In stories like, "How We Banned the Bombs," "Criminal in Utopia," and *The Computer Conspiracy*, Reynolds was engaging with global politics in ways that now seem commonplace.

If was Pohl's playground. There, he introduced new authors, including the first stories of Larry Niven, Gene Wolfe, and Gardner Dozois; ran two series, Keith Laumer's *Retief* and Fred Saberhagen's *Berserker*; and produced special issues, such as the "All Smith" issue, which marked the return of E. E. "Doc" Smith, one of Pohl's favorite author's from his early reading.[47] Pohl also cultivated the return to SF of A. E. Van Vogt, after a decade of silence. Although *If* was, ostensibly, the lesser of the two magazines, Pohl received the best editor Hugo Award three times for it in 1966, 1967, and 1968.

Pohl's editorial relationship with Robert Silverberg in the 1960s is worth recounting, as both Pohl and Silverberg attest that it was Pohl's editorial hand that brought Silverberg back into science fiction and led him to produce his most significant work. After an astonishingly prolific run in the late 1950s—at one point most of the contents of several magazines were virtually written by Silverberg singlehandedly, while he was also regularly appearing in *Galaxy* and *Astounding* and publishing novels for Wollheim at Ace—Silverberg had all but dropped out of science fiction, instead focusing on competent nonfiction works for the young adult market and softcore sleaze novels for William Hamling (also at a highly prolific pace). Pohl convinced Silverberg to come back to science fiction and made a deal with him, as Silverberg recounts the arrangement:

> In the late 1950s Fred had been vexed with me for my willingness to churn out all that lucrative junk, and he believed (rightly, as time would prove) that a top-rank sf writer was hidden behind the pyramid of literary garbage that I had cheerfully been producing over the past few years. So he made me an offer shrewdly calculated to appeal to my risk-abhorring nature. He agreed to buy any story I cared to send him—a guaranteed sale—provided I undertook to write it with all my heart, no quick-buck hackwork. If he wanted revisions, I would pledge to do one rewrite for him, after which he would be bound to buy the story without asking anything more of me. If I turned in a story he didn't like, he would buy it anyway, but that would be the end of the deal.[48]

This arrangement pushed Silverberg to become a better writer, by Pohl's refusal to consider stories that didn't reach the level at which Pohl believed Silverberg should be writing.[49] It went on for several years, and Silverberg contributed a bevy of major stories and serials to Pohl's magazines, beginning with "To See the Invisible Man." Silverberg credits their arrangement for forging his development from the workmanlike, although sometimes brilliant, work he produced in the 1950s into science fiction of literary quality. In this sense, Silverberg's trajectory as a writer is similar to Pohl's: an early phase of mostly pedestrian hackwork, followed by a mature blossoming into work of sustained merit.

As the 1960s continued, Pohl hired a young woman named Judy-Lynn Benjamin as editorial assistant. Benjamin would later marry Lester Del Rey, who also worked with Pohl as contributing editor, and together they would forge the Del Rey Books fantasy and science fiction line at Ballantine, the most significant publishing program in the field in the late 1970s and throughout the 1980s. In 1967 Pohl launched *International Science Fiction*, a magazine with the good intentions of expanding readers' horizons by publishing stories from around the world and expanding the overall scope of science fiction. Despite these good intentions, the magazine lasted only for two issues. But this was the start of Pohl's wider efforts for developing a cross-cultural dialogue among science fiction readers and writers from around the world, which would eventually lead to the creation of World SF, the brainchild of Pohl, Brian Aldiss, and Harry Harrison.

Pohl continued to produce a number of notable short stories, which he published in *Galaxy* and *If* throughout the 1960s. "The Abominable Earthman" (*Galaxy*, October 1961) is another alien invasion story where Sirians have invaded Earth and taken over the United States, setting up a breeding farm to make humans into slaves. The Sirians are defeated when ne'er-do-well Private Pinky Postal gets them drunk on carbon dioxide, destroying their ship and central computer. "The Deadly Mission of Phineas Snodgrass" (*Galaxy*, June 1962) is a delightfully nasty little story about overpopulation, recursively responding to L. Sprague de Camp's *Lest Darkness Fall*, that posits the notion of the time traveler going back to the time of Christ to try to eliminate the problem of overpopulation in his own era. Instead, Snodgrass makes the cycle of development happen much faster: by wanting to help the people, he transforms the living habits of Year One—"Everybody got healthy" (19)—and the human species burns out the planet, and ultimately the entire universe, by the year 1000. It is a stark meditation on the problem of human overpopulation written around the time Pohl wrote *Tiberius*, his short account of the brutal Roman emperor. "Father of the Stars" (*If*, November 1964) is something quite different, displaying a deep poignancy unusual in Pohl's work. One of Pohl's finest stories, it is a quiet, emotional piece about the man who paved the way for future generations to the stars, resonating with Heinlein's tales of D. D. Harriman. It is also a story about aging, and although Pohl was only forty-five years old when it was published, it anticipates the trajectory of Pohl's own life as he lived (and continued to work) into his nineties. In another variation of Pohl's mindswapping, the decrepit Norman Marchand is "smithed," a technique that puts his mind into the body of a chimpanzee, which allows him to voyage with the young colonists to a new planet on the ship he financed. Feeling that he somehow betrayed the lives of the people who committed to the long journey, but finding they have named the new planet after him, the simian Marchand wanders into the forest to die in peace: "'He gave us these planets. . . . Do you know what being a good man means, Ferguson? It means being better than you really are—so that even your failures carry someone a little farther to success—and that's what he did for us'" (96). "Earth Eighteen" (*Galaxy*, April 1964) is a bitingly humorous, satirical story presented as promotional materials for vacation tours for aliens to Earth. Very few humans remain on the trashed and nuked planet. Finally, "Under Two Moons" (*If*, September 1965), a parody and homage to Edgar Rice Burroughs's Mars books, is a good example of the fun Pohl was having with *If*.

Meanwhile, Pohl also continued to publish his own novels in both magazines. Over the course of the decade, *The Starchild Trilogy* (*The Reefs of Space, Starchild, Rogue Star*), written in collaboration with Jack Williamson, appeared in *If*. Due to writer's block and the demands of his academic position as professor of English at Eastern New Mexico University, Williamson had largely been absent from science fiction for a number of years, publishing just three stories and a fix-up novel of earlier stories since the last *Undersea* novel in 1958. It seems likely that *The Reefs of Space* developed out of an idea that Williamson had first worked up with Dr. Miles J. Breuer, a pioneering writer in the early *Amazing Stories*, with whom Williamson had collaborated in 1929. In the early 1940s, Breuer had tried to renew the collaboration, but it went no further than an exchange of notes.[50] In the early 1950s, when Williamson was suffering from writer's block, he approached Pohl, his agent at the time, about some ideas centered around a character deemed a criminal in a future society and bound by an "iron collar." Later, these ideas worked their way into *The Reefs of Space*. Although the three novels in the series are competent adventure novels, when compared to other Pohl or Williamson novels with interplanetary or galactic settings, they don't rise to the level of either author's best work. Pohl hired Algis Budrys to write book reviews for *Galaxy*, a post Budrys would hold through 1971, and in Budrys's first column in February 1965, he considered *The Reefs of Space*, pointing out that "it is not like a Jack Williamson novel, not like a Frederik Pohl novel, and not like a Pohl-Kornbluth novel."⁵¹ Budrys perceptively challenges some of the science—the novel relied on the now disproved steady-state theory—and the narrative structure of the novel, but he praises it for its "sense of wonder," something which comes across less successfully in the sequels.

In brief, *The Reefs of Space* presents an Earth that has become a global theocratic dictatorship under the "Plan of Man." No one seems to understand what exactly the Plan of Man actually means, as its origins have been forgotten. What it explicitly decrees is that humankind is not to strive into space; in the forgotten past something had happened, and, as in Clarke's *Against the Fall of Night*, humans have retreated to Earth in fear. The prisoner Ryeland believes that humans must go into space in order to survive. Criminals are controlled by unremovable iron collars and are harvested as body banks for "useful citizens," a more diabolical version of the idea of Full Medical that Pohl will later develop in *Gateway*. Ryeland escapes his fate, breaks the dictatorship of the Plan, and opens up a return to the solar frontier. The second novel, *Starchild*, takes place slightly further into the future, with humankind spreading out into the solar system but not having yet moved into interstellar space until the denouement of the novel. *Rogue Star* is much further into the future; humankind has spread throughout space, and Earth is mostly forgotten and abandoned, registering with the pattern established in *Search the Sky*.

Although *The Starchild Trilogy* is ultimately of only minor interest, one thing that makes these novels important in Pohl's creative trajectory is the move into plots set in space. Like *Search the Sky*, these novels anticipate the later period in which a number of his novels use the space adventure model, so Pohl can utilize the "big canvas" of outer space and future history to tell more sophisticated stories that explore cutting-edge ideas in speculative science and use the backdrop of space for political allegory. With that said, *The Starchild Trilogy* is best considered as a transitional work from the wry and cynical satires of the 1950s to the expansive, politically charged space adventures of the following decades.

More successful is *A Plague of Pythons*, another novel about mind control and paranoia—further variation on the theme Pohl mined previously in *Wolfbane*, "Mars by Moonlight," and *Drunkard's Walk*—which appeared in *Galaxy* in late 1962, not seeing book publication until 1965. Pohl later revised and retitled the novel as *Demon in the Skull* in 1984, but this analysis will consider the original paperback version. Here Pohl continues to expand his critique of power and corruption, focusing on how, given the means, the tendency for some human beings is to dominate, manipulate, and brutalize others. Returning to the near future, the novel is set at the end of the twentieth century; space flight has been abandoned, and Cold War paranoia has stagnated politics and the economy. Positing that the space program will fail by the end of the century is interesting, coming from Pohl, as this downbeat turn is most often associated with grim New Wave writers like J. G. Ballard and Barry Malzberg.

A Plague of Pythons initially appears to be a novel of alien invasion. At the beginning of the novel an alien presence, "demons," have arrived, wreaking havoc on the people of Earth and causing a pandemic of insanity:

> The real enemy had struck the entire world in a single night. One day the people of the world went about their business in the gloomy knowledge that they were likely to make mistakes but with, at least, the comfort that the mistakes would be their own. The next day had not such comfort. The next day anyone, anywhere, was likely to find himself seized, possessed, working evil or whimsy without ever having formed the intention to do so . . . and helplessly. Demons? Martians? No one knew whether the invaders of the soul were from another world or from some djinn's bottle. All they knew was that they were helpless against them (17).

The prospects of nuclear holocaust rears its head as the wave of possession leads the United States, suspecting the Russians are behind the possessions, to launch its entire nuclear arsenal, destroying the Soviet Union and killing a quarter of a billion people.

A Plague of Pythons is a downbeat and brutal novel, by far Pohl's most unrestrainedly violent and disturbing. Chandler, a former design engineer working on telemetry for the space program, is on trial for a brutal rape he committed while under demon control. His trial is not because he committed the rape—provisions have been made to exempt crimes committed while possessed—but because he committed it in a pharmaceutical factory, and the possessions simply do not occur in and around vital locations like pharmaceutical plants or agricultural areas. Thus, Chandler is suspected of faking. As punishment, the letter "H," for hoaxer, is tattooed on his forehead, making him a pariah. Taken in by a resistance group called the Orphalese, Chandler learns that the invaders are not demons or aliens but other human beings, somehow able to control the minds of others. In short order, the resistance is infiltrated, and in a brutal scene the entire community is gunned down by a young woman Chandler had befriended, a fat young man (who is one of the Orphalese leaders), and an arthritic old woman: "When every Orphalese except themselves was down on the floor, dead, wounded or, like Chandler, overlooked, the arthritic lady took careful aim at Ellen Braisted and the plump youth and shot them neatly in the temples. They didn't try to prevent her. With expressions that seemed almost impatient they presented their profiles to her aim" (50–51). Shortly after, Chandler is taken and delivered to the Los Angeles airport, where he takes a transport to the Hawaiian Islands and is enlisted as a technical laborer for the "Execs," the group of conspirators behind the mind control, all of whom are on the island. There he learns the full extent of the conspiracy: Russian researchers had created a coronet helmet that allowed the user to transmit "his entire personality" through high frequency radio and "invade and modulate the personality of any other human being in the world" (88). More coronets were manufactured; a select group of one thousand conspirators were recruited from around the world, disentwining themselves from conventional political loyalties, and they proceeded to take over the world, "killing for fun" (90) and otherwise creating mayhem to indulge their distorted synaptic pleasure centers. Like *Drunkard's Walk*, these elites consider themselves a "New Thing" (96), rationalizing their carnival of cruelty and lust by the fact that "the world was getting ready to kill itself anyway" (95). Chandler has been enslaved by one of the lead conspirators, Koitska, to build a second master transmitter so that the Execs can extend their control. As is typical in Pohl's fiction, an underground movement, the "Society of Slaves," gets into contact with Chandler. However, like the Orphalese before, the Society is infiltrated, and all members are massacred. Chandler again manages to escape through the help of a female Exec, Rosalie Pan, who is attracted to him. Chandler becomes Rosalie's lover, and she eventually lets him experience the coronet, intending to initiate him into the Execs. At the end, Chandler infiltrates the machine facility, destroys it, rendering the coronets inert, then places the master transmitter he had made for Koitska on his own head, using it to kill all of the Execs: "For he had been wrong, he saw now, in thinking that the destruction of the machines would free the world from its tyranny . . . It was necessary to destroy the machinery, yes; but it was also necessary to destroy the plans . . . not only the plans on paper but the plans that might linger in the brain of the members of the Exec. It was, in fact, necessary to kill them all" (155). The novel ends on a bitterly dark note as Chandler contemplates the task ahead:

> Yes, there was much to do. While he was waiting for the coffee to seep through its filter he slipped the coronet casually back atop his head. Only for a while, of course. A very little while. He pledged himself solemnly that there would definitely be no question about that. He would wear it just long enough to clean up all the loose ends—just that long and not one second longer, he pledged, and knew as he pledged that he lied (158).

Those following Pohl's trajectory as a writer up until this point might be shocked by this level of despairing cynicism, since Pohl usually ended his narratives with a semblance of hope for the prospects of the future (with the exception of "Let the Ants Try"). Indeed, *Analog*'s reviewer P. Schuyler Miller noted that Pohl had reached a darker turn with this novel: "There's no fun in what has hit the world he describes."[52] While still largely reflecting conventions of plotting and characterization typical of 1950s and 1960s magazine science fiction, the "darker turn" of *A Plague of Pythons* seems to anticipate the shift to Pohl's increasingly complex and sophisticated works of the 1970s and 1980s. An increasingly edgy and bitter cynicism would emerge in a number of Pohl's politically engaged science fiction novels from those years, such as *Jem* and *Black Star Rising*, although even in those bitingly cynical narratives, some degree of optimism remains. Along with Pohl's next novel, *The Age of the Pussyfoot*, and his masterful story "Day Million," *A Plague of Pythons* indicates a transition in Pohl's work, reflecting the transition of science fiction (and American culture at large) itself—a transition that can also be tracked in the pages of Pohl's magazines.

The Age of the Pussyfoot develops from then-current enthusiasm for cryonics. When Pohl received Robert Ettinger's manuscript "Life Extension through Freezing" (published in book form as *The Prospect of Immortality* in 1964), he published it serially in *Worlds of Tomorrow* and publicly championed the cryonic movement on the Long John Nebel all-night radio show in New York City, and later as a guest on Johnny Carson's *Tonight Show*.[53] In the novel, the unforeseen consequences of cryonic suspension lead to a problem that continues to surface in Pohl's work: overpopulation. The story has much in common with Wells's *When the Sleeper Wakes*, as Charles Forrester wakes up to find himself in a future where compound interest has left him with a substantial sum of money. But unlike Wells's famous novel, the cost of living has increased to the degree that Forrester is more or less broke from the moment he is revived. It is worth mentioning that Pohl explores this conundrum from a slightly different angle in the short story "A Visit to Belindia" for the 1994 shared-theme anthology *Future Quartet: Earth in the Year 2042*.

Like other nineteenth-century precursors—*Looking Backward, A Crystal Age, News from Nowhere*—Pohl establishes a contemporary connection before thrusting Forrester into the future. Forrester died in 1969 and was one of the first to be frozen; he has been revived in the year 2527. The story takes place in the city of Shoggo (Chicago). Forrester awakes at the cryonic facilities—with echoes of *Preferred Risk*, although when Pohl and Del Rey wrote the latter, the science of cryonics had not yet developed. Population has reached seventeen billion, and there are twice that number in cold storage. Once again, Pohl introduces an underground political movement, the Ned Lud Society, who preach that people are sheep, expropriated by their machines.

One of the most interesting elements in the narrative is how Pohl shows that Forrester doesn't understand how things work in the culture of the future—and the culture is not very helpful in showing him the ropes. The newly revived are called "greenhorns," and throughout the beginning chapters Forrester must sort out the varying social customs that distinguish the future from the present. One such custom is the practice of taking out hunting licenses against others. Forrester does not understand what this means, and when a license is taken out against him, he fails to defend himself and is killed. He is immediately revived by the ever-present machines, plunging him further into debt and reinforcing the painful lesson that in a world of advanced medicine where death is easily reversed, life itself is trivial. Part of the reason no system is in place to orient the newly revived is because people have become utterly dependent on their handheld machines, called joymakers (something quite different from James Gunn's classic novel of the same title)—a startling anticipation of the smart phone, that they no longer have the ability to take initiative, solve problems, offer assistance, or simply think for themselves—the joymakers do all that for them: "The principle of it was clear enough. It was a remote input-output station for a shared-time computer program, with certain attachments that functioned as a pocket flask, a first-aid kit, cosmetic bag, and so on. It looked something like a mace or a jester's scepter" (11). Thus, the novel is particularly notable for exploring the cultural changes that such a technology might instigate—issues that are of pressing importance as we push forward into the digital environment. The baffled Forrester is given a *Guide to the 26th Century*, which explains how the joymaker works but no further explanation, almost like the frustratingly inadequate "Help" feature on our computer software. The joymaker provides the user with an "interests profile," something that sounds a lot like Facebook or other interfaces on the Web. As Forrester's female sponsor Adne explains, "'Have you filed an interests profile? . . . Oh, do! Then it will tell you what programs are on, what parties you will be welcomed at, who you would wish to know. It's terrible to go on impulse, Charles,' she said earnestly. 'Let the joymaker help you'" (37). Later, when Forrester observes Adne's children, he does a double take when he encounters their simulacrum toys, similar to those in "The Man Who Ate the World," one of them modeled on Burroughs's Martian Tars Tarkas, leading him to reflect on how advanced technologies leave the uninitiated behind:

> It had always seemed to him wonderful and exciting that he should be living in an age when electricity came from wall sockets and living pictures from a box on a bench. He had thought sometimes, with irony and pity, of how laughably incompetent some great mind of the past, a Newton or an Archimedes, would have been to follow his own six-year-old's instructions about tuning a television set or operating the electric trains. So here I am, he thought wryly, the bushman in Times Square. It's not much fun (71).

The children demonstrate the mentality that occurs when ubiquitous information technology makes everything instant access: "You don't have to understand it, just do it. What do you think the joymakers are for?" (74).

Another timely thematic thread explores the rising cost of medical care: "Forrester gasped and coughed and cried, half strangled, 'Two and half million *dollars* for medical—Sweet Jesus God! . . . Holy AMA! Who can afford that kind of money? . . . The whole thing's crazy. Millions of dollars for doctors! People just can't *have* that much money'" (56–57). Pohl was ahead of the curve in thinking about the spiraling healthcare costs in the future, a crisis we currently face. Of course, everything else has inflated as well; even the unskilled Forrester can work for minimum wage at $25,000 a day. And the standard of living has escalated along with costs and wages: "His quarter of a million dollars would have bought him—and in fact *had* bought him—something very like a quarter million dollars' worth of goods and services, even by twentieth-century standards. It was not the dollar that had been inflated. It was the standard of living. There were so many things that a dollar could now buy" (93). In *Analog*, Miller observed that Pohl effectively combines the notion of compound interest with "the gradual increase of the standard of living and the cheapness of life that becomes inevitable when death is no longer permanent," noting further that there is a "smoothing out of individualism" within a "computerized economy."[54]

Moving from the wanderer-in-utopia plot, Pohl shifts the focus to an alien invasion subplot. As humanity moved out into space and encountered another colonizing species, war broke out with the Sirians, and eleven were captured. Having exhausted his financial resources, Forrester gets a job telling his life story to one of the Sirians and researching Earth's historical past, which gives the Sirian insight into human psychology. But Forrester refuses to follow the line of research the Sirian wants him to pursue and is fired. Unemployed and unable to maintain expenses, he is kicked out of his apartment, becoming one of the "Forgotten Men," those who have to live on the street and who are easy targets for assassination. Meanwhile, the Sirian has escaped from Earth, with the unwitting assistance of Forrester, and everyone fears he will return to Sirius and trigger all-out war. People panic and go into the cold sleep chambers, fearing that the Sirian invasion fleet is on its way. Forrester is rescued from anonymity by Adne and finds that he has inherited the Sirian's wealth—$91 million. After killing his nemesis Heinzlichen, the man who keeps taking hunting licenses out against him, and finding out about the Sirian's escape, Forrester fears he will be arrested and goes into hiding for nineteen days. Returning to the empty city, he's brought before Taiko, the leader of the Lud Society, who has aligned himself with the Sirians and plans to destroy the machines once most of humanity has gone into the freezers. Realizing that the Sirians' real plan is to destroy humanity once they are completely incapacitated, Forrester slits his own throat so that the machines will deliver him to the medical facilities where he will be revived and there be able to expose the invasion plan. In the final chapter, Forrester is awakened, the Sirians' plan has been thwarted, and people are being revived from the freezers. However, anticipating concerns now surfacing in our digital age, Forrester pensively reflects on whether Taiko and the Luds were right that humanity "took a wrong turning" in giving itself over to its computer technologies—to which Hara, his sponsoring physician, rebuts: "Chuck, there's no such thing as a wrong turning. You can't rewrite the history of the race; it happened; this is the result. If you don't like it, there's no reason why you can't try to persuade the world to change again. To something different—anything! Whatever you like. But *you can't go back*" (172). Such advice deeply resonates with the accelerated pace of technological change in the twenty-first century.

In a final Author's Note, Pohl stresses the extrapolative nature of science fiction, how it draws upon existing developments in science and technology and extrapolates them into the future: "Almost every aspect of it [*Pussyfoot*] is visible right now, in July of 1968, as a cloud no bigger than a man's hand; and I too am forecasting rain" (174). Extraordinarily, among these tiny, cloud-like extrapolations, Pohl anticipates the internet and the miniaturization of digital devices: "The joymaker? . . . At M.I.T., two big IBM 7094s, plus half a dozen or so servant computers, are available to anyone with a remote-access console in his home or office. The console right now can be anywhere a telephone line will go. . . . My only additional assumption is that it will be convenient to do the same thing by radio. The MAC consoles are presently the size of biggish electric typewriters; my only change involves microminiaturizing them into portability—and, while you're at it, fitting them with a few such necessities of modern urban life" (174). Such prescient observations, as SF writer David Brin points out, makes *The Age of the Pussyfoot* "one of the only science fiction stories of the fifties through seventies that envisioned computers becoming household tools, owned and used, avidly, by everybody" and that foresaw "citizens carrying about portable, computerized assistants that would fulfill the functions we now see gathering together in our futuristic cell phones."[55]

In both *A Plague of Pythons* and *The Age of the Pussyfoot*, Pohl's narrative voice is moving toward a new aesthetic, one reflective of the changing times and cultural mores, although that development has not fully manifested itself as it will in Pohl's fiction of the early 1970s. This shift is best exemplified by the short story "Day Million," published in *Rogue* in 1966, which is now considered by many to be Pohl's masterpiece in short fiction. This change in Pohl's aesthetic is a culmination of at least four things: his absorption of the changing science fiction aesthetic from the writers he was publishing in *Galaxy* and *If* (Delany, for instance); his increasingly sophisticated engagement with real science; the fact that Pohl was simply growing older himself, becoming more mature; and a greater freedom within the genre as writers, editors, and publishers no longer restricted themselves to the formulas of the 1950s magazine market.

"Day Million" has become Pohl's representative short story, appearing in dozens of anthologies and taught in countless college courses. It anticipates later discussions of posthumanity and gender, and shows a mastery of form and style that helped change the shape of science fiction. "Day Million" uncompromisingly posits that people will be far different in one thousand years, not only in their social relationships and customs but also in their physical form.

"Day Million" thrusts the reader into an accelerated posthuman future, where gender is malleable, the human form is altered according to environmental condition or individual choice, cybernetic humans are exploring the stars, and love relationships are stored in data receptacles to be experienced at the user's desire. Pohl takes a refreshingly approving viewpoint in the story: rather than balk in horror, Pohl here chooses to marvel at the people of day million's capacity to experience on levels beyond that of contemporary humanity. Pohl's point is that we stand at the beginning of an era of accelerated technological and biological change, and that if such technological progress continues, the posthumans of the future will be far different from us, while still maintaining the passion for life and experience that defines humanity.

Set a thousand years from now, "Day Million" is the love story of Dora, a seven-foot-tall woman who has a "tail," a "silky pelt," and "gill slits behind each ear," and smells of peanut butter, and Don, a 187-year-old cybernetic man who travels among the stars. Pohl challenges the masculinist assumptions of his original men's magazine audience by the fact that Dora is transgender, "the reason the girl was not a girl was that she was a boy" (11). Further emphasizing the malleability of the physical form in the future of day million and, more important, the cultural change that goes along with it, "It didn't matter to her audiences that genetically she was male. It wouldn't matter to you, if you were among them, because you wouldn't know it . . . and it didn't matter to them because they didn't care" (12). When Dora bumps into Don on "an elastic platform" outside "call it her rehearsal hall," they instantly fall in love (13). Don travels in interstellar space on a ship that requires "thirty-one male and seven genetically female human beings," by method reminiscent of Cordwainer Smith's Go-Ships (see, for instance, "The Lady Who Sailed the Soul") or Frank Herbert's Guild Navigators in *Dune*. Further, Don's cybernetic alterations, which allow him to survive on his journeys through the starlanes, anticipate the cyborg Roger Torraway in *Man Plus*, Pohl's award-winning novel about the first manned mission to Mars. To consummate their love, Dora and Don meet "at the encoding room" where "their identities [are] taped and stored," whereupon "they exchanged their mathematical analogues and went away," and henceforth "they never set eyes on each other again" (15). In the future world of Dora and Don, love comes through the exchange of data packets. But Pohl does not condemn this practice as cold and empty; rather, he emphasizes that it is a far richer sensual exchange than anything imaginable by beings like us, limited and contained as we are by our bodies and our private selves. Pohl hammers home that it is not for us to judge the people, customs, and mores of the future. The future *will* be different. Perhaps better than any other story in the genre, "Day Million" succinctly illustrates this point.

During the mid- to late 1960s, science fiction, like American and European culture, was changing, and these changes were making themselves manifest in the pages of Pohl's magazine. While Moorcock's *New Worlds* was establishing the New Wave in Britain and Harlan Ellison's *Dangerous Visions* anthology was stirring up outrage and delight in North America, Pohl was also changing the face of science fiction in the pages of *Galaxy*, *If*, *Worlds of Tomorrow*, and *International Science Fiction*. In retrospect, the segment of the New Wave that Pohl was publishing in his magazines had a greater impact and, perhaps, a more lasting value than what Moorcock published in *New Worlds*; with the exception of the work of J. G. Ballard, Brian Aldiss, and Moorcock himself, plus a few works by Americans (for example, Thomas M. Disch, John Sladek, and Norman Spinrad), most of the British New Wave has not aged well. With that said, future developments in the field would take into account what was opened up by all three crests of the New Wave—Moorcock's *New Worlds*, Ellison's *Dangerous Visions*, and Pohl's magazines—aesthetic innovation, inner space, sexual frankness, and reflective recursivity among them. Pohl's own fiction would come to exemplify these developments.

⋆   ⋆   ⋆

By the early months of 1969, Pohl's editorial energy and enthusiasm was beginning to flag. While he joined J. G. Ballard, Robert Sheckley, Harrison, Aldiss, and many other SF writers in Rio De Janeiro for the World Science Fiction Symposium, *Galaxy* and *If* were sold to Universal Publishing.[56] When Pohl returned home, he decided that this transition was a good moment for him to step down as editor, although he would remain on the masthead as editor emeritus for the remainder of the year.

The *Galaxy* years had been enormously productive and fulfilling, but, at age fifty, it was time for Pohl to move forward to the next stage of his life and career.

CHAPTER 3

GATEWAYS, 1970–1987

After Pohl stepped down from *Galaxy*, he went into a funk, and though he now had time to write, he wasn't writing. Having turned fifty at the close of 1969, Pohl attests that he was experiencing a midlife crisis.[1] Though he was absorbing all that he had learned as editor of *Galaxy* and reflecting on the changes that were happening in American society and in science fiction, other matters were keeping him from his work. Instead of buckling down and writing fiction, he took time to travel with his family, with trips to London and Paris, Bermuda, and Japan. Further complicating matters, the first signs of trouble in his marriage to Carol were beginning to show themselves.[2] Like many science fiction writers in the wake of the Apollo mission to the Moon, Pohl had become a highly sought-after speaker at universities, think tanks, and corporations, and he was a frequent guest commentator on late-night radio and television.[3] In an interview with Charles Platt, Pohl reflected with irony on some of the dissonance he experienced when speaking to corporate America:

My impression is that the corporations and management groups that employed me wanted me to shake things up a little bit and perhaps give them some new perspectives, but they were not inclined to heed what I said very seriously. I remember talking to a group in Chicago once and saying that the primary requisite for achieving a viable relationship between our society and the planet's ecology was individual self-control. They stood up and cheered me. Then the next speaker said exactly the opposite and they stood up and cheered him too.[4]

Pohl's busy travel schedule and frequent excursions into the city not only made it harder for him to start his writing engine, but with Carol and the kids at home in Red Bank, it exacerbated his family difficulties.

As if he were not already busy enough, Pohl made several trips to Eastern Europe, underwritten by the State Department, making connections with writers within the Soviet Bloc.[5] This direct interaction with writers from behind the Iron Curtain was to inform the sophisticated interplay between the superpowers that we see throughout his Cold War narratives of the coming decades. Pohl was also getting involved in grassroots politics, in 1968 working on the Eugene McCarthy campaign in New Jersey.[6] His political experiences are articulated in his first book of the 1970s, *Practical Politics 1972*, published at the end of 1971, which later contributed to his wife Elizabeth Anne Hull's congressional campaign in 1996 in Illinois's Eighth District.[7]

In *Practical Politics*, Pohl analyzes how American politics works (and doesn't work) and sets out to give advice for grassroots political activism. He is both cynical of the system as it has developed but also hopeful that through grassroots activism the electorate can make a meaningful difference. The book is informed by the earlier novel *Presidential Year*, and its political insight will continue to funnel into Pohl's fiction in subsequent decades in novels like *Jem*, *The Cool War*, *Syzygy*, and *Black Star Rising*. In early chapters, particularly chapter 3, "Patronage and Other Forms of Stealing for Fun and Profit," Pohl diagnoses some of the persistent faults in American electioneering and politics. There is some classic Pohl wry irony: "And what you must realize before you get very seriously involved in politics is that *for professional politicians this is what politics is all about.* They aren't in politics to safeguard American democracy or to fight communism. They are in politics because that is how they make their daily bread, and as things stand they make an awful lot of it" (37). Pohl dedicates the book to "all who know something's wrong but have been too embarrassed to do anything about it." What's most troubling about *Practical Politics* is that politics hasn't seemed to have changed for the better since Pohl offered his analysis.

Pohl's political views were linked to his engagement with science as, what he called, a "spectator sport." Observing policymaking decisions involving science, the space program, and the environment as he visited labs, university research facilities, and observatories, Pohl concluded that political maneuvering too often interfered with scientific advance. As manifested in *The Space Merchants* and his other works, Pohl was deeply concerned that overuse of planetary resources and overpopulation would have drastic environmental consequences in the future. In the 1960s these issues had been brought forward in the public mind by Rachel Carson's *Silent Spring* and Paul Ehrlich's *The Population Bomb*. But Pohl and the science fiction community in general had been looking at these problems through the extrapolative lens of SF since the inception of the genre[8] and Pohl had bought and published many stories about eco-crisis in his magazines throughout the 1960s. He brought a number of these stories, and some from other magazines, together in a brilliant anthology in 1970, *Nightmare Age*, one of several eco-catastrophe anthologies produced in the period—although *Nightmare Age* anticipates the others by a year or two. In *Yesterday's Tomorrows*, Pohl reflects on the book: "*Nightmare Age* was an eco-freak book. It sold out its one printing and was seen no more, but it still remains an anthology of which I am proud. It seems to me that the world ecology movement really began in the science fiction stories—especially in the 1950s, but actually going back as far as science fiction itself does."[9] Both *Practical Politics* and *Nightmare Age* articulated Pohl's ideas on the American political scene and the environment, and over the next four decades, these perspectives would be central to his fiction.

Practical Politics got Pohl writing again, but before he could settle into fiction once more, he needed to sort out what kind of writer he was going to be. Luckily, Ballantine reissued most of his back titles at this time, which afforded him the financial flexibility to regroup without feeling that he had to get back to work immediately. But by the fall of 1971 he began looking for editorial work. After John W. Campbell's death that September, Pohl was interested in taking over *Analog*, but the publisher decided to go with Ben Bova. Pohl then received a call from Charter Communications, which owned Ace Books. His old rival Don Wollheim had recently severed ties with Ace after twenty-plus years and set up his own paperback line, DAW books. Pohl joined Ace in December 1971—and soon found out that it was a disaster. Ace had money troubles, and their writers were furious; having gone through this before with his own agency, Pohl's sympathies lay with the writers. During his first three months at Ace, he tried to mend fences and resolve grievances with a number of writers who felt as if Ace was ripping them off. By July 1972, as his new stories were breaking out in the magazines, he'd had enough and left the company—which in turn was soon sold and gotten back on solid financial footing.[10]

The time off before the editorial grind at Ace, however, had afforded Pohl enough leisure to get it all put back together both creatively and at home, and he hit the field like a storm in 1972, producing such innovative and substantial novellas as "The Gold at the Starbow's End" (*Analog*, March 1972) and "The Merchants of Venus" (*If*, July–August 1972), followed the next year by "In the Problem Pit" (*FSF*, September 1973).

The first story to emerge in this flowering of new productivity was "The Gold at the Starbow's End," which marked Pohl's first solo appearance in the pages of *Analog*. This was one of the first stories selected by *Analog's* new editor Ben Bova, and the story not only marked a return to writing by Pohl, but it also set the tone for what *Analog* was going to be like under its new editor. Along with Joe Haldeman's *Forever War* stories, the sexual frankness and left-leaning politics of Pohl's tale indicated a change in the magazine's editorial policy. As Edward James remarks, "It is difficult to imagine Campbell publishing Frederik Pohl's 'The Gold at the Starbow's End.'"[11] But Bova did. And as if to quietly usher in this change, Bova left out the usual "In Times to Come" preview for the February issue, instead writing an editorial eulogizing Campbell, discussing the second-wave of emerging technologies, and telling readers that "inevitably, *Analog* will change."[12]

Reminiscent of Poul Anderson's novel *Tau Zero* (1970) (the shorter version, "To Out Live Eternity," appeared in Pohl's *Galaxy* in 1967), "The Gold at the Starbow's End" involves a starship voyage to Alpha Centauri. Ostensibly conceived as a mission to explore and colonize a newly discovered planet, which turns out to be a fabrication, the real motivation for the project is to send a group of young, brilliant minds into deep space in hopes that they can think: "We have selected eight of the most intelligent human beings we could find—healthy, young, very adventurous. Very creative. We played a nasty trick on them to be sure. But we gave them an opportunity to *think*. To think for *ten years*. To think about basic questions" (28). Meanwhile, the entire world becomes politically destabilized—even the United States, where a coup occurs and the president flees Washington. Although the planet at Alpha Centauri was a lie, the project has worked all too well: the crew forms a gestalt while practicing the *I Ching* and tap into higher states of consciousness, which gives them the power to manipulate time, space, and matter, allowing them to create a planet for themselves. Having determined that the political situation on Earth is resolvable only through drastic, cataclysmic action, the explorers send a message that says they are sending a pulse of heavy particles that will knock out all installations of the global military-industrial complex involving nuclear weapons. After which they will begin colonizing the new planet with people from Earth: "WE HAVE CREATED THE PLANET ALPHA-ALEPH. IT IS BEAUTIFUL AND GRAND. WE WILL SEND OUR FERRIES TO BRING SUITABLE PERSONS AND OTHERS TO STOCK IT AND TO COMPLETE CERTAIN OTHER BUSINESS" (71).

The story is a mindbender, blending Pohl's sardonic political imagination with the pop meditation and consciousness-raising fads of the early 1970s. As another story that evokes the political crisis of the Cold War, the novella reflects the political skepticism in *Practical Politics* and registers the overall cultural disillusionment during the Nixon years. It also demonstrates Pohl's shift to a hard SF orientation, as the story is deeply informed by emerging ideas in quantum physics and the sophisticated technical language arising from the complex engineering projects in the space sciences. The story is Pohl's first response to the promise of space, asserted by Neil Armstrong when he made his monumental one small step, and to the disillusionment with government bureaucracy that comes with it. The later novel *Starburst* (1982) is essentially just an expansion of the original story and seems incongruous as a product of the early 1980s, losing the important trendy topicality of the original publication in 1972. The condensed novella is more effective than the novel, demonstrating a more tightly controlled interplay of style, tone, and plotting.

Other important stories followed in 1972, three appearing in *Fantasy and Science Fiction*: "Sad Solarian Screenwriter Sam" in June, "Shaffery among the Immortals" in July, and another posthumous Korbluth collaboration, "The Meeting," in November, which won the Hugo Award for Best Short Story. "The Meeting" is a deeply moving story about a couple presented with the opportunity to have the healthy brain of a boy killed in an accident transplanted into the body of their "cerebrally damaged" nine-year-old son. Kornbluth's fragment developed from the difficulty he and his wife were facing with one of their sons as they put him in a school for children with special needs. Pohl found the fragment deeply moving but was unable to come to terms with it for some years, as his own daughter Kathy struggled with developmental disabilities. As Pohl attests, the story "was a kind of therapy for both of us."[13] Pohl effectively conveys the anguish of the parents but leaves the ending open, as the father picks up the phone to call the doctor with his decision: "The two of them stood next to the outsize crib that held their son, looking in the night light at the long fair lashes against the chubby cheeks and the pouted lips around the thumb. . . . Vladek stayed there for a full half hour and then, as he had promised, went back to the kitchen, picked up the phone and began to dial" (115). "The Meeting" stands as a poignant testament to the challenges and joys and abiding love Pohl had for his daughter—and Kornbluth had for his son.

But perhaps Pohl's most important story of 1972 is "The Merchants of Venus," which would begin his most sustained achievement, the Heechee saga. In "The Merchants of Venus" humans have found a vast network of tunnels on Venus left long ago by extrasolar visitors called the Heechee: "The Heechee built these tunnels a long time ago—maybe a quarter of a million years. Maybe more. They seem to have occupied them for some time, anything up to a century or two, give or take a lot. Then they went away again. They left a lot of junk behind, and some things that weren't junk" (22). This triggers a rush to prospect the planet in search of Heechee artifacts, the most prominent being what are called "prayer fans," though what these prayer fans actually are is not revealed until the second novel in the series. Like *The Space Merchants*, "The Merchants of Venus" uses a first-person narrator. Experienced guide Audee Walters is hired by Boyce Cochenour, a wealthy ancient who has been kept alive and physically robust through multiple transplants (introducing the concept of Full Medical, which is fully fleshed out in *Gateway*), to take him and his attractive girlfriend Dorrie out prospecting. Walters himself is in dire straits: his liver is failing, and he needs to strike a big score in order to afford a transplant. Unfortunately, nothing new has been found for twenty years. However, Walters has a pretty good idea where an unexplored Heechee tunnel may be and, after they are fully outfitted, he takes Cochenour out to look for it. As the story moves forward, they investigate the tunnel, but nothing pans out, as it has already been searched. Walters's hopes for a transplant are dashed when Cochenour reveals he's broke, having spent his money on keeping himself alive; he's heading toward bankruptcy, which means death. In desperation, Walters leads them into territory reserved by the military, where they find a treasure trove of Heechee machinery. To cover his tracks, Cochenour tries to kill Walters and Dorrie, but Walters, on the brink of liver toxicity, is able to overcome the attack, killing Cochenour in the process. As the story ends, Walters is in hospital tended by Dorrie, where he receives Cochenour's liver, thus ending up not only with the old man's liver but with his girl as well. The military has confiscated the discovery but has offered Walters a small finder's fee, which allows him and Dorrie to keep offering guided tours to Venus tourists. The lesson here is that the small guy can't beat the military-industrial complex, but he can, perhaps, beat the big-shot financier, and, hence, life goes on.

"The Merchants of Venus" indicates a shift from the satires of the 1950s, where the viewpoint character was primarily a member of the elite. Here, and in a number of works in the ensuing decades, Pohl is more interested in the economic life of the average Joe who is just trying to make a living. These characters are not scientists, corporate executives, politicos, or other elites; rather, they are everyday citizens, laborers, and pioneers—people either caught up in extraordinary circumstances (such as Reverend Hornswell Hake in *The Cool War*) or brave souls looking for better opportunities (such as Robinette Broadhead in *Gateway* or Audee Walters here). In some ways, Pohl advocates a spirit of entrepreneurship and pioneering vision, most often associated with Heinlein, which could be the road to space. As with "The Gold at the Starbow's End," Pohl's focus has shifted toward an increased interest in the possibilities of space, undoubtedly stimulated by the space program, and he would continue to set an increasing number of his novels in the firmament of space as the decades moved forward.

A third major novella, "In the Problem Pit," appeared in the September 1973 issue of *Fantasy and Science Fiction* in a special issue devoted to Pohl. In addition to Pohl's story, the magazine included an essay by Lester Del Rey summarizing Pohl's career and their long acquaintance, and a bibliography of Pohl's works.[14] The cover of the magazine features a painting by Carol Pohl, depicting a longhaired, bespectacled Pohl meditating on a mountaintop, conveying the cultural mood of the early 1970s and the general theme of the story. Like "The Gold at the Starbow's End," "In the Problem Pit" is hip, frank, topical, and informed by contemporary pop psychology, drawing from Pohl's experience with encounter groups, think tanks, and psychotherapy. The story is particularly notable for Pohl's employment of a complex narrative structure involving multiple viewpoints. Set twenty-five years in the future, the state of the world appears relatively free of cataclysm and hardship—a contrast from the desperate chaos in most of Pohl's fiction. In the story, the Arecibo Observatory in Puerto Rico—a setting Pohl utilizes at the beginning of the later novel *Syzygy*—is no longer used for radio astronomy (as that is now conducted on the far side of the moon) because of too much interference from "radio-dispatched taxicabs" and "radar ovens." Instead, it has become the location of the Problem Pit, where volunteers and draftees are sequestered in groups of sixteen to spend a period of isolation and group encounter to solve problems. These sessions have produced "more than 1,800 useful discoveries or systems" (42). The story traces one such group without a great deal of narrative tension. Instead, Pohl seems to be more interested in offering up an idea for positive interpersonal thinking that could facilitate useful personal, social, and industrial outcomes. The interest in the story lies more in Pohl's narrative technique and how he unfolds the purpose and methodologies of the Pit than in the characters and their specific problems. As a fictional exercise in industrial psychology, the story succeeds in imagining a future where exercises in democratized problem solving can lead to positive results.

By the time "In the Problem Pit" was published, Pohl was working as the science fiction editor for Bantam Books, a position he accepted at the beginning of 1973. Under the series banner "A Frederik Pohl Selection," he would bring out some of the most significant and innovative works of the 1970s: Joanna Russ's *The Female Man* and Samuel Delany's *Dhalgren* and *Triton*. These stand as landmark texts that engage with issues of gender and sexuality, among other things, and it is a credit to Pohl that he saw them through to publication. As Pohl relates, the story of *Dhalgren*'s publication is particularly significant: "When the manuscript was submitted to me at Bantam, it started out with three strikes against it. 1) I knew it had been rejected by most of the major publishing houses. 2) I had in fact been one of the rejectors—at least, an extract of an early version had been offered to me at *Galaxy* and I had turned it down very fast. 3) The son of a gun was huge. Two popping-full manuscript boxes—way over a thousand pages." As Pohl prepared the mammoth manuscript for publication, it became known as "Fred's Folly" around the Bantam offices.[15] But the digressive, virtuoso *Dhalgren*, which runs 879 small-print pages in its Bantam edition (some two hundred pages longer than John Brunner's *Stand on Zanzibar*), was a huge success, selling more than a million copies while Pohl sat in Bantam's editorial chair. *Dhalgren* came out in January 1975 and was soon followed by Russ's *The Female Man* in February, a multilayered narrative examining female sexuality, gender identity, and the adverse effects of patriarchal hegemony. Both novels have become canonical texts within academic criticism, not only in science fiction studies but also within other modes of cultural inquiry. Pohl's own writing was undoubtedly stimulated by these books.

Meanwhile, *Farthest Star* (1975), another collaboration with Jack Williamson, was Pohl's first novel since his return to writing—although it was not quite a novel in the proper sense, being a fix-up of a novella and serial published in *If* and *Galaxy* in the spring of 1973. Nonetheless, it marked Pohl's return as a novelist and henceforth he would produce at least a book a year for the next twenty years. *Farthest Star* is a bit of a warm-up for *Gateway* and the Heechee saga, having some parallel story elements, particularly a BDO (Big Dumb Object) and a Galactic Civilization. In this case, humans have recently been contacted by an alien race called the T'Worlie, and Ben Pertin, along with an uplifted simian named Doc Chimp, are sent by tachyon transmission to investigate Cuckoo, an object accelerating through the Galaxy. Tachyon transmission duplicates a person, who is then reconstituted at another new location, while the existing person remains on his or her own planet. This leads to interesting interplay between multiple selves as the stories proceed. Pohl and Williamson returned to the Cuckoo saga in a 1983 sequel, *Wall around a Star*, where it is revealed that Cuckoo is a vast Dyson Sphere. The Cuckoo novels are inventive, especially in the development of alien species such as the T'Worlie, but they mostly come across as planetary adventure utilizing updated scientific suppositions and xenobiology that distinguish them from the planetary romance of the past while remaining firmly embedded in that tradition.

As Pohl produced the novellas and stories that forged his comeback, he also wrote a number of key essays grappling with the history of the field, the business and craft of writing, and the theoretical underpinnings that distinguish SF as a genre. Science fiction had also found a new, hungry audience: academia. College courses were springing up on campuses across the country, writing workshops (both in science fiction and literary fiction and poetry) were modeling themselves on the Milford Writers' Conference, founded by Damon Knight, Judith Merril, and James Blish in 1956, and academics were writing articles and books that outlined genre history, explicated texts, and developed theories. Pohl's reemergence as a writer of substance parallels the rise of SF in academia, and he had strong ties with this emerging field of criticism—even before his marriage to Elizabeth Anne Hull, past president of the Science Fiction Research Association—partly through his deep connections to Jack Williamson and James Gunn, both seminal figures as SF academics and writers, but not exclusive to them. The most successful writers' workshop aside from Milford was Clarion, originally held at Clarion State College in Pennsylvania. For the first *Clarion* anthology in 1971, Pohl contributed the essay "SF: The Game Playing Literature," where he argued that "science fiction gives us a sort of catalog of possible worlds. From the wish-book we can pick the ones we want. Without it we can resent and deplore, but our capacity to change is very small" (193). For Pohl, science fiction is "more than fun, it is a way of looking at the world that cannot be duplicated by any other way, or improved on in some very important respects" (190). Alluding to "Let the Ants Try," Pohl concludes, "Perhaps the world at large can learn from sf. And perhaps then the ants won't have to replace us after all" (193).

For the *Clarion II* anthology, Pohl contributed "Golden Ages Gone Away," acknowledging that by 1972 science fiction had attained the "Age of Respectability," as "university libraries beg the privilege of collecting the papers of science-fiction writers" (95). The essay is a foray into the origins and history of the field, surveying the development of the genre in the magazines. Pohl's essay responds to the growing academic interest for SF, showing the large interface between the practitioners in the field and academic discourse, a trait the field still maintains. At this time, several major science fiction writers were writing retrospective essays and histories of the genre: Lester Del Rey and Theodore Sturgeon in the pages of *Galaxy*, William Tenn in *FSF*, Brian Aldiss in his history *Billion Year Spree*, and James Gunn in *Alternate Worlds*, among others. In *Hell's Cartographers*, a collection of retrospective memoirs and reflections on the writing process featuring Aldiss, Harry Harrison, Alfred Bester, Damon Knight, and Robert Silverberg, Pohl contributed the memoir "Ragged Claws," the first step toward *The Way the Future Was*.

Pohl also contributed to anthologies about the craft of science fiction writing. In Robin Scott Wilson's *Those Who Can* (1972), a teaching anthology of stories with essays by their writers analyzing the techniques used in creating the piece, Pohl was featured in the section on style with the essay "On Velocity Exercises," discussing the tightly packed stories "Grandy Devil" and "Day Million," both included in the volume.[16] In Reginald Bretnor's *The Craft of Science Fiction* (1976), Pohl's essay "The Science Fiction Professional" chattily gives advice on aspects of the writing profession beyond the writing itself—agents, marketing, contracts, and publicity.[17]

Pohl's friendships with Jack Williamson and James Gunn, both of whom were professors of English at midwestern universities, played a key part in Pohl's participation in the growing world of academic teaching and study of science fiction and science fiction writing workshop courses. In 1975, Pohl began participating in Gunn's writing workshops and teaching institutes at the University of Kansas, where he would stay for a week and take part in in classroom discussions of science fiction stories and novels. As Gunn recalls, "It was a great opportunity for a total immersion experience, and many of the students felt transformed by it."[18] His relationship with Gunn and SF at KU extended well into the twenty-first century, and Pohl would return every summer until he was unable to travel. Writer and current director of the Center for the Study of Science Fiction Christopher McKitterick recalls his first encounter with Pohl during the summer workshop in 1992:

> I first came to the University of Kansas in 1992 to take James Gunn's sf writing workshop, and was astounded to discover that we had the privilege of working

not only with Gunn but also Frederik Pohl. Enjoying the serious attention of *two* literary heroes set me upon a path that could only lead to a career in sf. . . . Fred made an impression on everyone he met. Despite his clunky glasses, non-athletic build, and despite smoking like a chimney (until his doctor told him to knock it off in his eighties), he was exceptionally charismatic. His deep, strong voice entranced listeners. He commanded audience attention and prompted thought. . . . That workshop changed my life. I felt I had to do my best to become a *real* sf writer to deserve such access and attention.[19]

Before becoming a regular summer visitor at KU, Pohl gave an important lecture for Gunn's *The Literature of Science Fiction* film series in 1973, where Pohl discussed "Ideas in Science Fiction."[20] In addition, he was a regular participant at the Jack Williamson Lectureship at Eastern New Mexico University in Portales.[21] Later, he joined Gunn and Judy Merril on the jury of the Theodore Sturgeon Memorial Award for short fiction, serving until the year of his death in 2013.[22]

Pohl's professional activities were extended by a term as president of science fiction's professional organization, the SFWA, in 1975–76. His tenure as president was complicated by the Stanislaw Lem affair. On the advice of George Zebrowski, prior president Poul Anderson had offered an honorary membership to Polish writer Lem, who was then very much in vogue among the academic critics. But Lem had made disparaging remarks about American SF, upsetting Philip Jose Farmer and the financially strapped Philip K. Dick, who believed Lem had diverted some of the money for the translation of Dick's *Ubik* to himself, and they wanted the membership revoked. Checking the bylaws, Pohl noted that Lem was eligible for regular membership, due to his substantial American publication, allowing Pohl to pull the honorary membership and offer a regular membership instead, which Lem ultimately declined.[23] Pohl's solution was not without controversy; Zebrowski and Ursula Le Guin, among others, were outraged by the treatment Lem had received. Striking a note somewhat incongruous with the outcome of the Lem Affair, in 1976, along with Harry Harrison and Brian Aldiss, Pohl helped found the World SF Society, an organization devoted to building relations between writers around the world, especially with those in China and Iron Curtain countries. Pohl served as president from 1980 to 1982.[24] During this time, Pohl also served on the governing council of the Author's Guild.

* ★ *

One would think that with all these professional activities and his editing job at Bantam, Pohl would be faced with the same writing dilemma during the second half of the 1970s as he had experienced at the decade's beginning. But in spite of this heavy workload, Pohl managed to write a trio of novels that stand along with *The Space Merchants* as his most significant work: *Man Plus* (1976), *Gateway* (1977), and *Jem* (1979). In between, he added his definitive memoir *The Way the Future Was* (1978). In an otherwise acerbic reading of Pohl's work to 1980, critic David Samuelson suggests that the three novels forge a kind of trilogy that "make an impressive case for his intellect and his mastery of different approaches to the central subject of SF, embracing or confronting the unknown, the 'alien.'"[25] As the 1970s concluded, Pohl was at the top of the science fiction field.

Man Plus was released in August 1976 by Random House after a serial publication in *Fantasy and Science Fiction* that spring, just prior to the World Science Fiction Convention, held that year in Kansas City, with native son Robert A. Heinlein as guest of honor. At that World Con, Pohl first met Elizabeth (Betty) Anne Hull;[26] the couple started dating in the summer of 1977, when Carol finally decided that their marriage was over. Pohl and Hull were married in 1984. Betty, a professor of English at Harper College in Palatine, Illinois, would play a significant role in Pohl's writing for the rest of his life.

Man Plus was a big success. Winning the Nebula Award, and among the finalists for the Campbell and the Hugo, it firmly placed Pohl at the top of the field. Published shortly after the Viking probes reached Mars orbit, *Man Plus* is a somberly brilliant novel of a possible manned mission to Mars, acutely extrapolating from the developments in the space program and the political crises of the Cold War. In a review in *Analog*, Lester Del Rey noted that Pohl "is one of the first to drop the old ideas of the planets and work honestly with what we've discovered them to be."[27] It is also a major novel exploring the concept of the posthuman cyborg, resonating with such classic stories as Anderson's "Call Me Joe" and Knight's "Masks," and anticipating the cyberpunk of William Gibson, Bruce Sterling, and Pat Cadigan.

The novel begins with astronaut Roger Torraway serving as keeper for the current subject in the special Mars development program called Man

Plus. This top secret exomedicine project is working to adapt men to the Mars environment by turning them into cyborgs. Torraway had gained fame for shuttle flights "after the freeze when the space program was just getting on its feet again" (4). But then the program became moribund: "As the space program declined rapidly from national priority to contingency-planning exercises, he had less and less that mattered to do" (5). Like with many of Pohl's works, there is an impending sense of doom: humanity needs this project, something that will inspire and transform; otherwise, the politics of the Cold War will lead to apocalypse. The energy crisis has reached critical mass, with power shortages and fuel shortages threatening stability. The Mars landing must succeed, or all-out war, they fear, will happen in less than two years.

The reader is introduced to Hartnett, the first cyborg; the president of the United States looks on via closed-circuit television as Hartnett completes some warm-up tests:

> He did not look human at all. His eyes were glowing, red-faceted globes. His nostrils flared in flesh folds, like the snout of a star-nosed mole. His skin was artificial; its color was normal heavy sun tan, but its texture was that of a rhinoceros's hide. Nothing that could be seen about him was of the appearance he had been born with. Eyes, ears, lungs, nose, mouth, circulatory system, perceptual centers, heart, skin—all had been replaced or augmented. . . . He had been rebuilt for the single purpose of fitting him to stay alive, without external artificial aids, on the surface of the planet Mars (17).

The doctors claim that Hartnett can be restored to his human form when the mission is completed. But Hartnett's sensory inputs overload, leading to madness and then death. Torraway is next on the list.

As the world crisis builds, Torraway is transformed into a cyborg, in the process losing his human physiognomy but still having to cope with human needs and emotions. His wife Dorrie (curiously the same name as the love interest in "The Merchants of Venus") is called in to give him encouragement, but she is shocked and afraid of his monstrous new appearance. In reference to *Man Plus* and other stories, Gary K. Wolfe discusses the icon of the monster in his classic study *The Known and the Unknown*, remarking that "Even in the stories in which such characters are sympathetically portrayed, the point is made that others regard them as monsters, as frightening challenges to the concept of what it is to be human."[28] For his part, Torraway balks when he realizes he no longer has any sex organs but still has the emotions and desires of a married man. In this sense, the novel is about the human cost of technological transformation: Torraway still must cope with the anxieties and insecurities of a normal human being. Brian Aldiss has suggested that "Pohl was not concerned so much with what such a being could *do*, but with how such a changed being would *feel*."[29] Suspecting that Dorrie is sleeping with Bradley, a member of the research team, Torraway's distress threatens to derail the project. At this point, the president goes so far as to suggest that they might have Dorrie "killed" in a car accident, thinking that Torraway would be happier mourning his dead wife than worrying about her sleeping around. To quell Torraway's sexual tensions, they bring in psychiatrist Sulie Carpenter as his nurse, who flatters him and treats him as a human being, so as to make him feel better about himself. As the sexual crisis eases, Torraway is given freedom to roam about the facility, but one night he escapes to see Dorrie. This visit serves as catharsis, as Torrraway, recognizing that he is no longer human, accepts his transformation and embraces the mission. Here again, psychotherapy is a major theme in Pohl's work of the 1970s.

As the countdown for the mission approaches, Dr. Carpenter is scheduled to go along on the mission to maintain Torraway's psychological balance. Meanwhile, the pressure point of the world crisis is about to explode in the days before the launch. Once on the surface of Mars, Torraway begins exploring, and what he sees is transmitted back to Earth (an anticipation of the recent missions of the Mars rovers, although the rovers have not captured the imagination in quite the same way), which leads to a respite of political tensions. What Pohl here shows is that for the vast majority of people to get excited and inspired by space exploration, the missions must involve human beings, not just machines. Currently, the Mars rovers are making exciting discoveries and doing important scientific work, but people quickly lose interest and take it all for granted. As the novel draws to a close, Torraway decides to stay on Mars, the environment he has been adapted for, but his systems malfunction, causing a brief moment of crisis. The novel ends with a startling deus ex machina, cleverly hinted at earlier in the text: unknown to humans, computers have achieved artificial intelligence and have manipulated this situation to get human beings on Mars; the sentient computers are behind the Man Plus project: "We had gone to a lot of trouble at every point along the line, and we were well pleased. Of course, human beings did not know we were pleased. . . . Human beings did not know that machine intelligence was capable of self-awareness in the first place. . . . As long as they thought computers were no more than tools, like a pickaxe or a frying pan, they would continue to entrust to us all their computations and facts, and would accept without question whatever interpretations we returned" (242). Because humans are on the brink of mutually assured destruction, the AI's motivation is to save themselves through saving humanity, following the survival imperative built into the fabric of their sentience. The novel is an important precursor to recent SF about the Singularity and transhumanism, anticipating the work of Vernor Vinge, William Gibson, Charles Stross, and others. One of the classics of post-Apollo hard SF, *Man Plus* still packs a punch and leaves the reader contemplating the prospects of future space exploration and the necessary impact it will have on the physiognomy and psychology of human beings.

Pohl followed the triumph of *Man Plus* with an even greater triumph the next year. *Gateway* is, arguably, Pohl's best novel, and certainly the one most often cited as representative of his work. Serialized in *Galaxy* at the end of 1976 and published by Ballantine in 1977, it is one of only three novels to win the Hugo, Nebula, and Campbell Awards (the other two being Joe Haldeman's *Forever Peace* (1997) and Paolo Bacigalupi's *The Windup Girl* [2009]). The novel draws from the background of "The Merchants of Venus," here involving a station built into an asteroid in the asteroid belt filled with abandoned Heechee ships, where volunteer human explorers, with no knowledge of how the ships work or where they are programmed to go, chance risky voyages in search of Heechee artifacts and astronomical data. The fact that humans are mystified by Heechee technology, never really discovering *how* the Heechee ships work, even after several trial-and-error missions, not only leads to what Darren Harris-Fain calls "a humbler vision of humanity's place in the universe,"[30] but it also speaks to the mystification the average person might face in a human world of increasingly complex advanced technologies, as Pohl examined in earlier works such as "The Midas Plague" and *The Age of the Pussyfoot*.

Like his previous work in this decade, *Gateway* is also very much a novel about psychotherapy and angst, as the story centers on the psychological crisis of Robinette Broadhead, a Gateway prospector who has returned from an immensely profitable voyage, allowing him to retire in luxury to Earth "under the big bubble" of New York City (recalling the dome housing of *Gladiator-At-Law* and anticipating Pohl's other Campbell winner, the utopian *The Years of the City*). Broadhead can afford the benefits of Full Medical but suffers from enormous guilt for what transpired at the voyage's endpoint—two ships reached the same destination where they discovered, and were subsequently drawn into, a black hole; in order to free one of the ships, Broadhead blows the tanks to free himself from the gravity well, thus trapping his lover Gelle-Klara Moynlin in the event horizon. The narrative consists of Broadhead relating his entire Gateway trajectory to his computer-simulated psychiatrist Sigfrid von Shrink sixteen years after he struck it rich. The confessional narration allows Pohl to again utilize the first-person narrative voice to memorable effect.

The state of the Earth in *Gateway* is, as in many of Pohl's novels, a world in crisis. Similar to conditions in *The Space Merchants* in that the Earth is overcrowded—there are 25 billion people!—and facing a food crisis, few opportunities exist except to work drudge jobs in the yeast farms, and the only hope for the common citizen is to strike it rich on Gateway and secure Full Medical. While working at a yeast farm in Wyoming, Broadhead wins the lottery, which gives him enough money to ship out to Gateway on a one-way ticket. Readers of recent science fiction will recognize a parallel in Ernest Cline's *Ready Player One*.

Gateway itself is a quintessential Big Dumb Object, an alien artifact whose existence and use precedes the existence of the human species. The Gateway asteroid was discovered a number of years after the Heechee caves on Venus when a prospector named Sylvester Macklen found a Heechee ship, which took him to Gateway; before he died he transmitted a signal to Earth. Soon, an expedition was sent to the asteroid, where an abandoned Heechee docking port full of ships was discovered, initiating "the Star Rush," recapitulating the Gold Rush in nineteenth-century America. An important thing going on here is that Gateway is not controlled by governments or militaries; instead, Gateway has been set up as a commercial venture managed by the Gateway Corporation, a vast multinational. This ties in with Pohl's themes from *The Space Merchants* and elsewhere, where multinational corporations are the real power in the maintenance of the economy and the governance of the world.

There are 924 ships on Gateway: some two hundred are non-operational, about three hundred have been sent out. Prospectors sign on to take Heechee ships out into space, with 80 percent not discovering anything useful; 15 percent don't come back at all. What is discovered is primarily observational data, but occasionally additional Heechee artifacts are found, one being another station called Gateway Two, where an additional 150 ships are docked. Pohl's descriptions of these observational discoveries and the Gateway asteroids adds a hard science fiction element to the novel, which often gets overshadowed by the reader's attention to Broadhead's psychological trauma, but the formula has nevertheless been praised by physicist-SF writer Gregory Benford for depicting "stellar astronomy, scrupulously rendered."[31]

Throughout the novel Broadhead's narrative is interspersed with advertisements, news reports, personals, public notices, data streams, and other textual breaks that effectively build the environment, conditions, and social interplay at Gateway. This technique was successfully brought into SF in the sharp, near-future novels of John Brunner, beginning with *Stand on Zanzibar* (1968), which in turn had borrowed the method from John Dos Passos's modernist masterpiece *U.S.A.* But it also owes something to the interstitial quotes from the *Encyclopedia Galactica* in Asimov's *Foundation*. Pohl utilizes the technique to build a rich social tapestry that places Broadhead within the broader context of the Gateway community and the economic forces in play, both on the asteroid and on Earth.

In *Gateway* Pohl masterfully blends hard science and compelling sense-of-wonder adventure with depth of characterization in the unfolding of the damaged psyche of Robinette Broadhead. This makes Broadhead Pohl's most individualized and memorable character since Mitch Courtenay, although Broadhead is far more richly drawn than his predecessor. At the same time, while it is the rich characterization coupled with the sense of wonder that makes *Gateway* particularly memorable, the reader must concede that in some ways *Gateway* lacks the relevance and power of the social satires, and even of *Man Plus* (not to mention *Jem*, which follows). This is not to say that *Gateway* doesn't rank as one of the genre's essential works. It is a virtuoso expression of the sense of wonder, leaving the reader wishing that such solar and interstellar exploration were, indeed, possible. *Gateway* is a major achievement in the science fiction field, though arguably, given its foregrounding of psychotherapy, it remains a product of the cultural and psychological *zeitgeist* of the decade in which it was written. But the same can be said of any masterwork. More so than its predecessor *Man Plus*, *Gateway* allows the reader to dream on the edge of the possible.

Following *Gateway*, Pohl released *The Way the Future Was* under Ballantine's Del Rey imprint; it is his memoir of his life in science fiction, chronicling his discovery of science fiction, his life in fandom, his career as agent and editor, his writing, and other aspects of his busy life. The book was the first of its kind, with the possible exception of the autobiographical essays that made up *Hell's Cartographers*. As noted earlier, the 1970s began the era of science fiction's self-reflection. Genre histories were written from both inside the genre—Aldiss's *Billion Year Spree*, Gunn's *Alternate Worlds*, Del Rey's *The World of Science Fiction*, David Kyle's *A Pictorial History of Science Fiction*—and by academics—Robert Philmus's *Into the Unknown*, Robert Scholes and Eric Rabkin's *Science Fiction: History, Science, Vision*, and Paul Carter's *The Creation of Tomorrow*. Several science fiction encyclopedias were produced, including the first edition of the monumental Nicholls and Clute *Science Fiction Encyclopedia* in 1979. Retrospective anthologies such as Asimov's *Before the Golden Age* and *The Early Asimov*, and the *Best of* series by Ballantine (and another by Pocket) traced genre history through stories and commentary. Released in 1977, Knight's *The Futurians* told the story of that quintessential fan group. And several prominent writers began putting together their memoirs: following Pohl by a year, the first volume of Asimov's mammoth autobiography, *In Memory Yet Green*, checked in at 732 pages, followed the next year by the even more massive volume two, *In Joy Still Felt* at 828 pages, both rivaling Delany's *Dhalgren* as the longest works in the field. All of this reflection was a symptom of the field's aging. James Blish had died from cancer in 1975, and that might have been a signal point that it was time for his generation to reflect. Plus, there was a burgeoning market for such reflections: readers wanted to know about the lives and careers of these literary pioneers. In an *Analog* review, Spider Robinson confirmed this hunger by stating that *The Way the Future Was* "is a deeply engrossing book that will be discussed for years, and hopefully will induce more SF professionals to put their oral history down on paper."[32]

After the successes of *Man Plus*, *Gateway*, and *The Way the Future Was*, Pohl would score again with his next novel, *Jem* (1979), which won a National

Book Award (then called the American Book Award), the only time the award was offered in the science fiction category. *Jem* blends the hard-edged political tone found in *Man Plus* with the sense of wonder and adventure of *Gateway* and returns to an unrestrained cynicism that makes the satires of the 1950s and the brutality of *A Plague of Pythons* look mild by comparison.

In *Fantasy and Science Fiction*, Algis Budrys praised *Jem* by proclaiming that "rarely has an SF author immediately followed a major triumph with as major a triumph as this."[33] Budrys rated *Jem* not quite as good as *Gateway*, but better than *Man Plus*—in his view all three were nonetheless masterful.

Jem also marked Pohl's last appearance in *Galaxy*, as the magazine ceased regular publication while *Jem* was being serialized, finally folding after a much delayed final issue in July 1980, after *Jem* had already long been published in book form. *Jem* is Pohl's first solo novel exploring another planet with sentient beings (the Heechee of *Gateway* do not make their appearance until later in the series), a scenario that would dominate much of his SF for the next thirty years. In *Jem* and many novels to follow, Pohl created compelling extraterrestrial environments and plausible encounters with alien species wherein he could continue to explore political situations, thus becoming increasingly allegorical in his analyses of earthly politics.

Jem is a very bitter, starkly political novel, where, as Thomas Clareson puts it, "the dark side of Pohl's imagination gained perhaps its fullest expression."[34] Like *Man Plus*, *Jem* is deeply engaged with the political tensions of the Cold War and the growing crisis in the Middle East. In 1979 those geopolitical tensions were reaching a tipping point, and *Jem* reflects that tension perhaps better than any other work of fiction written during the period. In much mundane fiction, for instance, the political crises of the period were only vaguely reflected, if reflected at all. A difficult book to summarize, as Pohl uses multiple viewpoints and plot threads, all leading to a devastating apocalyptic crescendo, *Jem* combines nuanced political commentary and satire with the planetary adventure Pohl mastered in *Gateway*.

Set in the near future, circa 2020, where an aged Carl Sagan serves as the honorary chair of the World Conference on Exobiology, the political alignments on Earth have reconfigured into three power blocs: Food, Fuel, and People, mirroring the triad alignment in Orwell's *1984*. The United States and Russia are allied in the Food Bloc; the British Commonwealth and the Middle

East in the Fuel Bloc; and India and China in the People Bloc. Since most nations have sufficient nuclear arsenals to blow each other up, the world is in a stalemate, and the political chess pieces are more or less in stasis: "'We can't afford to fight anybody, and nobody can afford to fight us. And everybody knows it'" (30). People Bloc astronomers have identified a star with a planet orbiting it. A probe has been sent and has identified the planet Jem (also named Klong and Son of Kung by the Chinese) as having a viable atmosphere and ecology, including three species "that seemed to possess some sort of social organization" (18). When exobiologist Danny Dalehouse meets Washington powerbroker Marge Menninger at the World Conference on Exobiolgy, where Jem is first revealed, she recruits him for a Food Bloc expedition to the planet. Using the prospects of contacting alien sentient species as a ploy, and desperate to break the political impasse between the three blocs, the ambitious Marge Menninger further convinces Congress that Jem has uranium and other fissionables that would change the balance of power if the Food Bloc—or the other blocs, for that matter—got ahold of these resources: "I think there are goodies on this planet. I want them for *us*" (30). One of the motivating factors is that China in the People Bloc is planning to raise prices on consumer goods, while at the same time the global oil supply is declining, leading to increased tensions: "There was something wrong in a world that let a handful of nations burn off energy so recklessly simply because they happened to be sitting on its sources. Sure, when it was gone, they would be as threadbare as the Peruvians or the Paks, but there was no comfort in that. Their downfall would be the world's downfall . . ." (106). One of the major themes of the novel is energy consumption and inevitable depletion.

There is a rush to Jem, the People Bloc arriving before the Food Bloc, which has allied itself with the Fuel Bloc for transport, though they build separate camps once on planet. The blocs make allies with the three intelligent species on Jem: the People Bloc with the Krinpit, a crab-like species that dwells in villages; the Fuel Bloc with the Burrowers, a tunnel-dwelling species living in a vast network of underground warrens; and the Food Bloc with the Balloonist Gasbags, an elegant species of airborne creatures riding the winds. At one point, the Food Bloc expedition is sprayed with Balloonist mist, their sperm, which is hallucinogenic and acts as an aphrodisiac, leading to an orgy, the results of which reflect a change between the free-love cultural moment of the early 1970s (depicted in "The Gold at the Starbow's End") and the more sober zeitgeist of 1979, as the participants awaken to embarrassment and shame, rather than to the groovy, swinging exhilaration that characterized the previous era.

As in many science fiction works, Pohl examines the idea that the space frontier offers new beginnings, an opportunity to start again, articulated when Ana Dmitrova, a member of the Food Bloc expedition, reflects: "On Son of Kung it could all be different . . . to be part of a new world where things could be done properly. Where the mistakes of Earth could be avoided. Where one's children would have a future to look forward to" (75). As in *The Space Merchants* and *Man Plus*, the theme that an expedition in space gives hope to a desperate world, hope for a place where old hatreds can be forgotten, is foregrounded. But here Pohl turns all this on its head: humankind will bring their wars and aggression with them and ultimately ruin Jem too. Marge Menninger's ambition is to make Jem one nation, modeled on the American melting pot: "They'll be all the same, all part of the same wonderful . . . well, dream. I don't mind calling it a dream. But you and I can make it come true, Ana. We can learn how to live on Klong. We can build a world without national barriers and without the kind of senseless competition and rapacity that have ruined this one'" (160). But behind Menninger's rhetoric is an undercurrent to eliminate the other blocs and even other nationals within her own bloc and make Jem an "American" world. This undoubtedly reflects Pohl's continued suspicions of American nation-building and the politics of the Cold War.

The dangers of the frontier mentality are made evident when Menninger arrives on the planet with heavy artillery and a nuclear bomb, bringing new meaning to her earlier statement to her father, "I guess you don't understand what it means to have a whole planet to play with" (89). Menninger has utopian ambitions here, as if the problems of Earth would not follow her to Jem. Indeed, later she declares, "I want the United States to send enough firepower up there to make the place fit to live" (169). She claims to want to develop trade goods for the Krinpit in particular, as they seem to be the species most equipped to use what she has to offer: weapons of war. Such are the "trade goods" that Pohl is mocking here, having a lot of cynical, bitter fun with the political chess game of the world powers that involves selling arms and other martial technologies to smaller states, fomenting war and instability in order to create "markets." Meanwhile, the expeditionary groups representing the three blocs hold a meeting, hoping that they can come to some cooperative truce and perhaps agree to ignore the mandates from Earth. This is also an element of the frontier theme: once away from the power players on the home planet, the people who are actually there can make their own decisions that fit with the circumstances of the new environment. But before this utopian compromise can get underway, Marge Menninger arrives on Jem with her weapons and soldiers. As in other Pohl novels, Earth's political situation implodes while the ship is en route, with anarchy and riots leading to cataclysm. The ever astute Menninger saw this coming, so she packed her ships up with all the supplies of civilization she would need (including nuclear warheads), with ambition to reinvent Jem in her own image.

While all this is going on, Pohl also effectively builds the planetary environment and compellingly portrays the first contact efforts of Danny Dalehouse as he learns how to communicate with the Balloonists. Further, one of the viewpoint characters in the novel is the Krinpit "social worker" Sharn-Igon, who, after being captured by the Food Bloc, escapes and becomes somewhat of a messianic hero to his species, rallying them to rise against the human intruders, whom he calls the "Poison Ghosts," because they are destroying the social order of his planet. Meanwhile, the Fuel Bloc subdues the Krinpit by nearly wiping them out, and, with the help of their Burrower allies, finds a mother lode of fossil fuels on the planet—fuel Marge Menninger desperately wants to control.

As the struggle for Jem continues between these small constituencies of colonists, all-out war erupts on Earth. The nukes have been launched, Washington has been obliterated, and Earth is mostly turned to wasteland. This seemed a very real threat in the late 1970s and throughout the Reagan years of the 1980s, when the underlying cultural zeitgeist was that it was almost inevitable—generally a given in science fiction narratives. In tune with this zeitgeist in this incredibly bitter and cynical book, Pohl seems to be saying, "Folks, here it comes, get ready." While Pohl would critique Cold War politics in a much more light-hearted manner in *The Cool War* and whimsically play around with the Reagan years in *The Coming of the Quantum Cats*, here he unleashes his bitterness to the full extent; after *Jem* his cynicism is a little more tempered with long-term optimism, the prospect that humankind will make it to the other side of its follies.

Ever the uncompromising Cold Warrior, Marge Menninger perpetuates the war on Jem, prompting Ana Dmitrova to cry to Danny Dalehouse, "It upsets me that what has happened on Earth is now to happen again, here. It upsets me that my—that my friend is dead. It upsets me that the colonel intends to kill a great many more persons. Can you imagine? She proposes to tunnel under the Fuel camp and explode a nuclear bomb, and that upsets me" (272). Menninger justifies her genocidal intent by arguing that "the Greasies are going to come to the same conclusions I did, only it will take a little longer. One of us has to run things. The only way to do that is to knock the other out" (275). However, she doesn't account for the indigenous sentients on Jem. Sharn-Igon attacks her on the beach just as the Greasies launch their own strike on the Food camp. Pohl draws an analogy to how Cold War powers fight their wars in other places, catching indigenous people in between the warring powers. Like the colonized elsewhere, Sharn-Igon finds that his assault is in vain: Marge Menninger survives, crawling out from under the roasted husk of his carapace.

After the Fuel camp's air assault, they call for a truce. Readings reveal that Kung's Star is unstable and about to flare, which will bathe the planet in lethal solar radiation. All remaining humans must move immediately to the base on the far side of the planet. With Earth in apocalypse, they may be what is left of humanity: "It is clear that for all practical purposes we on Jem are alone in the universe at this time. We think we will need all the resources we have to prepare our camp for this flare. If we continue to fight, we suppose we will all die" (284–85). Marge Menninger has other ideas, deciding to go on the attack and hit them as hard as she can. Leading the remaining members of the Food contingent to the Fuel Bloc camp, while lost in the labyrinth of the Burrower warren, Menninger lets loose her atomic bomb, killing herself, and most of the Burrowers and Balloonists.

Fortunately for the remaining humans, the tactical bomb was out of position and misses its target, the fallout mostly contained within the underground warrens. The survivors of the Food Bloc refuse to attack the camp. Led by Danny Dalehouse, who was inspired by the words of Ana Dmitrova, they set their rifles down and surrender themselves to the Fuels. The finale shows that the human race carries on in later generations, all descendants of the survivors. These descendants, however, have been transformed (evolved) by the planet and now live in a new state of being. They are no longer quite human—no longer *H. sapiens*—with all the ridiculous politics of the twentieth century long behind them. Through this transformation into a new kind of humanity, into transhumans, they have achieved real utopia, having harmoniously integrated themselves into the cultures and lifeways of Jem's native intelligences. Here Pohl breaks through his dark cynicism to offer a rather radical solution: to overcome our Cold War (and, alas, post–Cold War) craziness, we must transcend, become something else, and, indeed, in order to live on another planet might require that we become something new.

*   *   *

Pohl left Bantam in 1979 to concentrate on his own writing. Throughout the 1980s he was highly productive, usually producing at least two books a year and editing a number of anthologies, while continuing to build his reputation as one of the central figures in science fiction. Pohl reaped the benefits of the SF boom of the 1980s, producing a number of sequels and follow-ups—some fresh and invigorating, others seeming to be mere moneymaking opportunities. While these books were coming out, Pohl continued to write standalone novels and compelling short stories, including *The Cool War*, *Syzygy*, "Spending a Day at the Lottery Fair," *The Years of the City*, "Fermi and Frost," *Black Star Rising*, *The Coming of the Quantum Cats*, and, in 1987, his timely mainstream novel *Chernobyl*. But Pohl's most successful books of the decade further developed the Heechee saga in several sequels to *Gateway*, the first of which was *Beyond the Blue Event Horizon*.

Not as satisfying as the first novel, but still quite readable, *Beyond the Blue Event Horizon* moves away from the first-person narration of *Gateway* and uses multiple viewpoints (similar to *Jem*), one of which is periodic first-person narration by Robinette Broadhead, maintaining that compelling voice from its predecessor. In an *Analog* review, Spider Robinson praised the novel as "the most satisfying sequel I've ever read," further lauding it by claiming, "Certainly very few books have ever held my attention in such an iron grip right up until the last paragraph." Robinson thought it also just as worthy of the major awards as its predecessors.[35] Tom Easton felt much the same, marveling at this stretch of Pohl's career when Pohl emerged as the genre's leading writer: "Pohl is gifted well beyond the ordinary with the ability to conceive novel ideas, to assemble them into rich packages, to add in ideas contributed by others, to make them fit together in a way that lets his vision simulate the real world in complexity and interrelatedness. . . . I must call that vision holistic and integrated."[36] Indeed, here Easton pinpoints Pohl's greatest quality: as a grand synthesizer, able to make complex connections between science, politics, society, and the individual.

Beyond the Blue Event Horizon outdoes *Gateway* in its plot, which centers around the exploration of a Big Dumb Object, in this case a Heechee Food Factory processing cometary hydrocarbons in the Oort Cloud. Having overcome his psychological problems and become a wealthy magnate on Earth, Robinette Broadhead has commissioned an expedition to investigate the BDO, where the explorers discover a young man named Wan and a tribe of anthropoid apes, who are the descendants of a sample of anthropoids the Heechee took from Earth back in the predawn times (later described in the first vignette in *The Gateway Trip*). Following Marge Menninger, Wan is one of Pohl's most despicable and unlikable characters, becoming the central nemesis in the rest of the Heechee saga. Pohl employs another old science fiction trope to great effect, perhaps borrowing it from John D. MacDonald's *Wine of the Dreamers*, when Wan uses a Heechee dream machine to quell his loneliness, which in turn projects his adolescent dreams upon the world, causing periodic plagues of madness on Earth and the other human settlements in the solar system.

As was implicit in *Gateway*, and a recurring theme throughout Pohl's work, Earth is on the brink of a food crisis, and Broadhead hopes he can move the Food Factory closer to relieve the problem: "We can end this kind of poverty forever, Bover, with Heechee technology," he says. "Plenty of food for everybody! Decent places to live!" (179). But the Food Factory will also open up the stars for humanity: while exploring it, Broadhead's expedition learns from Wan that the "prayer fans" are actually storage devices, Heechee zip drives, and from them they uncover blueprints for building Heechee ships and designs for other Heechee technology. Another discovery on the Food Factory are the "Dead Men," lost Gateway prospectors who have been uploaded into the factory's computers. This gets into an interesting speculation on uploading of consciousness, bringing to bear developments in computer technology upon the ideas first introduced in *Wolfbane* and the story "The Knights of Arthur" and conjoining these ideas with Pohl's earlier interest in cryogenics in *The Age of the Pussyfoot*. Pohl continues to explore the concept of uploaded consciousness throughout the rest of the Heechee novels, amounting to a series of wide-angle, sense-of-wonder adventure novels that are compellingly topical through the engagement with theories of brain, mind, and consciousness in the context of emerging computer technology in the 1980s (and beyond), as the books were being published concurrently with the cyberpunk of Gibson and the singularity fiction of Vernor Vinge. Pohl's Dead Men anticipate Gibson's Dixie Flatline in *Neuromancer*, for example. Adding to the inventiveness he displayed in the creation of Sigfrid von Shrink in *Gateway*, here Pohl adds another computer-simulated construct, Albert (read: Albert Einstein), who is expert on all things science. Through Albert's discussions with Broadhead, Pohl can introduce the reader to the cutting-edge astrophysics and cosmology that inform the novel while also examining the concept of artificial intelligence.

After a number of crises involving Wan, the anthropoids, and the expeditionary team, Broadhead himself arrives on the Food Factory to take control. After Albert's analysis of the prayer-fan storage devices, the location of the black hole where Gelle-Klara is trapped is determined; it comes to light, too, that the shadowy Heechee themselves retreated into a black hole millennia ago, for a reason not yet understood. This resolves the mystery of the Heechee: where they are, why they haven't ever been encountered, and why they abandoned their outposts. But it opens up a new mystery: what led them to do this? That will be the subject of the next book in the series. With *Beyond the Blue Event Horizon*, readers can more clearly identify Pohl's exuberance for "chasing science" and perhaps gauge the trajectory of this particular path of his multivalent career.

Pohl followed *Beyond the Blue Event Horizon* with another novel of the Cold War, *The Cool War*, which harkens back to the political intrigue of *Slave Ship* and *Jem*. Portions of the novel appeared in *Isaac Asimov's Science Fiction Magazine* in late 1979, with the first book publication in April 1981. The story involves Reverend Hornswell "Horny" Hake, a Unitarian minister from Long Branch, New Jersey (a township not far from Pohl's home in Red Bank), who is reluctantly recruited into Cold War espionage by a group called the "Team." *The Cool War* is set in the very near future and has the tone of a contemporary spy thriller with a dash of sardonic comedy, although, like *The Space Merchants* and others, throwaway clues reveal to the reader that things are definitely different—socially, politically, and economically—than the world as it is. First, the novel begins with Reverend Hake counseling a married couple who are part of a legal plural marriage, evoking an extrapolation from the sexual revolution of the 1970s. The state of the world, though not on the brink of apocalypse as in so many of Pohl's other fictions, is nonetheless in a state of general decay, as Hake ponders:

> Wasn't there something in the essential grinding, grim grittiness of the world that was destroying social fabrics of more kinds than marriage? The strikes and the muggings, the unemployment and the inflation, the jolting disappearance of fresh fruits from the stores in summer and of Christmas trees in December, and the puzzling and permanently infuriating dislocations that had become the central fact of everyone's life—wasn't that where the cause was, and not in his failure? (7)

This establishes the overall tone of the novel: things are "coolly" coming apart, a slow decay into stagnation, mediocrity, and austerity; not enough to cause a major upheaval, but just enough to leave the average citizen frustrated and slightly confused, leading to what David Brin calls "a gradual death-spiral of lowered expectations and degraded hopes." For Brin, in *The Cool War* Pohl created "a chillingly plausible failure mode for human civilization."[37]

Other clues that inform the reader that the future in *The Cool War* is slightly off-center appear throughout the novel. At one point, Hake travels on a gigantic, one-thousand-passenger airplane tended by a "topless bar-stew" (50). To protect their embattled sovereignty, the Israelis have destroyed Arab oil, but this has precipitated a much deeper energy crisis than the one rearing its head in the late 1970s: Hake's parishioners drive a charcoal-burning van. On the global political front, the CIA has been disbanded, replaced by the "Team," and there hasn't been a shooting war for twenty years.

Most of the novel follows the shenanigans of global espionage as Reverend Hake is sent to spy for the United States. Much of what Hake is expected to do is to foul things up, put a wrench into the works; since he has no real clue what he is doing or why he is the one doing it, he serves the goals of his employers brilliantly. The goal is to keep things in disarray through acts of sabotage and theft; through manipulating distribution and fostering social ills; because there is no war anymore, there has instead to be chaos—in short, "nations playing trip-up games with one another" (38). Pohl uses the word "games" throughout the novel to describe the clandestine activities Hake gets caught up in, at one point adding the qualifier "adolescent," to suggest the calculated inanity of it all. Hake's first task is to unwittingly spread a flu virus in Europe. From there, he gets entwined in the drug trade in Rome and the "slave market," where European and American women are being sold as concubines to Arab sheiks. Indeed, Italy largely features in *The Cool War*, bringing Pohl back to the landscape and cities that played a central role in his developing imagination during his service in World War II. Vesuvius, Pompeii, and stories of the Emperor Tiberius inform Hake's intrigues on the Italian peninsula. The novel also topically poses questions regarding crises emerging in the Middle East and the instability of a global economy centered on Arab oil.

Although Hake is, at times, an intriguing character, the novel is often just too "cool." As Pohl thrusts Hake into one situation after another, the narrative flags and becomes tiresome, and the conclusion, in which Hake unwittingly exposes the conspirators to the world, is rather flat. Perhaps this is Pohl's point: in the "cool" war of the future, nothing of any real import happens; things just tick right along, leaving the average citizen slightly baffled and mildly uneasy, and thus easier to control and manipulate. But at the same time, good citizens like Hake can make a difference; if they just pay attention, they may be able to keep the powerbrokers and exploiters in check. Along with Pohl, we can only hope.

Syzygy is even closer to mainstream fiction than *The Cool War*. Beginning at the Arecibo Observatory in Puerto Rico, one of Pohl's favorite spots to "chase" science, the novel is a sustained narrative "what if" considering the "Jupiter Effect" posited by astronomer and sometime science fiction writer John Gribbin. In *The Jupiter Effect*, first published in 1974, Gribbin and his co-author Stephen Plagemann predicted that an alignment of the planets and the sun scheduled for March 10, 1982, would trigger a number of catastrophes on Earth, including a major earthquake at the San Andreas Fault in California. *Syzygy* is the term used to describe when planetary bodies are aligned. The novel was released by Bantam in January 1982, giving readers a few months to read it before catastrophe struck. Needless to say, nothing happened.

Pohl sets the novel in December 1981, just three months before the Jupiter Effect is predicted to happen. Although this allows *Syzygy* to be open ended, not knowing whether the effect will happen or not, Pohl's intention is not to write a catastrophe novel but rather to show how human beings get caught up in panic and hysteria when such prophecies gain public attention. While one can gather from the narrative tone of the novel that Pohl was rightly skeptical about the outcome of the planetary alignment—indeed, he explains in a blog entry, posted posthumously, that *Syzygy* came about through his reluctant dealings with a Hollywood production team who had gotten ahold of Gribbin and Plagemann's book[38]—nevertheless, it is evident that he was attracted to the idea as "speculative" science. When geologist Tib Sonderman reads *The Jupiter Effect* straight through on his way back to Los Angeles from Arecibo, Pohl has him reflect, "The book, to be sure, was *speculative* science. Much of what it suggested rested on presumptions and inferences. There was much in it that was unproved. But nothing that struck him as wrong" (41). From there, Pohl lays out the Gribbin and Plagemann argument step by step, from the planetary alignment to the authors' conclusions that this will trigger a massive earthquake in the Los Angeles area on March 10, 1982. The details of how science works—even, in this case, speculative science—is compellingly dramatized, not only here but also in the opening chapter when the Newton-8 spacecraft (a stand-in for Voyager), heading toward the outer planets after flybys at Jupiter and Saturn, goes offline just before it is to record Jupiter's transit of the sun, and mission director Rainy Keating must contend with a congressional committee wanting to pull her budget. Pohl knows his way around scientific conferences, having attended many over the years, and this portrayal of how science works and how scientists communicate with each other and the public at conferences gives *Syzygy* an authenticity similar to that seen in Gregory Benford's *Timescape*.

As the novel moves forward, the scene shifts from Arecibo to Los Angeles, where scientists are gathered for the American Science Federation meeting, where Pohl further tunes into the cultures and practices of science and the need for funding: "Like everything in the world of practicing scientists, attending meetings like this was an investment. You interrupted your real work to fill out grant applications, and to sit in on faculty senate meetings, and to go to Arecibo to plead before a senatorial committee, and to come here to be seen. It was part of the job. Science was not just a matter of finding facts and assembling them into theories. It was big business" (73). This too gives the novel a feel of scientific authenticity comparable to that found in *Man Plus* and *Jem*.

Pohl had spent some time in Los Angeles in 1980 and 1981 as he and his son Rick prepared their book *Science Fiction: Studies in Film*, and the novel captures some of Pohl's observations of the cityscape at that time. Themes of racial tension, young people seeking alternative subcultures, and fads associated with "California crazies" (109) and "psychotherapy junkie[s]" (like Rainy's ex-husband: "Tinker Keating was a psychotherapy junkie. Encounter group, bioenergetics, Primal Scream, Rolfing, Transcendental Meditation, orgone energy—all of them; first she had been startled, then it had seemed funny, finally pathetic" [137]) are abundant in the novel, capturing some of the cultural vibe of Los Angeles in the early 1980s. This includes a plot thread involving Danny Deere, an unscrupulous L.A. real estate developer. Deere picks up a flier calling for Californians to "Wake Up! The end is at hand!" (68). He realizes that this might be an opportunity to cause panic and buy up properties, then sell them dearly after the panic deflates. Joining forces with a group of young spiritual seekers, Deere ignites a campaign to stir up panic throughout the city, eventually incurring the wrath of gangster Buster Boyma, the real power behind California real estate. Rainy Keating and Tib Sonderman cross paths again when they are both enlisted onto a committee to prepare possible outcomes of the Jupiter Effect by the Pedigrues, an elite L.A.- area political family whose agenda is for the committee to shore up their waning political power and propel the next generation Pedigrue into office. As the hysteria rises throughout Los Angeles, one of those winter deluges of rain that periodically floods the city adds to the chaos. While Deere is set to meet with Boyma at his massive seaside condo project, a mudslide obliterates the condo and Deere along with it; for his part, Boyma avoids the avalanche but steps into the water and is electrocuted by a downed power line. All of the craziness sparked by the syzygy seems to be a larger metaphor for the broader craziness inherent in the L.A. megalopolis, articulated in a meeting between the principal scientists and the governor of California in the aftermath of the flooding by Sam Bradison, a professor of political science whose wife Meredith, a scientist, helped Sonderman and Keating study the

Jupiter Effect on the committee: "There's a climate of fear in this town, and it's been deliberately whipped up by people who make a profit out of it. Not just Danny Deere or the Jupes. I hold the Pedigrues responsible for a good deal of it. The whole committee was a fraud in the first place; there's no way to know whether the so-called Jupiter Effect is real or not, and the publicity given to it is dangerous. *Really* dangerous" (235). That final sentence appears to indicate Pohl's position.

But ever the science fiction speculator, at the end Pohl leaves off with another startling conclusion: what knocked Newton-8 offline was a communication from another star—the hope and dream of the Voyager missions. Humanity is no longer alone in the universe. At a press conference concluding the narrative, Tib Sonderman addresses the world:

> To discover that intelligence can arise is not in itself surprising, for we already knew that this is possible. It has happened here on Earth. What is surprising is to discover that an intelligent race can survive its technology. We now know that at least one other race has. It has passed the point of being able to destroy itself, as we are able now, and has gone on to some further stage; and that is new. This fact gives us hope. And it also gives us purpose, and certain obligations. For what we know now that we did not know before is that the human race is not necessarily under sentence of death, and so certain and dangerous follies can be abandoned (248).

This revelation that others are out there, giving answer to the Fermi Paradox, ends the novel on a note of hope, hope that humankind can overcome the craziness, of which the craziness of Los Angeles is only a microcosm. Here, as was not the case with *Jem*, Pohl suggests that we do not have to evolve into something else to survive. But we still must change. And perhaps it will take a message from "out there" for us to do so.

Since *Syzygy* is a novel that is, in part, about the cultures and practices of science, fittingly Pohl's contributions to science through his fiction and editing were recognized in 1982, when he was elected a fellow of the American Association for the Advancement of Science.[39]

Like Asimov, Heinlein, Clarke, and others, by 1982 Pohl began revisiting a number of his worlds or expanded shorter works into longer stories to cash in on the lucrative SF marketplace. This may in part have been because he now had the leisure to do so, no longer having editorial obligations—plus, such books had a built-in market. In this vein, Pohl added additional stories to the same consumer world as "The Midas Plague" and "The Man who Ate the World," bringing them together in a volume titled *Midas World* (1983); expanded "The Gold at the Starbow's End" into the less compelling novel *Starburst* (1982); wrote a sequel to *The Space Merchants*, titled *The Merchants' War* (1984); and, with Williamson, produced *Wall around a Star* (1983), a follow-up to *Farthest Star*. Somewhat later, one final novel in this register, *Mars Plus* (1994), a sequel to *Man Plus*, is ostensibly a collaboration with Thomas T. Thomas, though one wonders to what extent this was merely a sharecropped novel in which Pohl's involvement in the writing was limited. Some of these works are strong, all are capable, yet none quite lives up to the original. For instance, in *Midas World*, although the new stories have some interest, they do not leave the reader enthralled by the punch of Pohl's satire the way "The Midas Plague" and "The Man who Ate the World" do. As a result, this flattens the power of the masterpieces by embedding them between inferior stories in the larger narrative framework of the book, thus masking their individual effect. The same can be said for *Wall around a Star*. While it has some good qualities as a rousing science fiction adventure novel and displays Pohl's fascination with speculative scientific ideas and his skill at creating alien intelligences, the ground it covers is too close to that of *Gateway* and the Heechee saga, whereas its precursor, *Farthest Star*, at least feels like a warm-up to *Gateway*, rather than a bit of a retread.

The Merchants' War presents a different set of problems. In trying to re-capture the first-person voice of the original—Tenny Tarb is no Mitch Cour-tenay—the novel seems almost a parody rather than an effective follow-up to the world created in *The Space Merchants*. Tarb is a stooge working for Fowler Shocken Associates; apparently, Earth keeps ticking along after Courtenay and the Consies left for Venus, and the hegemony of the corporations is still firmly in place, while Venus has developed into a thriving utopian frontier colony. Unlike Asimov's 1980s *Foundation* and *Robot* novels—which have been decried by some—Pohl doesn't extend the extrapolation but merely reuses the setup of *The Space Merchants* to satirize consumer trends in the 1980s. Some of the humor is even broader than the original novel—in the register that some readers found objectionable in *Preferred Risk*—making some digs that would be apparent to a reader familiar with the original work and also making new digs at the contemporary scene. But this satire is less effective than the bitterness in a novel like *Jem* or even the cultural commentary found in *Syzygy*. Although there are some amusing set pieces—particularly the Moke-Koke addiction, a much more addictive brand than Popsie from the earlier novel, which seems to comment on both the rise in consumption of artificially manufactured beverages and the cocaine drug culture glorified in the 1980s—the novel at once is too much of a rehash of the original and veers too far from the conditions Pohl and Kornbluth brilliantly established therein. While a comment like "What made for a good consumer was boredom" (122) reflects the plentitude of the 1980s, it is inconsistent with the austerity of Mitch Courtenay's world. Given the expansion of the science fiction marketplace and a new generation of affluent readers clamoring for sequels to their favorite stories, *The Merchants' War*, ironically, comes across as a product of the consumer marketplace and its demands, making the book itself a conspicuous representation of the consumerism that its satire deplores. But, then again, no less a science fiction personage than Brian Aldiss remarked that "if it lacks the impact of the earlier volume, that has to do with the fact that the real world has caught up with the fiction of *The Space Merchants*. Advertising *does* now dominate our lives—does, indeed, create Presidents, sink causes, promote subtle chains of dependencies."[40] Nearly thirty years later, Aldiss's point is ever more apparent.

On the other hand, Pohl's further extensions of the Heechee saga, *Heechee Rendezvous* (1984) and *The Annals of the Heechee* (1987), maintain much of the original appeal of their predecessors, extend and develop the plot put into motion when Robinette Broadhead first stepped upon the Gateway asteroid, and richly world-build the galaxy that once was the playground of the Heechee while resolving the mysteries left dangling at the end of *Beyond the Blue Event Horizon*. In *Heechee Rendezvous*, Pohl returns to a narrative structure similar to *Gateway*, featuring Robinette Broadhead as the voice in most of the chapters, with occasional interruptions (structured like the interstitial advertisements, reports, and so on) by the Albert Einstein simulacrum. *The Annals of the Heechee* is primarily narrated by Broadhead, with a few chapters either narrated by Albert or using an omniscient third person. Pohl uses Broadhead's voice to great effect at the beginning of *Annals* with an explicit pastiche of *Huckleberry Finn*: "You don't know about me without you have read some books that was made by Mr. Fred Pohl. He told the truth, mainly. There was things which he stretched, but mainly he told the truth." But then Broadhead adds, "My friendly data-retrieval program, Albert Einstein, says I'm too prone to obscure literary references anyway, so the *Huckleberry Finn* gambit is out" (1). Here is another prime example of Delany's science fiction sentence: when one of the most familiar fictive voices in American literature has become an "obscure literary reference," the informed reader recognizes what Delany calls "the specific tension, with our present concept of reality."[41] The interstitial breaks are also gone in *Annals*, making the structure a little more like *Beyond the Blue Event Horizon* than *Gateway*. In both novels Pohl takes an increasing interest in the question of machine intelligence—so much, in fact, that by the end of *Heechee Rendezvous* Broadhead himself has been uploaded into a computer; therefore, for the entirety of *Annals*, Broadhead no longer has physical form, is no longer "still really *meat*" (4). This focus on machine intelligence is quite interesting, given that William Gibson's quintessential cyberpunk novel *Neuromancer* came out a few months after the hardcover edition of *Rendezvous* (which had been serialized at the beginning of 1984 in *Amazing*). Because of the overarching first-contact, galactic adventure theme in the Heechee novels, it is possible to overlook the fact that Pohl was engaging with ideas coming out of the burgeoning computer culture that, if not exactly congruent with, at least run parallel to the cyberpunk thematic focus. What elevates these later Heechee novels above similar galactic adventures (such as *Farthest Star*) is this exploration of the possibilities of human-machine interface; and, further, it simply chronicles the blossoming of computer technologies and their possibilities as they were emerging in the 1980s. This is not merely Pohl's jumping on a trendy idea but seems rather like a natural progression from the ideas first encountered in "The Tunnel under the World," *Wolfbane*, *The Age of the Pussyfoot*, and *Man Plus*. Pohl has gone from robot constructs to bio-components to cryonic rejuvenation to cyborgization, and here, finally, to uploading—in a way coming full circle, as both "Tunnel" and *Wolfbane* were imagining forms of uploading before the language existed to describe it. Consequently, this entire thread of Pohl's fiction contributes to the larger questions now being debated regarding the Singularity, god-like machines, bioengineering, and posthumanism.

Although Pohl's engagement with computer technologies are an important facet of the novels, their primary intent is to reveal the Heechee mystery and follow the human quest to find them. And, for Broadhead, his personal quest to rescue Gelle-Klara Moynlin from the black hole is also a significant thread in *Heechee Rendezvous*. In order to do so, he has to deal with the socio-pathic Wan again. Like Broadhead, Wan is also on a quest, seeking his long lost father by searching for him in black holes. He also has a vendetta against the Heechee. While on his search, Wan rescues and abducts Gelle-Klara; eventually, they are met by another Heechee ship and initiate first contact: "And so it was Gelle-Klara Moynlin who was the first human being to stand in the presence of a Heechee" (223). As the novel concludes, the reason the Heechee went away is revealed: another intergalactic species, known as the Assassins, beings of pure energy, "had killed off every technologically advanced civilization in the universe—at least in our own Galaxy, and in some nearby ones" (253). Fearing that the Assassins would destroy them, the Heechee retreated into a black hole until such time had passed that the Assassins had left the Galaxy. The Heechee send Gelle-Klara to warn humanity with the decree that humankind must stop all interstellar travel lest they attract the Assassins. In the end, the holographic Robin—"I practiced my best holographic smiles and designed my best holographic surroundings and waited for her" (272)—is reconciled with Gelle-Klara, finally able to fully let go of his guilt.

The Annals of the Heechee begins on the centennial of the discovery of the Gateway asteroid. This is a momentous occasion, causing Broadhead to reflect on the progression from the first, random voyages in the Heechee ships to the human mastery of the galaxy: "But every successful voyage in a Heechee ship taught us something, and by and by we could go anywhere in the Galaxy" (10). As one might expect, the focus of the novel is the confrontation between humans and Heechee with the Assassins, called the Foe by human beings. As the novel progresses, Broadhead tours the galaxy in search of evidence of the Foe, hoping to stop them when they do reappear. The Foe make contact and take control of two children, making their way to Earth, where they penetrate the human computer network. As the narrative reaches its conclusion, with the help of the simulacra Albert Einstein and his uploaded companions, Broadhead is able to confront the Foe and negotiate an understanding by which the Foe leave the galaxy to humans and Heechee so they can evolve over time into energy beings themselves, thus also being able to circumvent the eventual cooling of the universe. Extending his exploration of machine consciousness, *Annals* also raises questions about immortality, again paralleling Pohl's earlier interest in cryonics. The novel concludes with Albert observing the difference between "meat" and immortality: "When all the humans and Heechee who are alive decide to be *more* alive, and *permanently* alive as we are—then maybe there'll be a chance to carry on a real dialogue" (338). Thus, the future of humanity (and Heechee) lies in the evolution of the machine interface.

Although the main sequence of the Heechee saga was completed, Pohl returned once again to the franchise at the start of the next decade with *The Gateway Trip*, a collection of Heechee tales and vignettes, beautifully illustrated by Frank Kelly Freas. About half the book is devoted to "The Merchants of Venus." The additional material fills in some gaps in the Heechee saga, so in some ways it serves as a companion to the prior volumes rather than a collection of standalone stories—in fact, the vignettes were published in serial format in *Aboriginal Science Fiction* magazine as *The Gateway Concordance* in the months prior to book publication in November 1990. The first piece, "The Visit," tells how the Heechee first came to Earth and encountered the australopithecines, in a similar manner to that of Clarke's *2001* monolith, and then in a quick ten pages summarizes the history of humans up until the time of the discovery of the Venusian tunnels. "The Gateway Asteroid" details how Sylvester Macklin took passage on the first Heechee ship found on Venus to the Gateway asteroid, hence leading to the Gateway Star Rush. "The Home Planet" is a refrain on Pohl's familiar theme that the environmental, economic, and political conditions on Earth are dire: "So there were two kinds of human beings on Earth. If you owned a few thousand shares of PetroFood or Chemways you didn't lack for much—not even health, because then you could afford Full Medical. But if you didn't . . . If you didn't, the next best thing was to have a job. Any kind of job. Having a job was a dream of Utopia for the billions who had none, but for those who did have employment their work was generally a demeaning kind of drudgery that drowned the spirit and damaged the health" (161). Once Broadhead secures the CHON-Food Factory and figures out how to build Heechee ships, Earth experiences a Golden Age, described in "The Age of Gold": "Detroit led the way in the old United States, with its three-hundred-story New Renaissance megastructures that covered everything from Wayne State University dormitories to the river; a hundred and seventy people lived in the crystal ziggurat" (230). The final story, "In the Core," helps the reader conceptualize the Heechee within the black hole: "The place where the Heechee hid was in the core of the galaxy, within an immense black hole—a black hole so enormous that it contained thousands of stars and planets and satellites and asteroids, all orbiting together in a space so small that their combined mass had pulled space in around them. The Heechee were all there—several billion of them, living on some 350 roofed-over planets inside their core" (236). In his *Analog* review, Tom Easton felt "like Pohl is riding his own coattails here," like other famous writers having to make his way "through some of the hoops the marketers hold up before them,"[42] and though there is some truth to this, *The Gateway Trip* is not meant to be a continuation of the series but rather to serve as a kind of companion piece. The core of the book is, of course, "The Merchants of Venus," which, unlike "The Midas Plague" in *Midas World*, is here brought into context with the rest of the saga; the rest is meant merely to fill in some of the gaps of the series. In that, the tales in *The Gateway Trip* are pleasant additions to the Heechee saga, helping to fill out some of the details only suggested in the main sequence.

★   ★   ★

That ominously anticipated year 1984 was a particularly active one for Pohl. In addition to *The Merchants' War* and *Heechee Rendezvous*, the collection *Pohlstars* and the utopia *The Years of the City* both appeared in October. And in the summer, skipping his annual visit to Lawrence, Kansas, for Jim Gunn's summer programs, Pohl married Betty Anne Hull and moved to Palatine, Illinois, a Chicago suburb. Lester Del Rey flew in to be his best man. Pohl would, however, return to Lawrence the next year to receive the Campbell Award, his second, for *The Years of the City*, making him the only two-time winner until Joan Slonczewski matched the feat in 2012.

The Years of the City is an episodic utopian novel, and it is also Pohl's loving farewell to New York City. Two sections appeared as novellas in *The Magazine of Fantasy and Science Fiction* just prior to the book's publication. Pohl opens the book with an introduction wherein he writes of his relationship to New York City, its importance to him as a writer, his anxieties for its survival, and his hopes for the city's future. He fears the city might become an endangered species, which seems to be taking him back to *Gladiator-At-Law*. This was before the period of urban renewal and gentrification that revitalized many American cities—and made rents more expensive. He traces the genesis of the novel to a cocktail party in 1973 when he left the party at the same time as New York City's then-mayor John Lindsay and they talked about city politics. *The Years of the City* works through a number of ideas put forward in *Practical Politics* and approaches problems within the urban environment that recall *Gladiator-At-Law* and *Syzygy*.

Although *The Years of the City* won the Campbell for best science fiction novel, it is really a sequence of five interlinked novellas. The first story, "When New York Hit the Fan," involves a city planner, Shire Brandon, a single parent who works for the mayor and advocates a plan that will renew the city. As the story begins, Brandon's apartment has been burglarized, and he and the police suspect the young "Pins"—"Persons in Need of Supervision"—who live across the street. A garbage strike has left the streets piled up with refuse, and citizens in general are on edge because they feel powerless to advance positive change: "Behind most of the strikes and unrest in the city, in fact in the world, lies a perception of unfairness and helplessness—people believe that they are not getting a fair share of the world's goods, and at the same time that they have no good way to change that" (26). Here Pohl seems to anticipate the Occupy movement. Brandon's idea is to restructure urban politics around the concept of the Universal Town Meeting (a format that now appears in much diluted form occasionally on news networks), allowing for greater political participation. In other words, through televisual media, the common citizen can have a voice in urban planning decisions: "'You didn't listen!' he shouted. 'The UTM isn't an exercise in brain-washing! It's a way to give the people real control over what's happening! Not a chance to hear more bullshit from the Mayor. Not a way for the special-interest people to divide up the public treasury'" (71). Other ideas are brought to the table, such as putting correctional facilities underground and building a dome over Manhattan, both of which are featured in later sections. While Brandon makes his case at City Hall, a major snowstorm puts the city at a standstill. Meanwhile, with the power out, Brandon's daughter wanders from their apartment, thinking she can easily find her dad, and is lost in the city. Gwenna Anderson, a prostitute with the street name Vanilla Fudge, who plays a key role in the next story, finds the distraught child and takes her to shelter at a bus station, where the girl is rescued by one of the Pins, giving Brandon a lesson about judging others. The story effectively blends the arguments for the political ideas with the human story of a father trying to raise his daughter as they both cope with his wife's suicide.

The second story, "The Greening of Bed-Stuy," first appeared as a cover novella in *Fantasy and Science Fiction* in July 1984. The story examines the idea of underground prisons brought forward in the first story. The concept returns to some ideas Pohl first explored in the 1950s in the story "My Lady Greensleeves." Atop the underground facility, the urban environment has been renewed into a lush park, allowing for greater green space within the city. One of the key components of the renewed city is that it will be energy self-sufficient, no longer importing power from somewhere else. The novel as a whole, and this story in particular, begin an exercise in proposing urban sustainability:

> When Bed-Stuy was done it would not have to import one kilowatt-hour of energy from anywhere else. . . . Winter heating would come from the thermal aquifer storage, in the natural brine of reservoirs under the city, nine hundred feet down. Summer cooling would help to warm the aquifers again, topped off with extra chill from the ice-ponds. By using ice and water to store heat and cold the summer air-conditioning and winter heating peaks wouldn't happen, which meant that maximum capacity could be less. . . . Bedford-Stuyvesant was a demonstration project. If it worked there would be more, all over the country (95–96).

Some of these ideas will reemerge in a different way in Pohl and Asimov's environmental book *Our Angry Earth*. Parallels with *Gladiator-At-Law* are evident here also, but the additional thirty years of thinking about these questions has improved Pohl's argument, if not always the dramatic effect. The thrust of the drama revolves around a boy (Vanilla Fudge's son) who has been unknowingly enlisted to aide the escape of a group of convicts from the underground prison. The escapees seize the city power plant, holding the entire city hostage, threatening the viability of the sustainability project and thereby exposing a need to have failsafes in place in public works to protect against acts of terrorism. The convicts are thwarted when the police detonate a small bomb in a food package, and in an act to protect his mother, the hostage boy pushes the ringleader over a precipice, thereby saving the governor from assassination. Like its predecessor, the story blends political ideas with a story of parent and child.

"The Blister" also graced the cover of *FSF* in September 1984 with an intriguing cover illustration by Thomas Kidd, foregrounding the Statue of Liberty as construction of the dome over Manhattan is underway in the background. The story centers on a construction worker, Jeff Bratislaw, who, after a near-fatal accident on the scaffolding above Manhattan, is reassigned as the assistant to the union leader Ella Jennalec. Again Pohl uses the drama of Bratislaw's relationship with Jennalec as a vehicle to explore the architectural and political questions involved in doming the city, arguing that "doming the city was going to change the way the city worked" (149). For one thing, cars would be eliminated; public transit would be the only mode of transportation, cutting down on emissions and preempting the crisis that will occur when the dwindling fuel supply reaches its tipping point. Pohl revisits cryonic suspension when Bratislaw's sister-in-law, a police officer, is severely beaten and makes little progress in rehab (also recalling "The Meeting"). One option is to put her on ice at great risk, but in the end Bratislaw and his wife decide to accept her circumstances as they are. Political crisis ensues when Bratislaw realizes that Jennelac and the union want to put a stop to the Universal Town Meeting. In a tense fight high atop the dome construction, Bratislaw records Jennelac's ex-lover admitting to the union conspiracy, leading to trial and Jennelac's conviction. Throughout the episodes, common sense and the democratic system work. Pohl here demonstrates a faith in American politics and justice far different from his usual cynicism. This makes *The Years of the City* come across as something entirely different than the usual fare, but what is evident is that a number of Pohl's central concerns from previous novels and stories work their way into the narrative of *The Years of the City*, though from a different angle. So while *The Years of the City* is at once something quite different and new in Pohl's oeuvre, it is also clearly recognizable as a Frederik Pohl work. This in turn shows the versatility of Pohl's science fictional imagination.

The final two novellas, "Second-Hand Sky" and "Gwenanda and the Supremes," depict how new lifeways have emerged in the context of the new urban environment. In "Second-Hand Sky," a young man treks from Atlanta to soar his glider illegally under the dome of Manhattan, recalling Philippe

Petit's 1974 highwire stunt and George Willig's 1977 scaling of the Twin Towers. "Gwenanda and the Supremes" depicts an era of utopian government when all citizens participate. To be a Supreme Court justice or a member of Congress is a selective-service duty, taking the task out of the hands of political favors and ideological agendas. The titular character (who, given her name, is perhaps a descendant of Vanilla Fudge) is serving a term on the Supreme Court. The central case brought before the court concerns cryogenic revivals, again returning to territory explored in *Preferred Risk* and *The Age of the Pussyfoot*. The domed cities, in turn, with their sanitized climates, have lost the ability to resist common viral infections, and when a flu outbreak begins to sweep through New York City, the cryogenic freezers cannot handle so many people. This jeopardizes the Universal Town Meeting, now part of the fabric of national politics. The story works mainly as a set piece to examine the challenges of a UTM involving half a billion people. As such, it works within the overall tapestry of the book but lacks some of the punch usually associated with Pohl's stories. Easton, once again reviewing in *Analog*, apparently wanted the kind of adventure story he enjoyed most but thought the novel read "too often like a tract," and he had a hard time buying into Pohl's utopian argument.[43] But such was not Pohl's purpose in *The Years of the City*. In his review in *Fantasy and Science Fiction*, Budrys had an entirely different perception: "The total structure is technically stunning, beautifully various, and the best book from Frederik Pohl in years."[44] As an exploration of alternative, utopian political ideas, and as Pohl's love song and farewell to New York City, the power of *The Years of the City* lies not in the dramas of the plot but in the way Pohl's ideas stimulate thinking about sustainability and reimagined political systems.

Pohl followed *The Years of the City* with *Black Star Rising*, a biting political satire in the same vein as *Jem*. His 1983 visit to China informs the novel: he posits a future in which China and India hold global economic supremacy. A century after nuclear war between the Soviet Union and the United States left the Soviets completely destroyed, the Americans just barely hanging on, and the rest of the world devastated as well, China and India have emerged as the world powers. China has claimed the remains of the United States and holds dominion. Americans, then, become the colonized and are now second-class citizens, an idea that emerges again in *All the Lives He Led*. Pohl creates a highly credible scenario that allows for an examination of future Chinese culture and politics, the environmental aftermath of nuclear war, and the decline of American exceptionalism. The novel opens as Pettyman Castor, having some training as an astrophysicist but reduced to common labor on the "Heavenly Grain Collective," discovers a severed head in a Biloxi, Mississippi, rice field, which entangles him in the investigation headed by Tsoong Delilah. Castor and Delilah become lovers, and when an alien spacecraft arrives in the solar system, demanding that the Chinese leave the United States at once or risk annihilation, and insisting on a meeting with the president of the United States, Castor is thrust into the role, since no such office exists anymore. The Chinese hope he can convince the aliens that they are not evil conquerors but that they only picked up the pieces in the aftermath of nuclear holocaust.

At the novel's midpoint, the aliens insist that they speak to the president in person, a rocket is prepared, and, with Delilah and crew, Castor makes rendezvous with the alien craft, whereupon they are instantly transported via hyperdrive to another star system. There they discover a bizarre culture on a planet called merely "World," made up of the descendants of American space explorers, who call themselves "Yanks," and their intrepid retainers, the comically swarming erks, lobster-like beings that find a cause in rah-rah Americanism. Raised on the mystified stories of American heroics and encouraged by the erks, the people on World have become the embodiment of gung-ho patriotism: "All Americans had uniforms, tailored to them as soon as they were ten. They were for parades on Veterans Day and the Fourth of July; they were for dress-up whenever anybody thought of a good excuse to do it" (154). The erks are the uplifted bioengineered remnant of the pets of an advanced alien civilization, with dogged determination and loyalty: "They help the causes of righteousness and justice wherever there is need, of course. And they do it because the Living Gods made them that way" (183).

Pohl brilliantly moves from the first half of the novel, where Chinese colonization of North America was the focus, to the intergalactic setting, which allows him to examine the "patriotic" American attitudes that led to the nuclear holocaust. When a Chinese ship, armed to the teeth and with a crew of ten, including the encephalitic, multipersonality genius Manyface, follows from Earth, the Yanks and the erks delightedly prepare for war. Eventually, Manyface uncovers "the war records of the past eight thousand years," which reveal that, like the pyramids of *Wolfbane*, the erks have gone from planet to planet, intervening in conflicts and destroying civilizations: "Over the stretch of eight thousand years the erks had acquired the military technology of nine separate civilizations" (254). Realizing that they must somehow return to Earth and destroy the erk hyperdrive ship, thus affording time to prepare for a future erk attack, Castor and company use war tactics unfamiliar to the obtuse erks: deception and guile. The narrative builds to an exciting climax, as the erk ship is obliterated; Miranda, a Chinese-American rebel who wanted the Han Chinese out of America, concedes that she hopes the Hans "do better than anyone ever did before" (293).

Black Star Rising stands, then, as Pohl's strongest statement on Cold War nuclear politics since *Jem*, and along with that novel, it certainly holds up as one of Pohl's finest political satires. As such, *Black Star Rising* is a timely critique of the political culture of the Reagan administration and the policies that at the time seemed to be moving closer to nuclear war. Pohl was not part of the Citizens' Advisory Council, made up of a number of science fiction writers (Heinlein, Poul Anderson, Larry Niven, Jerry Pournelle, Gregory Benford, Greg Bear, and others), scientists, astronauts, and engineers, which was advising Reagan on space policy, strategic defense, and the nuclear option. But as a central member of the science fiction community, Pohl was certainly in touch with what was going on. He would continue his critique of Reagan policy decisions in another triumphant satire the following year, *The Coming of the Quantum Cats*, which combines speculations from quantum physics with alternate timelines to offer up a pungently funny analysis of 1980s America.

Before looking at *The Coming of the Quantum Cats*, a few of Pohl's short stories from the decade are worth mentioning. One of the best, "Spending the Day at the Lottery Fair" (*FSF*, October 1983), again examines his shibboleth, overpopulation, from another angle. In a depressed and grossly overpopulated future where opportunities for a decent livelihood, let alone sufficient sustenance, are limited, families attend voluntary Lottery Fairs, where employment can be garnered through the lottery, although at the risk of instant euthanasia if the wrong ticket comes up. Desperate for work, Randolph Baxter takes his wife and three children to the Lottery Fair: "When you have a wife and three kids and no job, living on welfare, never thinking about tomorrow because you know there isn't going to be anything tomorrow worth thinking about, a day's outing for the whole family is an event to be treasured. No matter what the price—especially if the price isn't money" (96). In part a critique of the Right to Life movement, Pohl raises tough questions about the links between unexamined population policies, American consumer capitalism, and resulting environmental problems. In what might be one of Pohl's most bitter endings, as Baxter finishes debating the American policy with a Japanese tourist, his wife comes rushing up in desolate misery: the numbers of all three children were up.

Further commenting on the growing political influence of the Christian Right in America and the crises of the Cold War and the environment, the short-short "Second Coming" (*Omni*, November 1983) starts out with the startlingly droll sentence: "I guess, just as with the Kennedy Assassination, everybody can remember exactly where he was and what he was doing on the day the space people brought Jesus back to Earth" (105). Alas, Jesus doesn't like what he sees: "He doesn't like the way we've spoiled His planet. . . . Says He told us what to do and we haven't done it—we've messed everything up—,'" and so Jesus decides to go "back with the space people. They've got a better-class zoo" (107).

Pohl's most successful story from this period is, however, the Hugo Award–winning "Fermi and Frost" (*Asimov's*, January 1985). Undoubtedly in dialogue with the extraordinarily powerful television mini-series *The Day After*, which aired in November 1983 and was watched by 100 million people, "Fermi and Frost" is a bitterly poignant indictment of the nuclear arms race that, through stark realism, imagines the desperate human calculus of atomic holocaust. As the Soviets and Americans unleash their nuclear arsenals, astronomer Harry Malibert, who has spent his career working on S.E.T.I. (the Search for Extraterrestrial Intelligence), is given charge of nine-year-old Timmy Clary while panicked parents try to get their children on desperation flights away from the coming devastation. Malibert is offered a seat on a flight heading to the presumed safe zone of Reykjavik, Iceland, and he takes Timmy with him. Just as they leave the Icelandic capital, a final, errant Soviet missile intended to strike the U.S. airbase at Keflavik destroys the city. As a trained scientist, Malibert is enlisted into "the task of keeping Iceland warm," utilizing the geothermal geography of the island (454), while the rest of the world rapidly succumbs to the perpetual cold of nuclear winter. Pohl ends the story with two possible outcomes: the nuclear winter persists too long and even the survivors on Iceland starve, or the cloud clears in time, Timmy survives and fathers children, and over time humankind is contacted by beings from other stars. This is Pohl's desperate dream—that we have a different outcome. That we won't destroy ourselves through nuclear bombs or by some other means. That there are other beings out there among the stars.

After the grave tone of "Fermi and Frost" and the piercing satire of *Black Star Rising*, Pohl returns to a more jocular brand of satire in *The Coming of the Quantum Cats*, first serialized in the pages of *Analog* at the beginning of 1986 prior to hardcover publication in May. *The Coming of the Quantum Cats* develops from the then-popular interest in cosmology and quantum mechanics (epitomized by the success of Stephen Hawking's *A Brief History of Time* two years later) and in American politics during the Reagan administration. Pohl has a great deal of fun poking at the Reagan presidency while also looking cynically at Cold War policies. Ronald Reagan exemplifies the Cold Warrior whom Pohl had been critiquing for thirty years and thus is an ideal target for Pohl's satire—though all in good fun. The novel is particularly clever in its use of multiple universes and multiple timelines, allowing the story to unfold from multiple first-person points of view, all from variant Dominic DeSotas from alternate Earths.

In the first timeline, dated August 16, 1983, America is controlled by Middle Eastern Islamists and permissive social mores are no more, being replaced by repressive Islamic doctrines. It takes the reader a little bit of time to pick up these clues, but it soon becomes evident that this is an alternate world. Significantly, the setting is in Chicago, indicating Pohl's recent move. Chauffer Nicky DeSota is excited by the prospects of a late-night swim with his girl-friend Greta. The whole scene is set up around the promise of "going topless." The twist comes when Nicky reaches "down between us and slowly, slowly unzipped the top part of my bathing suit" (6). This surprise alteration of the reader's expectations significantly draws attention to the rise of Islamic conservatism and its impact on the open democratic societies of the West. Pohl also extrapolates a situation in which America's dependence on Arab oil might lead to an economic indebtedness resulting in cultural colonization, from a different angle than in *Black Star Rising*. The alternate reality is further revealed by a number of embedded clues. When Nicky is arrested for public lewdness by Agent Nyla Christophe, he notices she doesn't have any thumbs, a signal for a past indiscretion prosecuted by Islamic law. When Nicky is arraigned, he swears upon both the Bible and the Koran in court. Further, there are only forty-eight stars on the American flag—Hawaii and Alaska never became states—and the Dodgers are still in Brooklyn, both alterations signaling when the divergence took place. Gas is overpriced at sixty-nine cents a gallon ("sixty-nine cents a gallon! If I'd looked at the prices I never would have stopped there" [21]); by 1985 it was up to around $1.20 in our reality. Nor do women have the right to vote.

Obviously, the political landscape has shifted. After Nicky is accused of breaking into DaleyLab, "a hush-hush military research place" (11–12), his lawyer Larry Douglas (a descendent of "Grandpa Joe" Stalin: "He was a bank robber before he came to America and changed his name" [30]) takes him to see an old, blacklisted actor in Dixon, Illinois: Ron Reagan. Reagan never became president; he's just a retired, left-leaning has-been actor who had "got involved in unions and stuff like that" (31)—a jab perhaps at how Reagan broke up the air traffic controller strike. Still married to Jane Wyman ("Janie was all for 'women's rights,' whatever she meant by that" [34]), Reagan had been pushed out of politics by "the Arabs and that whole fundamentalist bunch in Congress" (34). As Douglas bemoans, Reagan is "just out of touch with the modern current of politics in America. He had some crazy, sentimental notion about Franklin D. Roosevelt or somebody—I don't know—anyway he simply didn't understand what was going on" (36). Later, when Reagan is arrested for slandering the United States and the FBI, an airplane pilot must maneuver around a "huge tower where none should have been" because "Chicago didn't have any of those hundred-story buildings like New York; it had something to do with the fact that the city was built on alluvial soil, no bedrock anywhere near" (44). The plane soon vanishes. This is the first clear indication that there is a slippage in the time stream.

The narrative then shifts to another timeline. In this one, Dominic DeSota is a United States senator and is having an affair with Nyla Christophe, who in this reality is a classical cellist, a skill, needless to say, which requires thumbs. In this reality, Reagan is president—the reader's first assumption is that this is our reality. Senator DeSota gets word, "They've this man in custody and he says he's you" (49), introducing another Dominic DeSota, a physicist from yet another reality. As before, clues are casually introduced that Senator DeSota's reality is not the reader's either. For instance, DeSota is married to a woman name Marilyn, Nyla to a man named Fred—one conjectures this is meant to be Marilyn Monroe and, perhaps, an alternate Fred Pohl himself. Indeed, there's a story behind this. In the magazine version, the man's name was Henry, not Fred. Apparently Pohl confused Henry Miller for Arthur Miller, Marilyn Monroe's ex-husband. When Betty Hull pointed this out as the novel was prepared for book publication, Pohl "huffed a bit, then for spite married the hypothetical Marilyn (presumably Monroe) off to the hypothetical Fred (Pohl). Fred *did* like blondes."[45] Further, the Soviets and Chinese have engaged in a nuclear war, giving the United States fully unopposed global superpower status. As things progress, a fourth DeSota appears: Major Dominic DeSota of the United States Army, sent to arrest those Dominics from the other timelines.

From here, the timelines get increasingly confused, and part of the fun is to sort out which divergences belong to which timeline. In the Senator's world, a throwaway comment about Jackie, another senator's wife, reveals that JFK is still alive and well and in the U.S. senate, his brothers having both been killed in car accidents. Further, the political landscape differs, in that Stalin had been assassinated, while England had a socialist revolution. Another throwaway has yet another DeSota, apparently from a postapocalyptic timeline, marveling at "the place where Chicago had once been" (70). Pohl does not return to this thread, apparently only wanting to suggest another possible reality. In the major's world, Adlai Stevenson served two terms as president, and Jerry Brown now holds the office. The major wonders "why a militarily active U.S. society like ours got a jelly-backed President like Jerry Brown, while this other one, fat and peaceful, had elected the fire breather, Reagan" (80). Pohl's big joke here is that this Reagan is not Ronald, but Nancy: "And the best way for old Nancy to protect you folks would be to let us do what we want" (82). By this time the reader is thoroughly convinced that their own reality is not even present in the novel, recalling the estrangement one gets from the conclusion of Philip K. Dick's *The Man in the High Castle*.

The ideas of Stephen Hawking and John Gribbin begin factoring into the story, and they in fact become characters. After *The Jupiter Effect*, which Pohl used as the pivot of *Syzygy*, Gribbin returned to popular attention with *In*

Search of Schrödinger's Cat: Quantum Physics and Reality (1984), which is clearly the sourcebook for Pohl's narrative. Similarly delightful is Pohl's imagining of his friend Isaac Asimov, who in one of the timelines is the best transplant surgeon in the world: "Dr. Azimof, best transplant man in world. Has done three hundred eighty-five hearts alone, not counting livers, testicles ... when world's first successful hemorrhoid transplant is done, Itzhak will do it!" (118). Still later, a Professor Greenberg, expert in political science, is called in to interview the duplicate DeSotas; astute readers will recognize that this is Martin H. Greenberg, prominent science fiction anthologist and a friend of Pohl's. As the novel winds down, multiple Hawkings, in various states of health, and multiple Gribbins are exiled on an empty planet, along with other "Paratemporally Displaced Persons," including all the DeSotas, so as not to continue causing disruptions in the timestreams. The novel has a great deal of humor throughout, sustaining a level of comedic flare not seen since *The Space Merchants*, though it also raises serious questions about contemporary politics and individual circumstances of living. Near the end, one of the Dominics ponders, "In a way, we *did* have to be what we were, because of the world we lived in" (239)—meaning our individual selves are, in large part, socially and environmentally constructed. Still, there are choices: "'Have to' might be too strong, because some of it was our fault—we took easy ways. There were better ways, even in our time" (239). Pohl's point is that it is through individual choices and actions that social constructions change and environmental imperatives can be overridden.

Pohl continued the analysis of the political landscape of the late 1980s in the minor novel *Terror*, which was published a few months after *The Coming of the Quantum Cats*. Perhaps more a thriller than a science fiction novel, in it Pohl closely examines the growing concern for global terrorism, which later becomes central to his last novels, *The Last Theorem* and *All the Lives He Led*. Unexpectedly, the terrorists are part of a Hawaiian nationalist movement, suggestive of a growing global postcolonial nationalism. The main plot focuses on Rachel Chindler, a thirty-five-year-old librarian whose flight is hijacked on the tarmac in Hawaii, and the resulting difficulties she experiences when she later returns to the islands and gets caught up in the terrorists' plot. An uninspired Soviet subplot becomes part of all this, involving a nuclear submarine, another manifestation of Pohl's Cold War extrapolations. Pohl's interest in current speculative science also surfaces when James Lovelock's Gaia hypothesis enters the plot. Although the characterization of Rachel Chindler is at times interesting, overall the novel falls flat. What appeared to be Pohl's initial intention of examining terrorism and postcolonial nationalism devolves into another narrative involving global power politics, the Cold War, and the nuclear arms race. It is almost as if Pohl saw the direction in which global politics was heading but was not yet able to break away from the Cold War model.

A more inspiring contribution in 1986 is the shared-theme anthology *Tales from the Planet Earth*. Pohl's involvement with World SF continued during this period, and by the early 1980s he had visited forty or fifty countries and was pleased to find science fiction readers and writers active in most of them. Inspired by discussions at the 1982 World SF General Meeting in Rotterdam, a few years later Pohl and Betty Hull encountered a story by Japanese writer Tetsu Yano, "The Legend of the Paper Spaceship," which had a similar theme to a story Pohl had recently written, "Sitting by the Pool, Soaking up the Rays." Both stories envisioned the idea of alien "passengers" using humans as surrogates—in the case of Pohl's story, to conduct business on Earth. This is a kinder, gentler development from Pohl's 1974 story "We Purchased People"; the idea also shows up in the Cuckoo saga. With the two stories in hand, Pohl and Hull conceived a shared-theme anthology, inviting writers from around the world to add stories on the theme of aliens using human hosts, to be set in their own countries. The anthology features stories by such familiar writers as Englishman Brian Aldiss, the expatriate Harry Harrison representing Ireland, Canadian Spider Robinson, and Australian A. Bertram Chandler, along with international writers such as Czech Josef Nesvadba, Swede Sam Lundwall, Uruguayan Carlos Federici, Thai-American Somtow Sucharitkul, and many others from around the globe. The editors wanted to bring non-English science fiction to the attention of the American SF audience, recapitulating Pohl's effort in this direction in the 1960s in *International Science Fiction*. Tom Easton had nothing but praise for the book in *Analog*: "*Tales* is thus the best—the only!—way you have ever seen or will ever see to sample *world* science fiction . . . and it does a marvelous job of supporting Pohl's assertion that you can find SF everywhere."[46]

Pohl's internationalism and his critique of Cold War politics are capped off in this period by the contemporary novel *Chernobyl*, published by Bantam in

September 1987, and it still remains the only novel about the disaster. Published in the year just after the meltdown, *Chernobyl* is an intensely realistic novel that brings to life the fumbling bureaucratic missteps, the science of atomic reactions, the heroics of plant workers trying to contain the accident, and the tragedies of common men and women affected by the disaster. The novel should stand as an important historical novel and as a testimonial on the latter days of the Cold War, serving as a fitting capstone to Pohl's overall examination and critique of global Cold War politics. What a reader unfamiliar with the history and literature of science fiction might not recognize is how the novel (and the real incident) echoes Lester Del Rey's early novella "Nerves" (1942), which realistically portrayed the battle to contain a nuclear plant meltdown three years before the dropping of the atomic bomb. As noted, Pohl and Del Rey were neighbors in the mid-1950s when Del Rey, encouraged by Pohl, revised the original novella into a full-length novel, published by Ballantine in 1956. Pohl visited the Chernobyl region a few months after the disaster. In *Chasing Science* he provides illumination: "I had two purposes for the trip. The nuclear power plant at Chernobyl in the Soviet Ukraine had exploded violently some ninety days earlier, and I wanted to begin the research into that terrible disaster which ultimately wound up in my novel on the subject, *Chernobyl*. And the Union of Soviet Writers had invited me to attend, as a foreign observer, the every-five-years convention of their trade union" (136). So *Chernobyl* should be read in the context of Pohl's efforts to forge greater understanding between the Cold War powers, through his engagement with other science fiction writers across the world.

Chernobyl's plot begins in the hours just prior to the disaster. While four thousand men and women work at the facility, rumors swirl that the plant is poorly designed and uses unsafe materials. Nonetheless, the Soviet authorities insist on keeping the plant online, despite the protests of engineer Leonid Sheranchuk. But the unexpected happens, and the reactor explodes. Pohl employs exacting scientific detail in describing the sequence of events that occur as the reactor reaches critical mass and the radiation cloud spreads across western Russia, even reaching Finland. But he also creates the human drama of real people facing extraordinary events. Pohl is particularly careful to humanize the Russian and Ukrainian characters, which in itself is reflective of the easing of the tensions between the Soviets and the United States, but it also reflects Pohl's own deepening connection with international citizens, writers, and scientists. Pohl explains the mix of fact and fiction in the afterword: "Some of the things done in the novel were in fact done by real people, as in the case of the three men who donned diving gear and entered into the flooded corridors under the reactor to open the drainage valves . . . but the characters in the novel are not in any way modeled on them." Pohl further explains his method: "The nature and chronology of the explosion and its consequences correspond closely to reality as has been possible, although I have taken a few minor liberties with timing" (355). While the extraordinary events that transpired at Chernobyl were not science fiction, as it were, to document these events in fiction required the imagination of a science fiction writer.

Chernobyl was the capstone of Pohl's engagement with the Cold War. Thereafter, his narratives largely moved away from Cold War politics, concentrating instead on other issues, such as climate change and rising religious fundamentalism, paralleling the global political shift that was beginning to manifest itself by the end of the Reagan administration.

But 1987 also marks a shift in Pohl's work for other reasons, including the conclusion of the Heechee saga. By the end of 1987, Pohl had reached age sixty-eight. A number of his science fiction colleagues had died over the previous three years: Theodore Sturgeon in 1985, Frank Herbert and L. Ron Hubbard in 1986, Alfred Bester, C. L. Moore, and Futurian Richard Wilson in 1987. Heinlein would die the next year. Pohl, like the genre itself, was settling into senior-citizenhood. With the death of Heinlein and soon Asimov (in 1992), Pohl would ascend to the role of grand old man of American science fiction. As the years rolled by and more and more of his generation passed away, Pohl would carry on, striking many as if he were a boy who would, perhaps, live forever.

CHAPTER 4

THE BOY WHO WOULD
LIVE FOREVER, 1988–2013

Chernobyl and *The Annals of the Heechee* mark a transition in Pohl's career. The books that follow focus less on the Cold War and more on new, pressing issues facing the contemporary world. For instance, *The Voices of Heaven* (1994) takes on religious zealotry, a rising phenomenon that was becoming increasingly problematic in the 1990s. *Homegoing* (1989) considers the environmental crisis; published two years prior to *Our Angry Earth*, Pohl's nonfiction environmental alarm written with Isaac Asimov, the novel informs the reader on the ecological problems facing the planet. *Outnumbering the Dead* (1990) addresses issues of aging and death, something that, as Pohl turned seventy years old and as many of his contemporaries were passing, was undoubtedly on his mind. Pohl also continued to write fiction that engaged with currently topical scientific developments, such as *Mining the Oort* (1992), where he posits a method for making Mars habitable. But after the intense realism of *Chernobyl*, Pohl's next novel, *Narabedla Ltd.*, was a work of lighthearted fun that demonstrated his love of music and also played with Betty Hull's background in dramatic literature. Indeed, Hull has said that it is her favorite novel among her husband's works, written to amuse himself as much as it was to cheer her up after her heart attack kept them from being able to attend the Lyric Opera in Chicago, for which they had main-floor seats.[1]

The basic premise of *Narabedla Ltd.* is that human artists and entertainers are shanghaied by aliens to perform for the Galactics, a conglomerate of advanced civilizations spread throughout the galaxy. The Galactics are not particularly interested in inviting humans into membership with the greater galactic civilization, because humans don't have anything to offer beyond the performing arts, but the Galactics do enjoy human entertainment—hence the colony of abductees. The task of Nolly Stennis, a failed singer, is to convince the Galactics that humans have more to offer than mere entertainment, and, inevitably, by the end of the novel humans are invited to join Galactic civilization. The novel follows Stennis as he makes his way through the nightclubs of the greater galaxy, affording Pohl opportunities to satirize the entertainment industry. The most compelling idea that Pohl plays with is that Earth is not that important: there has been no contact, beyond snatching a few entertainers, because the Galactics simply have no interest in Earth. While this is a good joke in SF, it is also a serious supposition for explaining the Great Silence—why we have had no apparent contact from the stars. Pohl utilizes the first-person narrative he consistently excels at. According to Hull, "He wanted to show off a lot of the stuff he'd learned about stagecraft and dramaturgy and what happens behind the scenes to people who perform in public."[2] Although the novel is entertaining and reveals Pohl's interest in the other arts in greater depth, it lacks some of the pungent criticism generally found in his work. Consequently, it is one of his happier comedies of galactic manners. *Narabedla Ltd.* is a light-hearted romp, more joyous than, say, *The Coming of the Quantum Cats* or *Black Star Rising*. Perhaps the subject matter demands it.

Two more books appeared in 1988: *Land's End*, another collaboration with Jack Williamson, and *The Day the Martians Came*, a fix-up collection of stories involving how the first contact with the Martians impacts the lives of ordinary citizens. The central story in *The Day the Martians Came* is "The Day after the

Day the Martians Came," which originally appeared in Harlan Ellison's *Danger-ous Visions* in 1967. Consumerism, media, the space program, American com-placency, and American egoism all are put under Pohl's microscope at various times throughout the book. And there is some clever interstitial material—one involving Oprah Winfrey interviewing various pundits commenting on the Martian discovery—that places the book in the same satiric mode of Pohl's 1950s material. But despite all this, *The Day the Martians Came* does not have the sustained satirical interest associated with the 1950s collaborations or the Cold War critiques of the 1970s and 1980s.

Land's End also falls a bit flat. After a promising opening sequence that establishes Earth compromised by environmental abuse, which has led to the construction of underwater cities where humans are adapting to the oceanic environment (a further development along the lines of the *Undersea* novels), Pohl and Williamson introduce a cosmic entity living in the heart of a passing comet—echoing "The Dweller in the Ice"—which takes away from the power of the original concept. It would have been far more effective if the eco-disaster had played out on its own terms rather than through the manipulation of a vast alien intelligence. The novel begins with a familiar Pohl theme: Earth is overcrowded; there are eighteen cities below the sea that are relatively utopian, while the teeming masses on the surface live in abject poverty in the wake of environmental attrition. The planet faces an "ozone summer," a topical term used in the late 1980s to discuss the climate crisis. As the story progresses, the climate problem reaches cataclysmic proportions, and millions die. Meanwhile, the comet containing the alien entity strikes Earth, causing more death and destruction. It is disappointing that *Land's End* generally fails in its engagement with the imminently important theme of environmental crisis.

Again, this ecological theme is potentially very powerful, but it gets mired in the plot, which involves attempts at communication between humans and the alien intelligence, distracting the reader from the powerful implications of the ecological disaster.

The underrated *Homegoing*, however, hits all the right notes between ecologi-cal and alien-contact themes, and satire, making for a particularly strong novel. The conditions on Earth that serve as the backdrop for *Homegoing*—drowned coastlines and global climate change—resonate more with the public consciousness now than when it was written, giving the novel a continued relevancy. *Homegoing*'s ecological themes work in conjunction with Pohl's ecological book, *Our Angry Earth*, to illustrate the environmental crisis facing the planet. *Homegoing* also seems to be, in part, a response to Larry Niven and Jerry Pournelle's 1985 bestseller *Footfall*; the political solution to a similar scenario at the end of *Homegoing* offers an alternative to Niven and Pournelle's human victory by force of arms. The characterization is good here as well. Both Lysander "Sandy" Washington and the somewhat comic frog-kangaroo-like Hakh'hli are particularly well drawn. In fact, the Hakh'hli are among Pohl's best-conceived aliens; comparable to the Heechee, the Krinpit Sharn-Igon in *Jem*, or the harebrained erks of *Black Star Rising*. Sandy is presumably a human foundling taken in by an alien starship while orbiting Mars whose parents had been sent into space as a safety net, in case all were destroyed as the Earth faced nuclear war and ecological disaster. In truth, as revealed at the end of the novel, Sandy is a genetically spliced combination of human and hoo'hik—the Hakh'hli meat animal. He was not, after all, a foundling, but was rather a creation in the Hakh'hli lab.

The story the Hakh'hli tell Sandy about when he was supposedly picked up is that the situation on Earth appeared inhospitable to first contact, so the Hakh'hli left the system. They return for supplies and to reunite Sandy, now an adult, with his own people. The Hakh'hli ship left their own planet three thousand earth years ago. Hakh'hli are a diverse lot, each individual specialized for his or her tasks, recalling Wells's moon people in *The First Men in the Moon*. They represent themselves to Sandy as traders; in exchange for replenishment of supplies—oxygen, carbon, hydrogen—they will supply Earth with advanced technologies. While Sandy has reached age twenty-seven on the Hakh'hli ship, as a result of time dilation fifty-six years have passed on Earth. Upon the return of the Hakh'hli to the solar system, fewer broadcasts have been emanating from Earth and a "garbage barrier" of dead satellites and other space junk circles the globe. The Hakh'hli note:

> We have been observing your planet since first approaching this system. There are certain facts of interest. First, those electromagnetic signals which originally attracted us to this system, and which increased exponentially in energy and in number all through our first approach, are now quite sparse. We do not have

good, complete, recent information either by *radio* or by *television*. This may be because your *Earth* people have become either numerically few or technologically backward, due to that *war*. (27)

An important exchange on the environmental questions occurs when Sandy is instructed on the conditions on Earth and the follies of humans by Major Senior ChinTekki-tho: "By and large they are spoilers. You know what they have done to their planet—to your home planet, Lysander! What would our ship be like if we permitted such uncontrolled emission of dangerous pollutants?" (22). For the Hakh'hli, humans need help, and Sandy himself is compelled to recite the reasons: "The human race has raised the heat-retaining capacity of its atmosphere, released acid-forming compounds into the ambient air, cluttered up its low-orbit space with debris, saturated the surface waters with reduced and organic materials, discharged long-half-life radionuclides into the environment, and permitted deforestation and soil erosion" (23). This exchange and others like it allow Pohl to voice some of his ire at human behavior that is destroying the planet: "Your Earth people are vain, idle, careless, and deceitful. They are spoilers. They have spoiled their planet. You must be like us and not like them in your actions on this Earth" (28).

The Hakh'hli prepare to send a party to investigate, including Sandy, landing in Alaska to assess the situation. Assuming subarctic conditions, the expedition is perplexed when they find their landing zone humid and hot:

> It was not at all the way it was supposed to be. Something was seriously wrong with the mission planning. This was certainly the part of Earth called "Alaska"; the navigation screens proved it. Then why didn't it look that way? Alaska, along with all the rest of the planet, had been thoroughly studied by the Hakh'hli on their first time around. Alaska was known to be cold—at least, mostly cold during all but a brief period in the summer, and then it was only at relatively low altitudes that it could ever be called anything else. The planners had definitely assured them of "snow"; if there was such a thing (and a thousand television programs had testified there was), it might be somewhere on the Earth, but it definitely was not here. What was here was mud, and a temperature high enough to make Sandy sweat unbearably inside his furs, and an intense, scary, blinding storm (57).

Here Pohl brings climate change to the forefront. A twenty-first-century reader is likely more equipped to visualize this scenario than the initial readers in

1989, as parts of Alaska are now, indeed, experiencing an unprecedented thaw. Similarly, the contemporary reader might better recognize the possibility that Miami Beach and other coastal cities are inundated: "Sharks nose hungrily through the gambling casinos of Atlantic City, and coral grows on the golf courses of Georgia's sea islands. New York Bay is three times its former size, pocked with islands, and the Statue of Liberty stands with her feet wet up to the ankles. . . . But even they were as nothing, nothing at all, compared to what happened when Antarctica lost the Ross Ice Shelf. So the edges of the continents were awash; and in their centers the searing, drying winds have left new dust bowls" (112). Such scenarios are now part of our common discourse.

Despite all this, the devastation is not the end of all civilization that more extreme visions depict. Human beings keep carrying on, and some technologies still function. For instance, the Hakh'hli are interviewed on television. Further, Earth's political geography has changed dramatically due to the attritions of global climate change: "We don't have big countries any more—things like nations, you know? We just have commonwealths. About ten thousand of them, all over the world. I guess the biggest commonwealth in North America is York, over on the east coast, and that only has about a quarter of a million people" (77). Yet the remaining population seems to get by well enough: "Still, the arable lands that are left are now quite adequate to feed the world's population, for the simple reason that the human population is a lot lower than it used to be" (87). The compromised planetary ecology can only support so many.

As it turns out, rather than being the benevolent traders they represented themselves to be, the Hakh'hli are lost in space and "getting desperate too" (194), unable to reestablish contact with their home star because of the vast distance. And they have been lying to Sandy about his origins. Their true intent is to settle on Earth and hatch their eggs. Similar to Niven and Pournelle's *Footfall*, the aliens have emplaced meteors to bombard Earth's population centers if their demands are not met. Further destruction of the planet seems inevitable, as humans have some remaining atomic bombs left over from the war. Again, seemingly addressing the conclusion of *Footfall*, Earth's security agency wants Sandy to turn the Hakh'hli lander over to them so that they can threaten the starship, ramming it if they have to. But Sandy won't do it. As the novel reaches its conclusion, Sandy suggests a compromise: let the Hakh'hli settle Mars instead, "Trust has to start somewhere" (207). Pohl, then, seems to be wishing to send a different message than a novel like *Footfall* does, where compromise was not an option. It might also be seen as a coming to terms with the end of the Cold War. This compromise leads to hope for the future, for both humans and Hakh'hli: "It'll work. Oh, it will take a while. Fifty years, maybe, before we finish cleaning up the Earth and make Mars worth living on—but it's all going to go the right way, don't you see? Every year things will get a little better, instead of a lot worse" (208). *Homegoing* is one of Pohl's most compelling later books, effectively mixing the environmental theme with political allegory, and nicely extending the trajectory of Pohl's career from Cold War to cool war to hot war to resolution.

Pohl's next novel, *The World at the End of Time*, was his longest to date, more than four hundred pages in paperback. Drawing from ideas in contemporary cosmology, *The World at the End of Time* posits that living entities exist within the heart of stars. More than Pohl's previous work, this novel is inspired by the sweeping, wide-scope science fiction epitomized by E. E. "Doc" Smith (for example, the *Lensman* saga), Edmond Hamilton (*The City at the World's End*), and later by Poul Anderson (*Harvest of Stars*). Darren Harris-Fain sees it as representing "quintessential science fiction work" through its utilization of "many traditional SF motifs" and its demonstration of "how science fiction can challenge conventional notions." For Harris-Fain, "readers of Pohl's *World at the End of Time* . . . can indeed learn something about science, be better prepared for radical change in the future, and simply expand their minds through encountering scientifically rigorous yet highly imaginative concepts."[3] There are two narrative strands in the novel, the first involving the star-being Wan-To, the second following a human colonial expedition on an interstellar starship heading to a new home on a distant planet.

Wan-To is a being composed of star plasma who lives inside a star, capable of moving from star to star as needed. Compared to the comet creature in *Land's End*, Wan-To is more fully realized and therefore leads to a far more compelling story. Usually, vast cosmic entities such as the Eternal in *Land's End* devolve into boredom, but Pohl here makes Wan-To interesting and believable, brought to life by Pohl's discourses on how stars are made and how their energies work. Wan-To is not the only star-being, though he is the oldest; other such star-beings exist, all creations of Wan-To. As the novel progresses, a rogue star-being begins killing off others and taking over their stars. Wan-To is compelled to hide from the rogue. His hiding place is the star where the human starship is heading.

The human storyline focuses on Viktor Sorricaine, first introduced as a boy on the interstellar starship *Mayflower*, the second to be sent out, six years behind the first, the *New Ark*. A third ship, the *New Argosy*, was being built when *Mayflower* launched: "The three interstellar ships, combined, had a single assignment: to populate a world, and thus to establish a bridgehead for the human race in its long-term destiny of seeding the entire galaxy with people" (23). The narrative takes Viktor through several awakenings over thousands of years as he witnesses various stages of human colonization at their destined star system. Throughout the novel Pohl alternates chapters from Wan-To to Viktor. Aboard ship, most passengers are in cold storage. As the narrative begins, Viktor has been a "corpsicle" for one hundred years but is awakened because his astrogator father must try to adjust the flight plan after a flare star threatens to push the ship off course—all family members are awakened together under such circumstances. After some adventures aboard ship (including a case of puppy love over an adult woman, Maria-Claude Stockbridge, another astrogator), Viktor is put back into the freezer, next awakened as the ship prepares for planetary orbit years later; nevertheless, "he was still twelve" (41). The process of thawing everyone out takes eight months, and finally they are sent to the surface of the planet, christened Newmanhome, where the colonists of the *Ark* await them.

As Viktor grows up, Reesa McGann becomes his life-companion (of sorts); everyone is expected to procreate to the fullest on the new planet, thus the new environmental conditions lead to new social conditions, and conventional love relationships are transformed to adapt to the situation. Viktor also unfulfillingly consummates his desire for Maria-Claude Stockbridge. In this early part of the novel, Pohl successfully creates a believable space-frontier scenario, in terms of how the colonists adapt to the new environment, the struggles they face with the planet itself, and how they deal with personal and political differences. Catastrophe strikes when the planet begins moving. Unbeknownst to the colony, Wan-To is moving the sun: "The data is clear. Relative to the rest of the galaxy, our little local group is moving—and accelerating. It looks like some other groups are beginning to move in a different direction, too, but we're not sure of that. As to why all this is happening—God knows" (120). To make matters worse, the colony experiences a plague that decimates the population; only thirty-three hundred people survive. Religion spreads among the survivors, and factions develop, reaching a frenzy on the day the *New Argosy* was supposed to arrive, an arrival made impossible after the star's movement: "'What is the matter with everybody?' Viktor exploded. 'The whole town's going queer! I heard people fighting with each other over, for God's sake, whether there was one God or three!'" (132). Further faced with the fact that the star is radiating less heat as it moves through space, an anti-science feeling grows among the colonists.

After a desperate journey to Nebo, another planet in the system, which they believe may be the source of the anomalous movement, Viktor is frozen again following an attack from the planet's surface (from another star-being believing the humans to be part of the rogue's attack). When he next wakes, four hundred years have passed, recalling the scenario in *The Age of the Pussyfoot*. A new government has formed, and conditions are significantly worse than when the colonists first arrived. Only twenty-two hundred people are scraping by with barely enough resources to survive because of the dimming of the sun—here reminiscent of *Wolfbane*. There has been no contact with Earth for hundreds of years. Apocalyptic religion threatens what little survivability remains to the colony, as desperate people cling to regressive creeds: "The Great Transporters hated to see even unbelievers profane their Sabbath. The Moslems lost their tempers when they saw anyone drinking alcohol; the Peeps were constantly irate about the wasteful, sinful 'luxuries' of the other three groups, while the Reformers simply hated everyone else" (206). Here Pohl shifts his lens from Cold War politics to the resurgence of religious fanaticism. Viktor is reunited with Reesa in this icy hell, as she too has been reawakened. Reesa remarks, "We're living with people on the edge of starvation, Viktor. That's what you have to remember. All the time" (232). With no place in this world—one of starving, warring zealotry—for an outsider from another era, Viktor is sent to the freezers again for heresy.

In the next cycle, when Viktor is thawed in the year 4251, the colonists have recovered and are now exploring space again, and they have renewed a rational, scientific worldview. Viktor finds himself on a space habitat orbiting another planetary body: "The human population on Newmanhome had not only recovered from its ice age (though not on Newmanhome), it had flourished madly. There were three hundred million people alive now, and they lived very well. Most of them were in what an earlier human would have called O'Neill habitats, and those were various but uniformly fine" (272). The evolved humans living on the habitats are vastly intelligent, "skinny, seven-foot tall . . . with huge eyes" (286), recalling Dora of "Day Million," and are particularly interested in Viktor because he was born on "Old Earth." Viktor becomes somewhat of a concubine for a Dora-like female scientist, and for a while he relishes it: "Viktor might easily have thought this third act of his life close to the best" (286). The sequence involving the O'Neill habitats is the longest in the novel, and as it works toward its conclusion, contact is made between humans and Wan-To. Wan-To revitalizes the planet, allowing the restored people of the freezers a viable place to live, as there really is no place for them among the evolved human beings of the habitats. Viktor's love, Reesa, is revived once again, and they are left with the promise that on Newmanhome's surface they can live full lives and die when the time comes. Pohl handles the extended love story commendably so that the reader cares about whether the relationship between Viktor and Reesa grows, develops, and survives over time.

In *The World at the End of Time* Pohl successfully brings together many of the prevalent themes within science fiction. Moving away from the satiric and politically charged near-future science fiction that characterizes most of his work, Pohl manages to tell a very human story amid the grand-scale setting of the universe. While having some affinity with Olaf Stapledon's *Star Maker*, in *The World at the End of Time* Pohl manages to retain the warmth of human emotion and love in the face of the cold calculus of the universe.

Pohl's last collaboration with Jack Williamson, *The Singers of Time*—their tenth—appeared in 1991. Whereas *Land's End* seemed to be a book more Williamson than Pohl, *The Singers of Time*, both stylistically and in terms of ideas is more recognizably Pohl than Williamson, although the strengths of both writers are present, creating a much more satisfying book than its predecessor. The novel is dedicated to Stephen Hawking.

In *The Singers of Time*, Earth has suffered from environmental degradation and has been colonized by a superior intelligent alien race of beings that look somewhat like giant turtles, except they are bipedal. The Turtles retain a servant race, the Taurs, who look like bipedal cattle—and they are indeed used for meat animals when their days of service are at an end. Because humans had brought the Earth to the brink of environmental apocalypse, the aliens are perceived not as invaders but as benefactors, having provided technology that cleaned up the environment and also gave the gift of the stars in return for human fealty to their empire. The Turtles do not believe in conquest but in mercantile trade instead—and of course, like most colonial powers, they set the rules. The Turtles are more or less benevolent, but their social structure and way of thinking is rigidly hierarchical and unimaginative. For instance, they suppress humanity's heretical ideas about space, such as "multiple dimensions in space-time" and "quantum reality" (14). They ultimately make humans feel inferior, a similar theme as that in *Narabedla, Ltd.*

There are a number of compelling aspects to the novel. The Turtles' central spaceport is at a place that "was called 'Kansas City'" (7), suggestive of the visits Pohl and Williamson regularly made to Lawrence, Kansas, for James Gunn's summer programs. The Turtles insert data disks into their minds, which help them with their technological work; this idea is consistent with developments in computer technology in the 1980s but also integrates a cyberpunk theme into a traditional galactic adventure. As a result of climate change, the Turtles have instituted large-scale engineering projects: "They wanted to make it possible to farm here again—to do us good, you see. So they built the undersea baffle that diverted a warm tropical current past the Aleutians and through the Bering Strait" (55). Pohl and Williamson also nicely show cultural shock and cultural difference through the alien point of view, as one Turtle administrator blushes, "The thought of an intelligent race with more than one active female was vaguely repellent" (13), further making believable differences between the aliens and humans based on biological difference.

The thrust of the story involves two humans; one is a man named Krake, who is one of the few humans taken to the Turtle homeworld, having been abducted while piloting a fighter plane during World War II, when the Turtles first scouted Earth: "The Turtles must have been cruising around the area," Krake recounted, "checking us out from a distance. Then, when everybody's attention was on the war, they came in for some sampling missions. That was when they picked me up. 1945. I was twenty-two years old. I'd been flying combat for nearly a year, and the war was almost over" (57). Krake has been adopted into Turtle civilization; in fact, he captains his own interstellar wavedrive ship. Following an accident, while his crew receives medical attention on an orbital station, Krake goes planetside to visit his hometown, Portales, New Mexico (Williamson's residence). But a few centuries having passed, and Portales no longer exists, the floods having wiped it out more than one hundred years ago. It is now a coastal region, which indicates a major climatological and geological shift, as Portales is well inland. The second lead human protagonist is a young girl named Moon Bunderan, whose pet Taur is up for harvesting (humans now regularly eat Taurs). She runs away with him to avoid the edict, enlisting the aid of Krake.

The Turtles have a curious biology. All are brothers born of a single mother. Tragedy threatens to destroy the fabric of Turtle civilization when the Turtle Mother is missing. The rest of the novel turns into a galactic adventure as Krake takes Moon and her Taur to the Turtle Planet, where they get involved in the search for the missing Mother—in fact, they are the only hope in the effort, as the rigid Turtles have given up, and it is the blasphemous cosmological speculations of humanity that can solve the mystery. As the novel concludes, Krake and company find the Mother through a wormhole and return her to the Turtle empire, where a new understanding is forged between Turtle, Taur, and human, leading to humanity being given a better seat within the Turtle empire. Although *The Singers of Time* is an engaging science fiction adventure, it is strongest in the beginning, where Pohl and Williamson set up the circumstances on Earth, develop the Turtle culture, and illustrate the complex relationship between Turtles, Taurs, and humans. Throughout, discussions of ideas stemming from quantum physics, cosmology, and astrophysics put concepts like Dyson Spheres and the Fermi Paradox into dramatic action. But in the larger frame of Pohl's work, some of the ideas become repetitive. For instance, as in the Heechee saga (and *Wolfbane*, for that matter), Pohl and Williamson introduce a race of ancient destroyers that have wiped out most everyone else. Further, the planet missing in a wormhole too closely echoes the black hole where the Heechee hid. Although, one could argue that *The Starchild Trilogy*, the Cuckoo novels, the Heechee saga, *The World at the End of Time*, and *The Singers of Time* come together as a group, in the same way that we might identify other novels as the "consumer cycle" or the "Cold War cycle," as Pohl intensely engages with new ideas in physics and cosmology. In any case, as a capstone of the Pohl-Williamson collaborations, *The Singers of Time* is probably the most satisfying, not only for its interplay with cosmological ideas and environmental subthemes but also for its rousing sense of wonder. Capping off their long association, Pohl paid tribute to his longtime friend in a delightful alternate history story, "The Mayor of Mare Tranq" for the 1996 *festschrift* anthology *The Williamson Effect*, which imagines a different life path for Williamson wherein, after a career as a jet pilot in the Air Force, Williamson fortuitously saves John F. Kennedy from assassination and then joins Neil Armstrong and Buzz Aldrin on the first moon-landing mission.

Later that year, Pohl joined another old friend, Isaac Asimov, in collaborating on the important environmental text, *Our Angry Earth*, Asimov's final book published in his lifetime. It was a book Asimov wanted to be sure got written, so he joined forces with Pohl in a last act of Futurian collaboration. Due to the circumstances of Asimov's final illness, Pohl wrote almost all of the book, with limited input from Asimov.

Our Angry Earth is a major work focusing attention on the ecological crisis, although, unfortunately, it did not reach as broad an audience as it probably should have. Despite Pohl's own disappointment with the text (as recorded in the interview at the end of this book), it was a timely analysis of the problems inherent in (and possible solutions to) the climate crisis by two of the foremost figures in science fiction. Written in the tone of practical assessment and advocacy that Pohl demonstrated in *Practical Politics* and that is familiar to readers of Asimov's popular nonfiction, the book reveals that Asimov and Pohl anticipate a lot of the environmental problems that we are now so glaringly facing. This is nothing new: both writers showed awareness of environmental damage in their work as early as the 1950s. Pohl, in fact, wrote an important essay, "Power Play," for the fledgling *Omni* in 1979, laying out the impending crisis of global climate change with the same sort of scrupulous rendering Gregory Benford praises him for in *Gateway*. Looking beyond his own mortality, Asimov states in his introduction: "This book is not an opinion piece. It is a scientific survey of the situation that threatens us all—and it says what we can do to mitigate the situation. It is not a hopeless cry of doom at all. It is a description of what we face and what we can do about it. And in that sense, it is a hopeful book, and should be read as such.

It is not too late—but it may become too late, if we wait too much longer" (viii). For a man whose own life was fast coming to an end, this concern for the fate of humanity is endearing.

Pohl corroborates Asimov's purposes in his introduction: "But if every one of us does all those things it still will not be enough" (ix). The book is framed by a discussion of the Persian Gulf War, being waged early in the year the book came out, and the environmental impact of the burning oil wells. The rest of the chapters in section 1, "The Background," survey various ideas in the earth sciences and discuss humanity's environmental impact. Keeping a tone of calm scientific objectivity throughout, the authors nevertheless also display a note of pleading urgency: "Please remember that all of the unpleasant environment destroying processes we've been talking about are unquestionably real" (20). Section 2, "The Problems," takes the reader step-by-step through global warming, air pollution, ozone depletion, water pollution and shortage, garbage, and space junk. The chapter on global warming now seems prescient. Pohl and Asimov were in tune with the latest science and could extrapolate what was coming, and many of their observations and guesses have now become part of everyday cultural discourse. Section 3, "The Technocures," offer up a variety of engineering projects and suggestions for alternative lifeways that could conceivably mitigate the human impact on the planet. In the final section, "The Way to Go," Asimov and Pohl call on their readers to take action, not only in their personal life practices but also in advocacy through education and political action.

The paperback edition concludes with an afterword by Pohl, titled "One Year Later," wherein he shares his thoughts on Asimov's death: "For more than half a century Isaac was my very good friend. We became friends when we were both barely seventeen years old, two teenage science-fiction fans and would-be writers who shared a burning, but as yet unfulfilled, desire to get published" (400). When Our Angry Earth was conceived, Asimov and Pohl met for dinner in New York at "Isaac's favorite restaurant, Peacock Alley in the Waldorf-Astoria Hotel." During the get-together, Pohl first became aware that Asimov was becoming ill: "The only thing to mar it came at the very end when, as Isaac was getting up to leave, he announced that he was beginning to feel a little unwell" (401). Asimov died on April 6, 1992, from complications from AIDS, which he had acquired during a blood transfusion during heart surgery in the early 1980s.[4] Pohl's poignant novella *Outnumbering the Dead* would appear in the magazine bearing Asimov's name later in the year in an issue dedicated to his memory.

Outnumbering the Dead has an interesting publishing history. First appearing as a limited-edition chapbook in Britain, the original edition has a 1990 publication date, although the book did not appear until early 1991; it appeared in the United States from St. Martin's in 1992 and in an Isaac Asimov tribute issue of *Asimov's Science Fiction* in November of that year. *Outnumbering the Dead*, a novella about aging and death in a future where immortality is the normal condition of life, is a particularly moving story, especially given that its U.S. publication was in conjunction with Asimov's death. All the more poignant is that the main character, Rafiel, is ninety-two years old—Pohl was nearly ninety-four when he died—almost as if Pohl foresaw his own nonagenarian future. Here is another piece wherein Pohl explores longevity, medicine, and the consequences of age in a future of medical advancement and advanced technology.

In *Outnumbering the Dead*, ten trillion human beings reside on Earth and other worlds. People live in vast arcologies; Rafiel lives and works in one in central Indiana that rises 235 stories and has a population of 165,000 people: "In a world where the living far outnumbered the dead, space was precious" (31). For dramatic actor Rafiel, whose triumphant performance in *Oedipus* is a motif throughout the story, aging has "been slowed down, but not stopped"—that makes him an oddity in this benevolent future, and because of "those amusing little occasional stumbles and slips," the world adores him (14). But Rafiel is dying in a world where death lies outside human experience. As Rafiel's lover Alegretta readies herself for the journey of the first interstellar starship, the *Hakluyt*, she asks Rafiel to father her child: "You don't have to die *completely*. There's a kind of immortality that even short-timers have open to them if they want it" (84). Like Marchand in "Father of the Stars," Rafiel's wish is to join Alegretta on the voyage, even though he will die in its early stages. As the story concludes, Pohl quietly builds the emotional impact of Rafiel's final moments, leaving the reader bereft and contemplating mortality and the catharsis of a life well lived: "She kissed the unresponding lips and retired to the room they had shared, to weep, and to think of what, some day, she would tell their son about his father: that he had been famous, and loved, and brave

". . . and most of all that, certainly, yes, Rafiel had after all been happy in his life, and known that to be true" (110).

At its heart, *Outnumbering the Dead* is a love story. The drama theme is clearly the influence of Betty Hull, whose academic specialty was dramatic literature. It seems apparent that Pohl was reflecting on the fact that he was some years older than his wife and would, most likely, precede her in death. Just as *The Years of the City* was Pohl's love song to New York City, the city of Pohl's youth and adulthood, *Outnumbering the Dead*, then, is his paean to old age and a loving meditation on what the future would hold for his wife as his own mortality approached. These meditations are handled with the sensitivity and grace of a septuagenarian who knows he'll never see that future he's longed for since those teenage years with his fallen Futurian comrade, but he still retains optimism that humanity will find its way.

A similar specialty-press chapbook appeared earlier in 1991 and was later published by Bantam. *Stopping at Slowyear* is much more bitter than the poignant *Outnumbering the Dead*. A curious short novel, which recalls *Search the Sky*, the premise is that colonial planets are seldom visited because they are so vastly distant. On this occasion the merchant ship *Nordvik* stops at Slowyear, the crew hoping to end their days of wandering the starways and settle on the planet. The ship first launched from Earth orbit, but Earth is a distant memory. The crew consists of fifty-six men, women, and children; adult males are a distinct minority. The central character is Mercy MacDonald, who has been aboard ship for twenty-seven years. Mercy is now age forty-five, but, of course, as a result of time dilation, a much longer time has passed planetside. She is the only remaining member of the original crew, aside from the captain. As the *Nordvik* makes its long, slow voyages from planet to planet, "the worse the places it visited seemed to be" (5), partly due to the fact that "the rage for colonization had worn itself out centuries (Earth-time centuries, at least) before" (6), leading to the kind of colonial isolation seen in *Search the Sky* (though without the Swiftian cultures). Slowyear has not had a ship call for a long time: "There was hardly a soul alive on Slowyear who remembered the last time a ship had called, apart from the tiny and dwindling handful of five- and six-year-old dodderers" (23). This last bit "five- and six-year-old dodderers" informs the reader that Slowyear has a long orbit around its sun, hence its name. Despite having made planetfall at least twelve generations ago, the population on Slowyear is only around half a million. The *Nordvik* crew slowly discovers cultural oddities among the Slowyear people. For instance, when people break the law, even for minor violations, they must select a pill from a jar containing some pills that are fatally poisoned and others that are benign—kind of like the lottery in "Spending the Day at the Lottery Fair"—the severity of the crime determines the percentage of poison pills. The narrative builds to a startling conclusion as the *Nordvik*'s crew swiftly succumb to the intense radiation that makes strangers to the planet age rapidly, thus explaining the meager population—only mutations survived. Mercy's hoped-for paradise turns out to be her coffin. The pessimism runs thick in this novella, making it a remarkably stark contrast to the moving optimism displayed in *Outnumbering the Dead*, and even in the broader trajectory of *The World at the End of Time*. Indeed, *Stopping at Slowyear* seems to come out of the same territory as *The World at the End of Time*, and one wonders if, perhaps, its genesis was from ideas Pohl had while at work on that novel that he wished to develop in another direction. It also looks forward to Pohl's 1994 novel *The Voices of Heaven*, but in between he published a novel set closer to home, *Mining the Oort*, a coming-of-age story that realistically imagines the colonization of Mars.

Mining the Oort is a strong work of near-future interplanetary SF that presents a possible human presence on Mars and in the solar system. There was a flurry of prominent science fiction novels published in 1992 that dramatize the possibilities of exploring and colonizing Mars: Bova's *Mars*, Williamson's *Beachhead*, and Kim Stanley Robinson's *Red Mars* immediately come to mind, and *Mining the Oort* is among them. *Mining the Oort* has the qualities of juvenile (nowadays YA) science fiction, where a young protagonist goes through an education program leading to discovery and success within the space environment. In the tradition of the Heinlein juvenile, *Mining the Oort* certainly has some parallels with *Space Cadet* and *Podkayne of Mars*, the latter seeing publication in *If* during Pohl's editorial tenure. But given the illness and death of Asimov in the same year *Mining the Oort* was published, perhaps Asimov's *Lucky Starr* novels are a more fitting comparison, as all of Lucky Starr's adventures took place in the solar system. Pohl's teenage protagonist, Dekker DeWoe, is compellingly drawn, and like Viktor Sorricaine in the early sections of *The World at the End of Time*, the reader is drawn into the problems set into play on Mars through Pohl's inviting portrayal of a youth coming into adulthood.

The first step in Dekker's education occurs when he gets hold of a copy of *Huckleberry Finn* and learns the Law of the Raft, which has parallels with the Martian colony's "docility training": "That's what docility training is all about. Not just getting along, but wanting everybody to be satisfied, and to feel good about the other people. Not just on the raft, everywhere. On our planet, too. That's what we do here on Mars, while the Earthies are always grabbing whatever they can grab and competing with each other" (27). Because of the circumstances of living in space, people are taught to cooperate, and there is no place for aggression, as it would put everyone at risk. This establishes the frontier theme and the necessity for space colonists to work together and get along. Colonists take the "Pledge of Assistance," which means they will offer aid when someone is in trouble, even at the risk of their own well-being. This is a good instance of Pohl's showing how circumstances change behaviors—that so-called "human nature" is shaped by environmental factors, that people living in societies learn to overcome primal impulses.

The central problem is that Mars needs an atmosphere. To facilitate this, comets are transported from the Oort Cloud and strategically crashed onto the Martian surface to build up an atmosphere. The Martian colonists primarily live underground, since there is as yet no stability topside. They are heavily in debt to Earth corporations because of the massive costs of importing goods to Mars. The corporate executives who do business on Mars treat the locals as low-class drudges while maintaining their own profligate habits: "Earthies kept pretty much to themselves, in their own luxurious quarters" (7). This sets into motion Pohl's major argument in the novel: a critique of the 1990s venture-capitalist paradigm.

The narrative follows Dekker through a number of adolescent experiences, foremost being an infatuation with a rich Earthie girl, Annetta Caudy, who invites him to a party, where he gets drunk, embarrassed, and is insulted by a rival Earthie teen. His feelings of inadequacy lead him to sign on with the Oort Corporation for Oort mining training on Earth, following in the footsteps of his estranged father, a pattern not unlike Jim Eden's in the *Undersea* books. When Dekker goes to school on Earth, the narrative develops along the lines of the school story, in science fiction recalling, again, Heinlein's *Space Cadet* and Charles Sheffield and Jerry Pournelle's *Higher Education*, but also having affinities with the *Undersea* novels. Meanwhile, the business practices of venture capitalism have led to another economic bust that threatens the stability of the Mars colony: "Haven't you been watching the news? The Earthies are screwing up again—strikes, and bank failings, and—now, we're going to have to find some more cuts to make, in fact" (47). One of Pohl's major themes is an anatomy of contemporary selfishness and greed in American economic life. By positing a space culture where selfishness won't work, Pohl challenges the growing hegemony of the American capitalist ideal that was beginning to be taken as sacrosanct following the end of the Cold War. Pohl reminds us that American economic supremacy within a global capitalist system is mutable: "Didn't it ever occur to you what was going to happen when the Russians and the Chinese, with all their people and all their resources, began to copy your economy?" (147). At the academy Dekker is reunited with Annetta Caudy, whose father lost his fortune due to the vagaries of a market economy built on speculation rather than on tangible productivity. There, he reiterates the social pact necessary in the space environment to his Earthie classmates, which illustrates the differences between self-interested venture capitalism and community: "Out in the Oort it's like Mars, only tougher. You can't throw your weight around. You can't afford to be jealous of somebody else, or try to get an advantage over him. You have to try to understand how the other person feels" (66). Most of the rest of the novel follows Dekker through his education, on Earth and in space, tracing both his technical training and his sexual awakening. While Dekker and his classmates train in the space environment, Mars becomes a pawn in the chess game of speculative investment. With the United States economy in shambles, several of Dekker's classmates plot to reestablish American economic dominance, and Dekker must put his docility training to the test to thwart their terroristic plan to threaten Earth (specifically Japan) with one of the Oort comets, recalling Heinlein's *The Moon is a Harsh Mistress*. In the end, Dekker saves Earth from a cometary strike by emptying the station of air, killing all the conspirators but Annetta. *Mining the Oort* extends Pohl's analysis of economics, the space environment, and politics, but without the Cold War frame that was so central to his previous work. As such, it is a natural progression, given the economic and political circumstances of when it was written. In it, Pohl's imaginative radar remained finely tuned to the political complexities of the post–Cold War world.

*　*　*

Between 1975 from 1992 Pohl published at least one book every year. No book appeared in 1993, and though Pohl continued to publish a number of novels throughout the 1990s, this gap suggests a slowing down of—or at least a change in—the science fiction marketplace. But 1993 was not altogether a year of inactivity, as Pohl was named science fiction's twelfth Grand Master by the Science Fiction Writers of America. Sorrowfully, his longtime friend, former neighbor, and onetime collaborator Lester Del Rey, the previous Grand Master inductee, died that year too.

Having a similar adventure backdrop as *Mining the Oort*, Pohl's next novel, *The Voices of Heaven*, returns to the heavy satire of books like *Black Star Rising* and *Jem*. This time Pohl sets his satiric sights on religious zealotry in a much broader register than in *The World at the End of Time*. Told in the first person, as are many of Pohl's best books, the psychologically damaged narrator Barry di Hoa is patterned on Robin Broadhead—in di Hoa's case, suffering from a form of schizophrenia and relating his story to an insect-like alien species called the leps. In contrast to the Hakh'hli of *Homegoing*, the leps have no evolutionary diversity; they are all the same, even more so than the Turtles of *The Singers of Time*. Di Hoa is a ship's fuelmaster stationed on the Moon, in charge of defueling and refueling interstellar starships. The narrative begins when di Hoa services the starship *Corsair* from the Pava colony, captained by Garold Tscharka. Only four interstellar colonies exist, and their impracticality is painfully evident: "You can't make much of a dent in ten billion huddled masses when you have to cart them away fifty or a hundred at a time. It didn't matter what they said; I thought the project made no sense at all. There was only one real reason for planting human beings in places so far away—and that was just to be doing something humongous. Showing off, that is" (6). Here Pohl deflates the dream of space.

Religion is the target of Pohl's satire throughout the novel. The political landscape on Earth is apparently functioning with its usual gridlock: "Delta Pavonis wasn't the only star with a planet that somebody once had thought was worth colonizing, and with the budget-cutters riding high in the Congress, all four of the extrasolar colonies were on shaky ground. Pava, as the farthest away, had just been the last to hear about it" (5). Religious fundamentalism has deeply infiltrated government and appears to have risen to levels of irrationality, self-interest, and factionalism comparable to what it is now (remember—Pohl was writing in 1994, when neo-conservatism was new and had not yet succumbed to the present levels of discord):

> You haven't asked me just how it happened that the religions ran the governments, but I'll tell you anyway. It wasn't always that way. They say that in the old days people used to vote for 'political parties.' But all the parties got to be pretty much alike. Whatever people said their 'political' principles were, it turned out that they were generally voting their religions and their social and ethnic backgrounds anyway—sometimes with a lot of violence. It was simpler to cut out the middleman. (20)

Curiously, such dissolution of Jeffersonian rational democracy leads to *less* factionally driven violence: "I wouldn't say that solved all the problems, but at least we don't have much 'car bombing' or 'kneecapping' or 'ethnic cleansing' going on anymore" (20). Here Pohl shifts from government being run by corporations (as in *The Space Merchants*) or by Wall Street stock traders (as in *Gladiator-At-Law*) to a return to theocracy.

Before he knows it, di Hoa is shanghaied by Tscharka, put in the cryogenic deep freeze, and finds himself on Pava: "When I saw him staring in bafflement down at me, and realized that what I was waking up in was a freezer-thawer capsule and a long time had passed, I got the picture fast" (71). Captain Tscharka is a Millenarist whose central "saint" is Saint Jones, the Kool-Aid drinking Jim Jones of the Guyana cult:

> The Millenarists believed that the Bible promised the world would come to an end a thousand years after the birth of Christ and then at that Millennium the earth would open and all the dead would rise—the living too, I guess—and they'd all be singing and praising God as they headed straight for heaven's eternal joy. It was as good a central dogma as any, if you didn't mind that actually it hadn't happened. The year 1000 A.D. had come and gone, and—oops, back to the drawing board—the Second Coming didn't come. The Millenarists had figured that one out, though. . . . The main tenet of their belief was that, although everything is sinful, some things were less sinful than others. In their view, about the least sinful thing any Millenarist could do in this sinful world was to die and get out of it before it got any worse. That was why you hardly

ever saw an old Millenarist . . . and the converts didn't usually stick around for more than ten or twenty years, tops. (12)

From di Hoa's point of view, Pava is overrun by churches and factions, but for the zealot Tscharka the colony has grown more secular since he left, and upon his return he's disappointed. The conditions on Pava have parallels with *The World at the End of Time* and *Stopping at Slowyear* in that scarcity is a fixture of the Pava colony, whereas, by contrast, this is no longer an issue on Earth, where expansion into solar space has solved the scarcity problem. Pava's scarcity has led to rampant apocalyptic creeds beyond those taken for granted on Earth.

As the narrative progresses, di Hoa learns that Captain Tscharka is a madman who plans to "rescue the planet earth from its sin" (298), intending to bombard it with atomic weapons on his next visit. Pohl opens up a very real possibility: in the wake of Cold War disarmament and instability, what happens when religious lunatics get hold of weapons of mass destruction? As is typical in Pohl narratives, di Hoa spoils the plan and detains Tscharka before he can depart to Earth with the bombs. Another recurring pattern in Pohl's fiction sees di Hoa reunited with his girlfriend, Alma, at the novel's end, repeating the pattern that goes all the way back to Mitch Courtenay's reunion with Kathy at the conclusion of *The Space Merchants*.

Pohl's critique of religious fundamentalism and factionalism in *The Voices of Heaven* is another departure into political trends rising out of the global realignments at the end of the Cold War. As such, the novel continues Pohl's intense engagement with twentieth-century global politics. Given the shape of global politics and the increasing challenge of fundamentalism in America and across the globe, like much of Pohl's fiction, *The Voices of Heaven* has a continued provocative relevancy.

Pohl's satiric wit continues in the novel *O Pioneer!* (notwithstanding the Willa Cather allusion), which gives the impression of an homage to Keith Laumer's *Retief* stories, the adventures of an interstellar diplomat, which Pohl published in the 1960s in *If*. Serialized in *Analog* in late 1997, *O Pioneer!* saw book publication in May 1998. The novel is dedicated to Betty Anne, "for among other reasons keeping me alive." According to Hull, while Pohl was working on the novel during the spring he fell ill with a serious urinary tract infection. When she fortuitously came home after delaying a dental procedure and found him shivering in bed, she called an ambulance; in the hospital Pohl was diagnosed with toxic shock.[5]

Pohl's satiric target in *O Pioneer!* is the art and practice of politics and the "business" of war. Evesham Giyt is a computer hacker, though not in the manner of a Gibsonian mirrorshaded console cowboy; rather, a more apt comparison is the aforementioned Retief, with a little of the wisecracking everymanism of Robinette Broadhead mixed in. As this is a novel that plays with the frontier theme and evokes Willa Cather's quintessential vision of the Great Plains, appropriately, Giyt lives in Wichita, Kansas—this setting again suggests Pohl's connections with Gunn's summer programs in nearby Lawrence. A computer genius, Giyt makes his living by hacking accounts and embezzling just enough funds to keep himself afloat without getting caught. As in *Jem*, no one fights wars anymore, though for different reasons. Instead, the battleground is commerce, reflecting the economic and political climate of the late 1990s.

Fourteen years earlier a habitable planet called Tupelo was discovered, and with Earth relatively at peace, human colonization gets underway. Giyt is intrigued by the prospect of starting out on a grand frontier adventure, and so he books transport to Tupelo. When Giyt arrives, he is quickly appointed mayor, thereby becoming the chief negotiator between humans and "five rather odd-looking races from other star systems" (22), all vying for the virgin territory on Tupelo. There is fierce competition to exploit it, and this allows Pohl to satirize the rapacious greed of competing colonial powers. The comic ironies register, albeit more whimsically, with the diagnosis of colonial enterprise put on trial in the early sections of Conrad's *Heart of Darkness*. Pohl draws the aliens as broadly comical—again, much in the style of the oddball aliens Laumer's Retief encounters in his diplomatic missions, although these comic aliens don't reach the menace found in the Krinpit of *Jem* or the erks of *Black Star Rising*. In this, *O Pioneer!* reveals the impish Pohl, making the novel more playful and less sardonically perilous than its predecessors.

At first Giyt finds mayoring easy enough, but then he realizes it's a sucker's job, because the mayor has to deal with all the crap. Aside from having to tiptoe through the maze of interspecies custom and listen to the demands and complaints of human colonists, the most pressing problem that Giyt must adjudicate is the fact that Tupelo is facing an energy crisis, and each race must reduce their consumption and demand. Notice how Pohl's novels of the 1990s often project current Earth problems onto extraterrestrial environments. Pohl uses these environments to raise important issues currently facing humans on Earth.

The narrative follows Giyt in his dealings with the comical aliens, especially regarding the challenges of communication, laughingly illustrated by an exchange in which a Delt tries to convey his familiarity with a work by the "earth-human liar Kepigay" (Ernest Hemingway): "Yes. Excellent liar, Kepigay. Greatly enjoy Earth-human lies; Earth humans such excelling liars. You know Kepigay old Earth romance lie, *Man Approaching Death in Relationship to Ocean?*" (88). While Giyt makes diplomatic progress in human relations with aliens, he begins thinking it rather peculiar that the only humans on Tupelo are from the United States. Then he discovers they have been importing weapons in mass quantities, even though hostilities are not likely to erupt among the alien species. The target criticism here is how the U.S. exports weapons throughout the world to foment conflict and in turn stimulate its own economy. The plan is that Tupelo can turn into a reasonably safe war zone, where Americans can wage war on the other species, stimulating the economy without the risk of damaging the home planet:

> There was no reason for any Earth human to possess Kalkaboo firecrackers, even little ones, to say nothing of these monsters. But the other things in the locked storerooms simply had no business existing on Tupelo at all. They were Earthside weapons, and there were hundreds of them. Handguns. Minicarbines. Assault rifles. Grenades. Mortars. Even shoulder-launched missiles, the kind that rocketed an enemy's position and then exploded with a shower of high velocity shrapnel. And when he looked more closely at the missiles he saw the answer to two puzzles. The missiles bore sniffer vents. They would follow the airborne odor of a target and explode over the target's head, and that explained why there had been that almost forgotten data file on the scents of the eetie races on Tupelo (227).

In typical Pohl fashion, Giyt stops the conspirators and negotiates an agreeable peace with the aliens. The novel serves as a commentary on American expansionism, particularly in terms of unregulated weapons manufacture. Written during the Clinton administration, it startlingly anticipates some of the policies of the twenty-first century: "Ex-Earth was a front for an American expansionist conspiracy that reached up into high levels of the administration. They were planning to take Tupelo over. The autofactory at the Pole had been secretly manufacturing weapons" (250). Pohl effectively questions the increased corporatization of military action, where war becomes good business, registering a different vibe than the Cold War cynicism of *Jem*'s Marge Menninger, but operating under the same diabolical principles.

The first volume of the *Eschaton Sequence*, *The Other End of Time*, appeared the year before *O Pioneer!*, to be followed by *The Siege of Eternity* in 1997 and *The Far Shore of Time* in 1999. Like most trilogies, the books are probably best read back-to-back, as the reader then can get the full scope of the adventure. And these books are pure adventure, in the manner of the gosh-wow! high-concept interstellar science fiction adventure seen in the Cuckoo saga and the later books of the Heechee. In fact, the *Eschaton Sequence* recycles the idea of multiple selves created through tachyon transmission Pohl first introduced in *Farthest Star* but works with it in different ways. In this case, the multiple selves are closer to home and must deal with their multiplicity on Earth. Throughout, the use of multiple versions of the central characters, NBI (National Bureau of Investigation) agent Dan Dannerman and his cousin, Dr. Patrice Adcock, a SETI astronomer, raises interesting questions about the self and also how humans diverge down different lines when new circumstances arise, in this sense paralleling some of the concepts in *The Coming of the Quantum Cats*.

The Other End of Time begins with the discovery of the first message from an alien intelligence: "It was definitely the very first time that the patient astronomers who tended the SETI telescopes, or for that matter anybody else, had received an authentic, guaranteed alien message from an extraterrestrial source" (8). The signal was received on Starlab, a once-manned orbital astronomical observatory, funded by the Dannerman clan; Dannerman and Adcock, with three others, are sent to find out what has happened. Again, Pohl comments on the decline of the space program: "As he was growing to become a man, the space program was dwindling almost at the same rate of speed—few human heroes but a lot of machines; then, as the money began to run short, fewer machines, too" (94). Pohl effectively captures the sense of wonder as the crew investigates the derelict observatory. Although this isn't an unknown object, it still has the feel of the classic Big Dumb Object exploration.

The expedition is captured by aliens, who look like "Hallowe'en trick-or-treat" characters (125), and the humans are transported to an alien vessel via tachyon transmission. The point of view shifts, though only slightly, because this Dannerman and this Adcock are in fact divergent duplications; their original selves still remain on Starlab: "We are all copies, are we not? How else could we have been transmitted here from your Starlab?" (168). The aliens are searching throughout the galaxy for intelligent races under the direction of a race called the Beloved Leaders who believe that the "eschaton," the rebirth of all intelligent beings, will happen as the universe contracts to the Omega Point: "What our friends from space have discovered in their scientific investigations—which are far more advanced than our own—is that at a time in the far future, a very long time from now, something very strange will happen. At that time every intelligent being who ever existed in the universe will come to life again, and then will live forever. In scientific terms this is called the 'eschaton'" (225). As the first volume draws to an end, it becomes apparent to Dannerman and Adcock that the Beloved Leaders eliminate those species who do not cooperate with them, setting up a problem to face in the sequel. Here Pohl recapitulates the galactic menace seen in the Heechee saga and *The Singers of Time*. He also extends his critique, although this time allegorically, of resurgent religious millenarianism.

Resonating with *The Voices of Heaven*, Pohl delves into the territory of religious eschatology using the concept of the Omega Point introduced in the writings of the Catholic scientific mystic Pierre Teilhard de Chardin, a variation of which was argued by Tulane physicist Frank Tipler in the 1994 book *The Physics of Immortality*, the apparent source for Pohl's speculations. The 1990s also saw a rise of Christian millennialism, and it is hard to imagine Pohl wasn't aware of the sensation beginning to stir with the publication of Tim LaHaye and Jerry Jenkins's *Left Behind* series, which began in 1995. A reader would not be wrong in making connections with Philip Jose Farmer's *Riverworld* series either; it is worth noting that Pohl published some of the original *Riverworld* stories when editor of *If*. Pohl includes an author's note at the end of *The Other End of Time*, where he explains how he uses speculative theory and science from which to build his stories. In this case, he received (from robotician Hans

Moravec) Tipler's original paper from which *The Physics of Immortality* derived. When posing the question "Are we indeed all going to be reborn at some remote time eons in the future?" Pohl admits, "I would be inclined to bet quite heavily against it." Nonetheless, he concedes it makes for a good science fiction story: "It is certainly pretty to think so" (348). This shows Pohl's method: take a rather far-out idea currently receiving some play in the sciences and use it for a vehicle to tell a rousing science fiction adventure. A savvy science fiction writer need not believe in the ideas for his imagination to be stimulated.

The Siege of Eternity involves the nonduplicated Adcock and Dannerman, the ones who remained on Starlab. This narrative, then, parallels events happening to the duplicates during their alien captivity by showing the impact the preduplication first contact events have on Earth. Fairly early in the novel, a message is received from the duplicate Dannerman, now back on Starlab, which complicates matters. The novel further discourses on the Eschaton theory, the intentions of the Beloved Leaders, and questions of individuality and consciousness when faced with multiple selves. Like its predecessor, it's a fun romp, but offers little new in the way of ideas, as its main purpose is to advance the plot of the trilogy. The final volume, *The Far Shore of Time*, uses one of the Dan Dannermans as a first-person narrator. With multiple Dan Dannermans and multiple Pat Adcocks, the reader has to sort out who is who in this novel, as in the later chapters of *The Coming of the Quantum Cats*. Again, the novel is great fun, but seldom rises to the level of Pohl's more substantial achievements. In some ways, Pohl is here harkening back to the days of superscientific exploits in the E. E. "Doc" Smith tradition. In that sense, the *Eschaton* books are rousing science fiction adventure, made compelling more for Pohl's playing around with multiple selves who have multiple, though congruent, voices, than for the ideas and political focus we are used to seeing in Pohl's fiction. The fact that the *Eschaton Sequence* consists of three volumes published one after the other should not go unnoticed. Is this a bow to the commercial pressures of the science fiction marketplace in the late 1990s, which too often demanded books in packages of three, the trilogy model? It's hard to say, since Pohl was always savvy when it came to the marketplace, but he also followed his own beat. Nonetheless, the *Eschaton Sequence* might have been a more profound contribution to Pohl's oeuvre if it were a little more condensed.

What is clear is that the *Eschaton* novels demonstrate Pohl's practice of "chasing science." Pohl, as he turned eighty years old, summarized his love affair with science as a "spectator sport" in the 2000 book *Chasing Science*. Pohl began the chase early on in the days when he was attending Brooklyn Tech and borrowing books from the public library. Working for *Popular Science* after the war, his appetite for science grew further. During the 1960s, Pohl often wrote with enthusiasm about the latest science books he had been reading in his *Galaxy* editorials. From *The Age of the Pussyfoot* on, Pohl's fiction became increasingly informed by new ideas in the sciences, in part because his own fame was putting him into contact with science professionals and his income was allowing him to travel to places where science was being conducted. In *Chasing Science* Pohl enthusiastically encourages his reader to find out about what is going on in the sciences in the way that he has—by visiting laboratories, facilities, and museums, by talking to researchers, and by finding out about new discoveries through reading, memberships, and lectures. Pohl calls himself "a fan of science," because although he has had no formal training in the sciences, he enjoys learning about science and seeing it at work in the the way others might follow their college football team or their favorite rock band: "I can't really understand why there are any human beings alive in the world today who don't share my infatuation with the subject" (11). The rest of the book is a survey of places where science happens (national laboratories, observatories, NASA facilities, dams, caves, public lectures), what the latest discoveries are, and what the interested person can do to find out more about what is happening in the world of science. Pohl marvels at the wonders of the night sky, urging readers to take up backyard astronomy; at the vast history of the Earth and of human beings as revealed by fossils and archeology; at the aqueous world of the ocean and other waterways. *Chasing Science* is, in part, an answer to that question writers often must deflect from inquisitive readers: "Where do you get your ideas?"

⋆   ⋆   ⋆

It would be another four years before the next Pohl novel was published, and when *The Boy Who Would Live Forever* appeared in 2004, it marked his return to the Heechee saga. In the meantime, Pohl finished editing the three-volume *SFWA Grandmaster* anthologies, begun in 1999. *The Boy Who Would*

Live Forever is Pohl's longest book, running 452 pages in paperback. At the turn of the millennia, Pohl, now in his eighties, began adding additional stories to the Heechee saga, which would make up portions of the novel. The first two chapters appeared in Robert Silverberg's *Far Horizons* in 1999; what became chapter seven, "Hatching the Phoenix," was published in the newly slick *Amazing Stories* that fall; and chapter 5, "A Home for the Old Ones," appeared in the *30th Anniversary DAW Science Fiction* anthology in 2002. The novel revisits the origins of the Heechee saga, depicting the first encounter between humans and Heechee from another angle. Pohl introduces a new character named Stan, who is growing up in Istanbul, the setting, as is often the case in Pohl's work, inspired by a recent trip to Turkey.[6] Stan wants to go to Gateway, to be like Robinette Broadhead: "The famed old explorer Robinette Broadhead, for instance, was rich beyond avarice with his Gateway earnings, and he was always funding space missions. Like the one that even now was gradually climbing its years-long way to the Oort cloud, where some fabulous Heechee object was known to exist but no one had found a way to get to it other than on a slow, human rocket ship" (12). Like his hero Broadhead, Stan has a financial windfall, which provides him with enough money for a ticket to Gateway, and enough funds left over to remain there for eighteen days. In some ways the early chapters of *The Boy Who Would Live Forever* are simply a recapitulation of the original *Gateway* but done effectively, showing that others try to make their mark, much like Broadhead. In that sense, the novel has recursive qualities, serving as a commentary and supplement to the earlier novels.

On Gateway, Stan meets Estrella Pancorbo, a girl with a lopsided face, injured while laboring in the Wyoming food mines (where Broadhead worked before his lottery winnings took him to Gateway), and they become partners and lovers. Stan and Estrella's story is happening simultaneously with the events in *Beyond the Blue Event Horizon*. As Stan and Estrella prepare to set out on one of the remaining Gateway ships, all Gateway missions are cancelled, but Broadhead now knows how to build his own Heechee ships from the information gleaned from the prayer fans on the CHON-Food Factory. Against orders, Stan and Estrella take the last Heechee ship anyway, which happens to be the master ship headed for the Heechee black hole, which also contains data on all human development. Stuck in the event horizon of the black hole,

Stan and Estrella emerge to meet the Heechee at around the same moment Robin Broadhead encounters the Heechee at the end of *Heechee Rendezvous*.

Later in the novel, the notorious Wan starts causing problems again. Wan claims he "owns" the Old Ones, the australopithecines from the Food Factory who have been given a preserve in Kenya from Broadhead, returning them to their natural habitat; and Wan comes to Earth to try to claim them. He eventually absconds with two and takes off, forcing Broadhead to chase him around the galaxy, because Wan has also stolen a significant cache of advanced weaponry. These events recapitulate some of the events from *Annals of the Heechee*, continuing the recursivity of the novel.

Enter Sigfrid von Shrink. He's called forth from Broadhead's "shipmind" and joins Stan and Estrella in tracking down Wan's ship. Wan himself has now become machine-stored and is causing all kinds of mayhem in the virtual world, which threatens the stability of the galaxy. Like its predecessors, *The Boy Who Would Live Forever* meditates on the possibilities of machine-stored consciousness, made all the more interesting and relevant by the fact that Pohl himself was outliving most of his generation of SF writers and was likely becoming keenly aware of his own mortality.

Like the *Eschaton Sequence*, *The Boy Who Would Live Forever* is good fun. The extent to which it adds anything significant to the Heechee saga, let alone to the overall scope of Pohl's career, lies in the postmodern playfulness demonstrated by the retelling of the entire Heechee saga through other eyes. Stephen King was doing much the same thing at the time, as he finished up his *Dark Tower* saga. If anything, it is a reflection of an aged writer who enjoys telling stories and loves his chosen field, science fiction. In this sense, *The Boy Who Would Live Forever* seems to have a deep-seated air of nostalgia: nostalgia for the golden days of adventure science fiction, nostalgia for an immensely popular science fiction franchise, nostalgia for a youth gone by. Such nostalgia, of course, defined a segment of the SF marketplace since the boom of the 1980s made bestsellers out of Asimov, Clarke, and the World as Myth novels of Heinlein. One would expect, then, that a collaboration between two aging science fiction titans would be just another walk down memory lane. But when Pohl joined up with Arthur C. Clarke for *The Last Theorem*, the result was a book that at times successfully engages with the political and social realities of the new century, showing the wisdom and insight of two lifetimes spent thinking about the future.

Just as Pohl co-authored the final book of SF titan Isaac Asimov, he did the same with Arthur C. Clarke, in Clarke's final novel *The Last Theorem*, published just prior to Clarke's death in 2008. Suffering from a a debilitating nerve disorder, Clarke had not written a novel on his own for nearly twenty years, often employing subordinate co-writers to work from his concepts. In this case, Clarke's collaborator was another grandmaster with an equally strong alpha personality, and as could be expected, the writing process was challenging. It was made more difficult by the fact that Pohl was losing function in his right hand, a result of spinal atrophy pinching the nerves.[7] Collaboration was long distance, as Clarke and Pohl were both getting to be too old to travel. Matters were not helped by the fact that at one point in the writing the long-distance exchange of manuscript drafts ran into word-processor compatibility problems. The circumstances of composition were similar to that of *Our Angry Earth*: Pohl wrote most of the book, with Clarke mainly reading Pohl's copy and giving feedback. Despite all these complications, the novel is often appealing and engages with a number of important political and cultural situations, though, admittedly, it flags at the end, as if the complications of age and long-distance collaboration were showing themselves.

On one level, *The Last Theorem* is about the quest by Sri Lankan math student Ranjit Subramanian to solve Fermat's Last Theorem. But it is also a novel about contemporary globalism, sectarian politics, government conspiracy, and the life of the mind. As such, *The Last Theorem* is a rich engagement with the global political landscape in the twenty-first century, fitting in well with Pohl's prior politically engaged fiction, marred only by the introduction of a "Grand Galactics" subplot, which seems to fall back into almost a pastiche of familiar Pohl (and Clarke) ideas about alien civilizations.

As the novel opens, Ranjit Subramanian is a freshman at Sri Lanka's principal university, where he becomes close friends with another student named Gamini Bandara. While at university, Ranjit becomes fascinated with Fermat's Last Theorem, and, indeed, a good part of the novel describes Ranjit's enthusiasm for mathematics, paralleling Pohl's own. At one point Ranjit recapitulates Pohl's 1956 essay "How to Count on Your Fingers" and later, while teaching at the university, Ranjit tackles binary numbers, drawn from Pohl's 1962 essay "On Binary Digits and Human Habits." Both essays appeared in the collection *Digits and Dastards*. Ranjit's father suspects a homosexual dimension to Ranjit's relationship with Gamini and forbids him to continue the friendship or else face being disowned—but he is not concerned about the sexual play; rather the concern is because Ranjit is Tamil and Gamini is Sinhalese, the two warring factions on Sri Lanka. Here the novel is examining the kind of political and ethnic factionalism that has become symptomatic in the twenty-first century, while also recognizing the conflicting attitudes toward sexual orientation. With this, Pohl moves into new political territory, beyond the Cold War politics central to his earlier work. This transition was already evident in such 1990s works as *The Voices of Heaven* and *O Pioneer!*, but here Pohl returns to a real-world, near-future setting, like that in *The Space Merchants* or *The Cool War*, using the Earth as his stage rather than whisking characters to other planets. When Gamini is sent to London to finish his studies, Ranjit can avoid a family crisis. Ranjit spends the rest of the year becoming deeply engrossed in mathematics, at one point getting himself into trouble when the dean of students catches him using the computer password of a faculty member so that he can cycle numbers for Fermat's Last Theorem.

From there, the novel traces the ups and downs in Ranjit's life. In this sense, the novel has the qualities of a literary novel, focusing on the unfolding of Ranjit's character—one is reminded to some degree of Salman Rushdie's *Midnight's Children*—more than on the science fictional ideas. And, in fact, the widescreen galactic science fictional plot element, which often seems like an intrusion in the early part of the novel, disrupts an otherwise effective character-driven piece. The more effective science fictional plot element (if we can call it that) is Ranjit's quest to solve Fermat's Last Theorem. During summer vacation, Ranjit is kidnapped by Somali pirates seeking ransom money and taken aboard a hijacked cruise ship. The scenes on the ship, where Ranjit amuses children with mathematical parlor games, are well drawn from Pohl's long familiarity with the Holland America cruise line. With a destroyer closing in, the pirates beach the ship along the coast. On the beach, Ranjit is mistaken for one of the pirates, imprisoned, and sent for interrogation. His imprisonment lasts more than two years. To stay sane in his isolation, Ranjit runs numbers and proofs through his head, eventually solving Fermat's Last

Theorem. For several months, he lives in terror, not of his captivity but that he will forget the proof. Then Gamini Bandara, now working as an operative for the UN, arrives to rescue him. Fearing he will forget the proof, Ranjit demands a computer first: "Can't you understand what I'm saying? I think I've got the proof! I need a computer, and I need it right now! Do you have any idea how terrified I am that I'll forget some part of the proof before I can get it refereed?" (108). Ranjit achieves a degree of celebrity and marries Myra de Soyza, a young woman he met at university.

As his life goes on, Ranjit continues to cross paths with Gamini Bandara, who is now a major powerbroker in UN intelligence. The familiar Pohl theme of a world on the brink of political catastrophe resonates throughout the first half of the novel, until UN forces use an advanced weapons system that neutralizes all electronic devices—recalling the wave-pulse from "The Gold at the Starbow's End"—to knock out the North Korean dictatorship. This leads to "Pax Per Fidem," or "World Peace Through Transparency" (171). At first, Ranjit and Myra are suspicious of this set of policies, comparing it to Orwell's 1984, but it does make for a better world. And, indeed, this end to human conflict leads the Grand Galactics to withdraw their edict to destroy the dangerous sentients of Earth, which, in turn, leads to humanity's being invited into the Galactic community. Ranjit is the recipient of first contact.

Some recurring ideas from Pohl's fiction, and Clarke's, appear throughout the novel. Ranjit's astronomy professor lectures on how volcanoes create lava tubes, which eventually leads to finding similar tubes on the Moon, allowing for colonization. A space elevator called Skyhook, a central concept in Clarke's work (see especially *The Fountains of Paradise*), makes Moon colonization possible. After Pax Per Fidem, in some countries judges and representatives are selected randomly by computer, an idea Pohl introduced in *The Years of the City*. Ranjit and Myra's daughter, Natasha, enters the solar regatta, using a solar sail, an idea Clarke explored in "The Wind from the Sun." Ranjit and Myra's second child, Robert, has the same childhood developmental condition that Pohl's daughter had. The anguished passages read almost identically with what Pohl wrote in *The Way the Future Was*: "And all this 'progress' in understanding Robert's condition had been bought at the price of some dozens of unpleasant episodes. Like strapping Robert to a gurney while they x-rayed his head. Or shaving his hair so they could wrap his skull with sticky magnetic tape"

(219). When the "Machine-Stored" aliens first appear to humanity, "the tiny church of satanists . . . decided that the spiky-furred humanoid was indeed the image of the devil"(259)—this seems to be a tease on the iconic scene at the end of part one of Clarke's *Childhood's End*, when Karellen is glimpsed by the human Stormgren. After a failed military incursion against the aliens, the benevolent aliens believe they must pay "reparations" by synthesizing gold out of seawater, an idea from Clarke's *White Hart* story "The Man Who Plowed the Sea." By the end of the novel the alien visitors have introduced machine-stored technology to humans, and after a fatal scuba diving accident (another familiar Clarke theme), Myra is uploaded; as in the later books of the Heechee saga, all humanity eventually uploads, giving access to the wider galaxy. The final scene, where machine-stored Ranjit is interviewed by a younger machine-stored human some thirteen thousand years later, who is to "play" him in an historical reconstruction of the first contact, alludes to the conclusion of Clarke's *Childhood's End*: "Ranjit sat up straight. 'Well,' he said, 'if the Grand Galactics aren't running things anymore, shouldn't somebody else be taking over for them?' 'Of course,' the stranger said impatiently. 'I thought you knew. Someone is. It's us'" (293).

Unfortunately, *The Last Theorem* is an uneven novel. Once the subplot involving the Grand Galactics and their minions becomes central toward the latter third of the novel, the story loses the unity of characterization and plot that makes Ranjit's life trajectory so gripping in the previous two-thirds of the narrative. Thus, an otherwise compelling novel of near-future politics, mathematics, and a young man growing into maturity becomes tarnished by the very galactic dream that is central to many of the works of both writers. On the other hand, as both writers had no illusions about the fact that this was, at least, Clarke's *last* novel (and quite possibly Pohl's), the recursive pastiche of the first-contact–"welcome to the galaxy" plot gives *The Last Theorem* a postmodern, self-referential flavor that, read in the context of the larger oeuvres of these SF titans, allows the reader to reflect upon the themes central to both and witness the harmonies.

Pohl's final novel, *All the Lives He Led*, is surprisingly fresh and contemporary throughout; an impressive final statement for a lion of the genre. Fittingly, it received a favorable review from Russell Letson in *Locus*; Letson observed that the novel harkens back to *The Space Merchants*: "Pohl builds a funhouse-mirror near-future that suggests that his vision of human nature and the ways of the world have changed hardly at all from the days of *The Space Merchants*. . . . Fred Pohl remains a cunning, astringent, and entertaining observer of our follies."[8] A politically charged capstone to Pohl's extraordinary career, as Letson suggests, *All the Lives He Led* recalls the early work of the 1950s and 1960s, but it also resonates with such 1970s and 1980s works as *Gateway, The Cool War*, and *Black Star Rising*. What's more, Pohl goes back to the roots of his writing by setting the story at Vesuvius, upon which he had composed that lost novel about advertising that morphed into *The Space Merchants*.

In *All the Lives He Led*, Brad Sheridan is a young American who signs on for Indenture in other parts of the world because a good portion of North America has been wiped out when the Yellowstone volcano erupted and left a swath of destruction across the central plains. Sheridan *was* from Kansas City, which is now buried in ash. As previously mentioned, Kansas City plays an important role in Pohl's experience: it is where he met Betty Hull while at the 1976 World Con; where he would fly every summer for James Gunn's workshops in nearby Lawrence; and where the 2007 Heinlein Centennial was held, when he was finishing up *The Last Theorem* with Clarke and contemplating this novel. Sheridan is another of Pohl's wisecracking, naïve, first-person narrators, and as with Robinette Broadhead in *Gateway* or Barry di Hoa in *The Voices of Heaven*, the novel serves as his confession. *All the Lives He Led* has the same "reveal" structure as *The Space Merchants*, where Pohl packs in several disruptions in the first two pages that clue the reader into the fact that they are not in a contemporary or historical setting. In the first chapter, "Introducing Myself," Sheridan states that he is going to "do this experiment in Telling All" (13). This is a typical Pohl ploy, as we've seen, and one that resonates with modernist and postmodernist narrative technique in the manner of Norman Mailer or Salman Rushdie. Sheridan is going to tell the reader "about the summer of '79"—the immediate assumption of the mundane reader is that this, then, must be a historical novel, perhaps about the Iran hostage crisis, in the manner of James Clavell's *Whirlwind*. But the science fiction reader knows better, and indeed it soon becomes evident that this is the summer of 2079. Here Pohl quite effectively returns to the technique of *The Space Merchants* discussed earlier in this study. A little further on, Sheridan casually mentions the "Pompeii Jubilee" where "Some thirty or forty million of you guys from the wealthy countries were" (14). This is another moment where the reader has to pay close attention—"wealthy countries" no longer includes the United States.

The circumstances in the United States are revealed by the fact that Sheridan, who by training is an engineer, holds a low-paying service job overseas because there are no opportunities in his own country. When Yellowstone erupted, Sheridan was eight years old. His parents had money but lost it: "The thing about my parents having money was that they stopped having it at the same time everybody else did. . . . I don't mean I hadn't noticed any changes. I certainly saw the difference between the eight-bedroom house overlooking the Missouri River where I'd lived since I was born and the tiny, shared-bath hovel that the government provided for us refugees on Staten Island" (17). Later sent to "New York A&M"—"Its purpose for being was to turn as many as possible of New York's wildblood youths into reasonably respectable citizens, capable of holding such minimally skilled jobs as waiter or, well, faculty member at NY A&M" (18)—and not inspired to "plant a Recovery Garden" or "to run earthmovers in Ohio or Kentucky for the Citizens Recovery Corps" (18), Sheridan signs on to become an Indenture, a contract laborer at the virtual theme parks that have transformed historical sites into an "authentic" experience.

Sheridan begins his work in Egypt, showing tourists around the virtualized Egyptian monuments, such as the pyramids, the sphinx, and Luxor. Advanced simulation techniques, called "virts," have been developed for entertainment purposes, which recreate archeological sites down to the minutest detail. Americans can get jobs at the various tourist spots because they are all poor and, more important, they speak English, and English is still the common global tongue. Soon, Sheridan transfers to Pompeii, which, probably because of the Yellowstone cataclysm in America, has been turned into the most popular theme park in the world. In *Chasing Science* the genesis of the novel is anticipated: "I don't want to make Pompeii sound like more than it is. It's not a theme park. Its facilities are no longer in working order. There is no wine in the jars of the fast-drink emporia, and even the jars themselves have generally been taken to some museum" (172). Pompeii has the best "virts" in the business, simulating life in the first century A.D. in all its Roman grandeur, including animals getting killed and Christians being crucified. Sheridan first works in the bakery at Pompeii, a nasty, smelly job, echoing Mitch Courtenay's time at the Chorella plant in *The Space Merchants*. Sheridan eventually works his way into a position as wine-seller: "All that virtual stuff was astonishingly convincing. Early on in my wine-seller career I tried to figure out just what parts of my own little cubbyhole were physically real and which were just insubstantial virts. I wasn't always right" (74). Pohl's research for his 1960 nonfiction study *Tiberius* comes into play here in his richly imagined Pompeii setting.

Meanwhile, the "Stans," the former Soviet states of Central Asia, are the rogue states of the future and have been expelled from what is left of the international community, supplying deregulated Soviet weaponry and biotechnology and providing terrorist training to disenfranchised zealots. Terrorism is a persistent problem, as every subgroup and faction resorts to terrorist violence in the name of their cause. While Sheridan works in Egypt, St. Peter's Square at the Vatican is truck-bombed by a group called "True Original Child of Christ Catholics," protesting the ordination of married bishops. Pohl posits that continued fractionated identity politics and escalating sectarian strife will define the twenty-first century as natural disasters, diminishing natural resources, and limited opportunity become increasingly globalized.

While working at Pompeii, Sheridan meets an attractive young woman named Gerda Fleming. As his relationship with Gerda progresses, a plague outbreak, called the Pompeii Flu, rightly assumed to be an act of bioterrorism, begins to spread across the globe, killing eighty thousand people each week. Gerda leaves to take claim of an estate that has been left to her—she was supposed to return but does not. Soon, a major terrorist attack on the UN building in New York occurs. Terrorism hits closer to home for Sheridan right in front of his Pompeii wine shop when park security shoot a woman who evidently has an atom bomb strapped to herself. However, Sheridan becomes suspicious after being told, "That wasn't any real goddamn terrorist. Security was *practicing* for the way they would take a real nuclear terrorist out if one of them ever showed up around here" (164). But it wasn't a nuclear bomb that she was carrying; instead, it was anthrax: "Atom bomb, my ass. Just killing her like that might have made some sense if that was what she had, but the grunt got it wrong. What Maris was carrying was a little glass tube full of anthrax bacteria. Are you hearing what I'm saying? Bacillus anthracis, that is, and I'm not talking about spores. I'm talking about the actual damn bacteria. . . . She was hoping to get them into the Giubileo water supply" (177). The reader here will recognize echoes of *Preferred Risk*.

Behind the Pompeii Flu outbreak and other notorious terrorist acts is the elusive international fugitive Brian Bossert, who, as it so happened, had a sex change to cover his tracks, turning him into Sheridan's lover, Gerda Fleming: "Do you feel bad because now you know that the woman you've been banging all these weeks started out as a man?" (198). As in *The Last Theorem*, Pohl is exploring the topical debate over gender identity. Sheridan learns the history of his erstwhile lover in the cleverly titled chapter 24, "Getting to Know the Man who Was the Woman I Love." Meanwhile, Gerda/Brian, for all appearances, has been caught and shot down. Inside her body is a coil with a recording of the cure for the Pompeii Flu.

As the novel concludes, Sheridan is back in the employ of Pompeii, supervising the live-action gladiatorial ring, here recalling the final scenes in *Gladiator-At-Law*: "Now my job was supervising some of the actual non-virt living combatants, which mostly meant seeing that they weren't too drunk or stoned to perform" (278). Sheridan also has in his possession a set of "plague marbles," left to him by Gerda/Brian. As years pass, Sheridan becomes rich, still keeping the plague marbles in reserve. In what might be some of Pohl's darkest reflections on the folly that is humanity (short of *Jem*), Sheridan considers releasing them upon the world, having concluded that humankind is a miserable lot. But in the end he decides to allow humanity to keep muddling along—"'Oh, hell,' I said, 'let the bastards live. Maybe they'll get better'"—and destroys the plague marbles, though keeping one in reserve, "just in case": "Oh, I don't think that that in case will ever be the case. But, you see, things don't always happen the way I think, and expect, they're going to. And in the remote and improbable event that fate goes in the wrong, in some terribly wrong, direction, I would like to have the option of changing my mind" (347).

All the Lives He Led caps Pohl's career as science fiction's most eminent Swiftian satirist. Within the larger context of Pohl's work, it seems to be at play with most of his previous work on some levels. Though more implicit than Heinlein's late World as Myth novels, like *The Boy Who Would Live Forever*, *All the Lives He Led* reflects back on Pohl's entire career in science fiction: from that moment at age ten discovering a copy of *Wonder Stories* to his battles in fandom, to his time at war, to his advertising and agenting days, to the triumph of *The Space Merchants* and the other 1950s satires, to his Cold War fictions of the 1970s and 1980s, to his latter years as Mr. Science Fiction, the aged patriarch of the field. These are all the lives that Frederik Pohl led.

★   ★   ★

While completing *All the Lives He Led*, Pohl began blogging in January 2009 on his Hugo Award–winning website *The Way the Future Blogs*. Between reminiscences of those he knew in science fiction, Pohl often wrote with acuity and passion about the political issues facing the twenty-first-century world. He embarked on this adventure into twenty-first-century social media shortly before he and Betty went on their last Holland America cruise in the South Pacific.[9] While travelling, both picked up a virus, which caused a number of health crises, culminating in Pohl's receiving a pacemaker that fall.[10]

In celebration of his ninetieth birthday, Betty prepared a Festschrift anthology, titled *Gateways* and published by Tor, which included new stories by old friends—Aldiss, Gunn, Harrison, and Frank M. Robinson; by writers Pohl nurtured in the 1960s—Benford, Joe Haldeman, Niven, and Gene Wolfe; and by current genre stars—David Brin, Neil Gaiman, and Cory Doctorow. Along with the stories, appreciations by writers and editors, such as Silverberg, Gardner Dozois, Joan Slonczewski, Connie Willis, and others, reflect on Pohl's impact on the field.

Pohl's health would go up and down, on more than one occasion nearly reaching terminus, in these final years. But under the caring hand of his loving wife, Betty Hull, and her daughter, Cathy, Frederik Pohl would carry on until nearly his ninety-fourth birthday. They say that sometimes when people are dying, they hang on until a particular person arrives, a conflict is resolved, or a particular event has come to pass. It is not surprising, then, that Frederik Pohl died on September 2, 2013, the concluding day of the 71st World Science Fiction Convention in San Antonio.

CONCLUSION

Frederik Pohl's death on September 2, 2013, leaves a chasm in the world of science fiction. His contributions to the field, as writer, editor, agent, and fan, are unmatchable. He truly was a giant in the field. Writing shortly after Pohl's death, Joe Haldeman summed the man up succinctly: "For all the lives Fred did lead, he did an amazing job. We'll never see his match."[1] James Gunn, among the last surviving major figures of Pohl's generation, shares "that [Pohl] was associated with almost everything good in science fiction that happened to me."[2] Scholar Mack Hassler paid tribute to Pohl in a poem titled "Pohl Hero," writing that "Fred Pohl was that / High hero. A man of great peace."[3] An era has ended.

But Pohl's legacy continues and will continue for many decades to come. Through the readers who discover his work for the first time on a library shelf or paperback rack (or these days on the Web), as I did when I found a copy of *The Cool War* at the grocery store one rainy afternoon in 1982 when I was fifteen. Through the writers who are influenced by his writing, his editing, his advice, and his mere presence in the field. And through the scholars who will find in Pohl an astute critic of the twentieth and twenty-first centuries and an advocate for future alternatives to the roads humanity now travels.

He *is* one of the founding "fathers" of the genre. I hope that this study has laid the groundwork for further critical, biographical, and historical work on the contributions of this science fiction master. I will return to Christopher McKitterick's recent piece in *Foundation*, where he offers this moving farewell, evoking the language of parenthood to assess the stature of Pohl's place within the SF community:

> Goodbye, Mr. Science Fiction. Thank you for helping build a community that has swelled far beyond First Fandom. You Are Not Alone. Thank you for demonstrating how a rational, inquisitive attitude—combined with determination and hard work—can change the course of history. Thank you for giving us hope for the future. Thank you for your ideas, for the laughs and tears, for the entertainment and uncomfortable contemplation. Thank you for your support and advice. Most of all, thank you for sharing your life with the community you helped give birth to, and for raising us, and for being the finest parent any child could hope for.[4]

Frederik Pohl lived a life in science fiction. Building it and shaping it for over three-quarters of a century. Warning us of our economic, social, and political follies, and of the damage we are inflicting upon the planet. But also inspiring us to do better. To strive for greater things. To marvel at the wonders of science. And to marvel at the universe. If science fiction matters—and I believe it does—and if science fiction as a mode of human inquiry can make a difference in how we face our collective future, then the contributions of Frederik Pohl will remain relevant for many years to come.

A CONVERSATION WITH FREDERIK POHL
AND ELIZABETH ANNE HULL

This interview was conducted at the home of Frederik Pohl and Elizabeth Anne Hull in Palatine, Illinois, on July 17, 2013, slightly more than six weeks before Pohl's death on September 2. By this time, as he was nearing the end, Pohl was only able to sustain conversation for about an hour, but he was still able to respond to further questions after some brief rests. Throughout our talk, he remained sharp, vibrant, and insightful. I especially wish to thank Betty Hull for inviting me to their home and allowing me to spend the morning conversing with her and Fred.

PAGE: Why is science fiction important? And why should it still be vital today?
POHL: The trouble is that science fiction is very good at telling us what is likely to happen given this assumption or that assumption. It gives us useful warnings, which no one pays any attention to. The destruction of the environment began fifty years ago, and nobody has really done anything

about it, including me. Unfortunately, I've flown in a lot of airplanes in that time and contributed seriously to the carbon in the air. Science fiction is useful in telling us what we should be worried about but just don't have enough sense to worry about it.

PAGE: Over the last couple of years in your blog, you've been concerned with global warming and global climate change. But this goes way back. In the 1979 interview with Charles Platt, you spoke about climate change, although you didn't call it that at the time, but you did say that this is the big problem that we are going to be facing, and further in *Our Angry Earth*, written with Isaac Asimov, which I believe is a vital book.

POHL: Well, it wasn't particularly perceptive of me. Anyone who looked at the evidence knew that was happening. But most people just didn't want to look.

PAGE: The climate change issue seems to be something that science fiction was becoming aware of as early as the forties and fifties, I think.

POHL: I think so. Well, the first fictional discussion of it that I remember was in a book called *The Space Merchants*, which I happened to have something to do with, and that was in 1952. But it was by no means the first that existed, but it was the first one I was involved in. But long before *Silent Spring* those questions were being discussed in science fiction. Now, that doesn't mean much, because everything else was being discussed in science fiction, too, it was a very all-reaching thing.

PAGE: Well, I think that's an important element of science fiction too. In the film you did with Jim Gunn in the 1970s, "The Ideas in Science Fiction," there's something you articulate that I use when I teach science fiction classes and point out to students that you said: "Science fiction doesn't predict the future, it shows us a variety of possibilities."

POHL: Yes, it shows us what *can* happen. But the trouble is, the area of debate is controlled by people who have axes to grind. The question of what fossil fuels are going to do to the environment has been known for a long time but it hasn't been discussed because such huge investments are bound up in fossil fuels. Most people are afraid to tackle that sort of thing. They're afraid the cure will be worse than the disease.

PAGE: And I'm sure those folks who have a lot of capital invested know exactly what they're doing when they are using fracking and other techniques.

POHL: Yes, and they don't really care what happens to the people who live where the pollution is most dangerous. Because they don't live there.

PAGE: And they don't really care about future generations and what they'll have to face.

POHL: No. The Koch brothers and our most recent Republican presidential candidate and all sorts of leading thinkers have decided not to worry about anything, because it will happen anyhow, but they won't have to be bothered by it. [Pohl says this with a mischievous smile; Betty Hull chuckles in the background.]

PAGE: Maybe it's always been this way, but it seems to me that in the public consciousness science fiction has retreated a little bit. When I encounter students they are familiar with science fiction media, but when you give them a real science fiction novel they ask, "What is this? I don't understand what this is." Or if you ask them if they've ever read science fiction they say, "No, I don't think so." And then if you ask them what books they have read, they say something like *"The Hunger Games"*—and that is science fiction! In other words, they don't understand what science fiction really is.

HULL: Well, for them, *The Hunger Games* gets grouped with things like zombies and vampires and stuff like that . . .

PAGE: Well, yes, all that stuff gets mixed into what they think is science fiction. So I guess, maybe, in some ways the fantastic genres have become indistinguishable for young readers. They don't distinguish science from magic anymore.

POHL: It's been diluted by magic. And armies of zombies . . . and vampires. All of which . . .

HULL: And steampunk.

POHL: This happened when the Science Fiction Writers of America made the bad decision of changing its title to Science Fiction and Fantasy Writers, as though they were related, and they are, but there is a big distinction to be made. I was against it, but I only had one vote, and we never voted on it anyway. It was a fiat of the administration at the time. But we are now in SFWA sort of out-voted by the fantasy writers. In the directory of the members about 25 percent of the names are people I never heard of, because I don't read anything they write. They pay their dues so I guess they're useful.

PAGE: It's interesting that as the larger culture has become more saturated with technology; it's almost like that technology is magic itself as opposed to that rational scientific vision that I think science fiction provides. They have the computers and they know how to use them, but they don't understand them sometimes, I think.

HULL: And they don't know that they don't know.

PAGE: You've said that science fiction is not just a form of storytelling, but it is also "a way of looking at the world."

POHL: It is a way of looking at the world, yeah. A way of observing time, thinking in various directions, and seeing how they all fall together, and fall in different ways. Science fiction is not predictive it is discussive [*sic*], shows what can happen, not what will happen, and that's a big part of it.

HULL: Ray Bradbury said, "I don't want to predict the future, I want to prevent it."

POHL: [*Laughs gleefully.*] That's a good one.

HULL: He's quite far right in his attitudes. He's nostalgic. His best known book is probably *The Martian Chronicles*, and he said, "I know that's not proven over time to be valid, but it sure is a good story." And most writers agree. He's a good storyteller.

PAGE: I think that's a key to what you said there that science fiction is discussive [*sic*] or it's been a conversation since 1926, and that's a lot of what you've done through your whole life is to be part of that discussion, even with the fan culture, and your development of fandom, et cetera.

POHL: I certainly hope that's true, yes.

PAGE: I don't know to what extent other genre readers discuss their stuff in quite the way science fiction people do.

POHL: Not that I'm aware of. There's a whole culture of science fiction that includes the reader and the writer almost on equal terms. Which is not true in any other kind of writing that I know of. In other areas of writing, writers think of things and people read them and are moved by them in one way or another. In science fiction, writers think of things, and readers think of exceptions or improbabilities or whatever . . .

HULL: And the writers challenge each other, like Kuttner and Kornbluth, as in "Mimsy Were the Borogoves" and "The Little Black Bag." Some object comes from elsewhere, and what happens? Each story gives a totally different view.

PAGE: Yes, there are a lot of texts responding to other texts. Maybe more so than in other genres. So we have something like *Starship Troopers*, and then Haldeman, well, even before Haldeman, I think, Gordon Dickson's *Naked to the Stars* is a response to *Starship Troopers*, and then you have Haldeman's *Forever War*, and also *Ender's Game*, and all these are kind of building on one another.

POHL: Have you ever tried to write any science fiction yourself? You should try it. It's a very liberating experience.

PAGE: Yes, Jim [Gunn] encouraged me to try it again at some point. Getting into some of your work a little bit, I've noticed a few recurring themes or images, one of them being Mt. Vesuvius, which shows up in *Preferred Risk*, for one, but also in *All the Lives He Led*.

POHL: I lived on Mt. Vesuvius. Volcanoes tell us what a fragile world we live in. Most of us are not aware of that. They're not in our backyard. But if you live in Italy and see volcanoes everywhere you look, almost always producing if not a real eruption at least a certain amount of throwing up sparks, leaves you to think, "I wonder how long this planet is going to hold together."

PAGE: I think this ties in with your theme of global climate change, not only from human beings, but the Earth itself can change. It has in the geological past and in the historical past and it will in the future. In fact, in *All the Lives He Led* what ends the power of the United States is that Yellowstone blows and goes through Kansas City and other parts of the United States.

POHL: It hasn't done it in the last million years; we're about due again.

PAGE: Just as I finished reading the novel, I saw a news report that Yellowstone was overdue.

HULL: It's been overdue for 150,000 years.

POHL: I made a list once, I don't know whether I ever published it or not, of the disasters that can confront us, whether it's earthquakes, or volcanoes, or tidal waves, or whatever, and there are so many of them that it sort of gets boring after awhile. Something goes off and everybody's dead. Which could easily happen in large areas of the Earth. I don't know if we're in a position—I don't if the Earth is in a position—for all the people to become extinct. But it's certainly going to reduce the numbers of the population.

PAGE: Well, speaking of that, one of the other themes that is consistent in a large number of your works is the concern with human population and its effect on the environment, possible food crisis, and global warming. You've been examining that for sixty years.

POHL: I wonder if anyone has ever noticed yet that people don't want to think about such things. And more than that, there is such a concentrated effort on [the part of] some people, who have a lot of money and are willing to spend it for their purposes, to divert people from things that matter. It distracts people from the important questions, even the ones they can do something about, like the fact that 1 percent of the population gets something like 80 percent of the income.

PAGE: So we live in a culture of distraction?

POHL: A culture where they are continually throwing dust in our eyes so we don't see what's really going on. I cannot believe that this is accidental. I think that they've made a practice of thinking of new things to divert people with, so that they will not notice that the rich people are getting richer all the time.

PAGE: And it distracts from those global, planetary issues.

POHL: It's really scary when you think about how much pain and danger people will go through to get the jobs that Americans don't want to do under any circumstances. I mean stoop labor is not something anybody anywhere likes to do. And people will risk their lives to try to do it here. Betty and I were being interviewed in Europe somewhere, I've forgotten where, and at the end of the discussion the interviewer said, "Dr. Hull what do you consider Mr. Pohl's primary objective in the world is?" And she said, "He just wants everybody to play nicely together." I'd never before thought of it in those terms, but she's so right!

HULL: And play is a big part of it too. We should work together, but we should also play together.

PAGE: And that's probably where the pleasures of reading and fiction come in. That ability to play. And science fiction is a very playful literature.

POHL: It is at that.

HULL: It is. It's an imaginative process and some people, their idea of imagination is to have a pretty light show, like a kaleidoscope.

POHL: I mentioned in my blog that I would not really want to be an editor anymore, but if someone came to me with proper funding, there was one job I would take, and that is a new magazine which I'd call *Super-Science Stories*, because that was the title of one of my early magazines, which would be devoted to reprinting science fiction stories from the early fifties. What marks science fiction stories from the early fifties is that they were all about individuals doing all sorts of brave and exciting things, and not only that, but they all wanted to make things better for themselves and for everybody. It was one of the things that made science fiction something people liked when they first encountered it, because human beings were depicted as the kind of people who wanted to make things better for everybody, and they want to go to a lot of trouble in order to do it.

HULL: Solving problems.

POHL: When science fiction first appeared as a magazine form, there was a wide sense of discovery by the people who read it and they thought, "Hey, I've been waiting for this all my life, but didn't know it!" And I think that is the quality of science fiction that makes people suddenly love it when they first find it. And I think that it is one of the things that has made science fiction fans and readers be homogenous. They may fight and they may disagree, but they always go to bed together. My idea for a magazine was to buy up stories from this period, early fifties primarily, late forties and early fifties, and reprint them, which could be done fairly cheaply, and would do much good. I think that actually could be something that brings people together.

PAGE: You mention the early fifties as your target area there. Prior to *The Space Merchants*, you were an agent, and you've written that you represented most of the writers in the genre. So in a lot of ways your role as agent from 1947 to 1952 did a lot to shape the field by representing those stories. In that, you were pretty significant in growing the field to a more professional level.

POHL: I was lucky enough to be in a position to do a lot of things. I did them for their own sake, but also they had good effects on the field, including raising the rates of all science fiction magazines. Writers would have written anyway, but I wanted them to be a little bit better fed while they were doing it. It's a dog's life being an agent, though. Somebody else gets all the credit.

PAGE: One thing I've noticed about your work is that in the seventies and eighties more of your fiction explored the idea of going to the stars, the dream of space.

POHL: The seventies was a lucky period for me. I had almost abandoned the idea of writing, and I put this story in my autobiography, but you might not remember it. An insurance salesman came to my door and he wanted to sell me insurance, and I didn't feel like I was a good candidate, and I said you're wasting your time but you can give me an exam. And he gave me an examination, or the doctor did, and it turned out that I was quite healthy. And I thought, that's interesting. So I sat down at the typewriter and I typed a little bit, and the words came out fairly well, and it was a whole period of a year, or more than that, when everything was working just the way I wanted it. *Man Plus*, *Gateway*, and four or five others that are really among my favorite parts of my production. All around the same time, which means that . . .

HULL: And all those were done before he met me, which means I can't take credit for any inspiration.

PAGE: With those books in the seventies and eighties, not all of them but a good portion of them, you got more interested in off-planet settings, space travel, some of these possibilities. To what extent did the hopes or dreams of the Apollo Moon landing have to do with that?

POHL: I'm afraid that the Golden Dream of science fiction that your spaceship that you jump into and fly to Alpha Centauri is never going to happen. There are reasons to think that it might possibly occur . . .

HULL: But not in the immediate future. Not in the next two hundred years.

POHL: Well, maybe not.

PAGE: And if it is, it would probably be more the uploaded Robinette Broadhead than the physical Robinette Broadhead.

POHL: And it is not likely to be a faster-than-light spaceship that gets you anywhere. But you could get to one solar system from another through freezing, where you'll notice no time pass—that's essentially as good as going faster than light. It has taken some of the spirit out of the writings of a lot of new people who don't have the same joyous freedom that all of us had forty or fifty years ago.

PAGE: Yes. The stories are still delightful even though we can't realize the possibilities.

HULL: I think human beings have an innate, really deep-seated need to tell each other stories or listen to stories. And at its very lowest level it's probably gossip. Maybe not very artistic. But it goes back a long way. Town criers and poets. I think the need to tell stories, in different ways, is just fundamental to what it means to be a human.

PAGE: And I suppose in science fiction, whether we will ever be able to do it or not, we still want to have stories about the universe and about the solar system. These places that are out there. What could it be like if we were out there as human beings?

HULL: The kind of stories we tell each other do matter.

PAGE: You've collaborated with a number of people. You've written quite a bit about your writing relationship with C. M. Kornbluth. I heard Greg Benford say a few months ago that he thinks science fiction is particularly ripe for collaboration because of its relationship with science, because science is a collaborative enterprise. I was curious about your writing relationship with Jack Williamson.

POHL: We started collaborating when I was his agent and I sold everything he sent me, and I said, "I want more." And he wrote back saying, "I have pieces of a novel that I can't put together. I'll mail it to you and you can see what you can do with it." So I opened it and read and thought, "Well there's a lot of nice stuff in there, but the pages don't seem to be having any relationship to each other." So I began reconstructing it and turned it into the first *Undersea* book. It wasn't great, but pretty good. Both Jack and I are fans of science, and we liked to read about what was happening in science. I enjoyed working with him. He was much better at seeing the intrinsic beauties in a scientific notion than I was. Oh, I loved doing that with him.

PAGE: Are there any underrated writers from the Golden Age?

POHL: There are a number of such writers. Number one on that list is Mack Reynolds. I don't know if you've read much Mack Reynolds?

PAGE: I've read a handful of his novels and a couple of dozen short stories.

POHL: He's a low-skilled writer, he's not good at making pictures and getting your emotions up. But I discovered years ago that when I talked about science fiction ideas that struck people I was talking to as of great interest and great ideas, and they were, they were almost always out of a story by Mack Reynolds. Things like the common Europe, and the minimum living income for everybody, and all those economic things that have become actually part of some people's political programs first appeared in a Mack Reynolds story. And when I was editing *Galaxy* and *If*, I hired Lester Del Rey to edit our fantasy magazine, and the two of us were talking one day and complaining about the injustice of the Nebulas, and I said, "Let's do our own best of the year award." So we worked out a fairly safe system that could not be easily perverted for counting up points, and we gave away a thousand dollar prize for the story our readers voted best, and Mack was dominating. All of his stories were rating really high. But if you ask somebody "Who is a great writer?" I doubt you will ever hear the name Mack Reynolds.

PAGE: But he wrote about a lot of political and social ideas.

POHL: He was not a great writer, but he was a great idea writer.

PAGE: Are there any other writers from those days we should be aware of?

POHL: There are a lot of in and out writers that sometimes are very good and sometimes are not. I wouldn't consider them underrated because they usually get fairly well rewarded for their good stuff. There are very few writers who are consistently at the top of their form. Bob Silverberg and Harlan Ellison are the two I find to be most reliably good. They're the writers that if I had three choices for writers to get into my magazine, I would pick those two first.

PAGE: Who are among the science fiction writers most important or influential for you?

POHL: H. G. Wells beyond doubt is the primary writer. I learned not just to write about certain kinds of things but to generate new kinds of things to write about from H. G. Wells. I've always considered myself his illegitimate son. But there are a lot of writers that I've learned things from, including almost every writer I published as an editor. One of the reasons I think my writing has worked out fairly well, because by being an editor and an agent, I've observed what writers do wrong, and it's a wonderful way to stop doing them wrong yourself. Every writer I know who has taken a turn as an editor has become a better writer as a result, and I think that's a good thing.

HULL: Fred, can I recommend some of the people that I've heard you talk about as influences on your writing?

PAGE: Well, I know he's mentioned Mark Twain. But, then again, he was occasionally a science fiction writer.

HULL: Also Stephen Vincent Benet.

PAGE: Oh, yes, "By the Waters of Babylon."

POHL: That's a nice old science fiction story, but he also wrote a long, long Civil War poem, which I memorized once, a lot of work too because it was long.

PAGE: I think you mentioned O. Henry, and how you read Gene Stratton Porter because her books were next to his on the library shelf, and it wasn't until sometime later that you realized they were different people.

POHL: I was just thinking about that yesterday, as a matter of fact, trying to remember what it was about O. Henry or Gene Stratton Porter that had attracted me so, and I can't think of a thing.

PAGE: Maybe the economy of his short stories?

POHL: Maybe. Maybe. There was something in there that made me like them.

PAGE: Well, you've mentioned the writers in the field influencing you while you were an editor. Like Isaac Asimov, I imagine Campbell influenced you, because you would visit him in his offices, even though he never published your stories. Could you say what that experience of visiting with John Campbell was like?

[At this point, Pohl was getting tired and was unable to continue for a few minutes. But then he roused up again and spoke a little bit about *Our Angry Earth*.]

POHL: Isaac and I had talked about doing a book on the environment without much seriousness, and then finally he said, "Yeah, let's do that," and he and his wife and Betty and I all had dinner together to celebrate that we were going to write this book together in Isaac's favorite restaurant, which is in the lobby of the Waldorf Astoria in New York City. We had a very nice dinner, laughing and joking and having fun, and as we were getting up to go Isaac sort of stretched and said, "I think I'm getting a case of I don't know what. I'm going back to the apartment to lie down for awhile."

And he did. He went back to their apartment on Park Avenue and went to bed and didn't get up for quite awhile, and it turned out he had cancer of the throat or something like that.

HULL: No. He was HIV positive.

POHL: Well that was the blood that they gave him when he had surgery. They gave him tainted blood and that's what he ultimately died of. And when he discovered that he was ill, he didn't know what was causing it and he went to the doctor and the doctor said, "You have HIV, Dr. Asimov." And he said, "I can't. I've never had sexual intercourse with a gay man." There are other ways of getting it.

PAGE: So you did most of the writing on that book?

POHL: No. All of it. Because he couldn't do anything. I'd show him a page or two that I'd written and he'd say, "Oh, yes," then he'd put it down and not even look at it again. But we had talked about what we were going to do, and I went up to visit him and told him what I'd written and showed it to him. He mostly said, "Okay, that's all right." He didn't even make any suggestions about it, which was very disappointing to me because Isaac knew a great deal more about some areas than I do, and I wanted his advice, and didn't get it. It would have been better had he been healthy.

HULL: Well, we had a similar experience with Arthur C. Clarke.

POHL: Arthur was dying when I started working with him. He knew he was sick. He didn't know quite how badly he was ill. He couldn't write it himself. So he hired me to finish it for him. The book didn't turn out badly, but it didn't turn out as well as I had hoped. But I'm not ashamed of it. Whereas *Our Angry Earth* I should not have finished it. I should have sold back the contract, because it's not as good as it should have been.

PAGE: Oh, really. Nevertheless, looking back on it you brought up a lot of important environmental concerns that twenty years later become a big deal.

HULL: Well, I think Fred's right that it could have been much better had Isaac been able to do his part. There's some synergy that happens between writers. I've watched it when Fred was working with Jack. The best examples I can give of it are the collaborations of Niven and Pournelle, and I think the collaborations they did together were far superior to their individual work. And you can see that with a lot of writing teams, that they were better together, all the way back to C. L. Moore and Henry Kuttner. And to try to figure out who did that part and who did that part is kind of useless. It's like when Fred and I collaborate on solving Wheel of Fortune. Ninety-nine percent of the time we solve it before the person there and it's because we collaborate. We don't try to solve it in isolation, we just kind of give the part we recognize and we put it together almost instantly. There's a synergy.

[Pohl was starting to slump in his wheelchair and was clearly in need of some rest.]

HULL: Are you ready for a nap Fred or do you want to eat first?

POHL: I'm getting very, very tired.

HULL: Do you want to lie down?

POHL: Yeah.

PAGE: Thank you very much.

POHL: Oh, you're very welcome. I wish I had been a little more awake.

HULL: Well, it is what it is. And I'm glad you got a chance to meet him, because who knows when you'll get back. And he isn't coming to see you.

PAGE: Yeah. (*Grinning.*) I understand that.

NOVELS

Indicated editions are those cited in this study.

The Space Merchants, with C. M. Kornbluth, 1953 (St. Martin's, 2011).
Search the Sky, with C. M. Kornbluth, 1954 (Bantam, 1977).
Undersea Quest, with Jack Williamson, 1954 (Baen, 1992).
Gladiator-At-Law, with C. M. Kornbluth, 1955 (Ballantine, 1969).
Preferred Risk, with Lester Del Rey, 1955 (Ballantine, 1980).
A Town Is Drowning, with C. M. Kornbluth, 1955, non-genre (Ballantine).
Undersea Fleet, with Jack Williamson, 1956 (Baen, 1992).
Presidential Year, with C. M. Kornbluth, 1956, non-genre (Ballantine).
Sorority House, with C. M. Kornbluth, as by Jordan Park, 1956, non-genre (Lion).
The God of Channel 1, as by Donald Stacy, non-genre, 1956 (Ballantine).
Turn the Tigers Loose, as by Col. Walt Lasky, Pohl ghosted, non-genre, 1956 (Ballantine).
Slave Ship, 1957 (Ballantine, 1975).
Edge of the City, movie novelization, 1957 (Ballantine).
Undersea City, with Jack Williamson, 1958 (Baen, 1992).
Wolfbane, with C. M. Kornbluth, 1959 (Bantam, 1976).
Drunkard's Walk, 1960 (Ballantine / Del Rey, 1982).
The Reefs of Space, with Jack Williamson, 1964 (Ballantine).
A Plague of Pythons, 1965 (Ballantine / Del Rey, 1978).
Starchild, with Jack Williamson, 1965 (Ballantine).
The Age of the Pussyfoot, 1969 (Ballantine / Del Rey, 1982).
Rogue Star, with Jack Williamson, 1969 (Ballantine).
Farthest Star, with Jack Williamson, 1975 (Ballantine).
Man Plus, 1976 (Bantam, 1977).
Gateway, 1977 (Ballantine / Del Rey, 1978).
Jem, 1979 (Bantam, 1980).
Beyond the Blue Event Horizon, 1980 (Ballantine / Del Rey).
The Cool War, 1981 (Ballantine / Del Rey).
Syzygy, 1982 (Bantam).
Starburst, 1982 (Ballantine / Del Rey).
Wall around a Star, with Jack Williamson, 1983 (Ballantine / Del Rey).

Heechee Rendezvous, 1984 (Ballantine/Del Rey).
The Years of the City, 1984 (Timescape).
The Merchants' War, 1984 (St. Martin's, 1986).
Black Star Rising, 1985 (Ballantine/Del Rey, 1986).
The Coming of the Quantum Cats, 1986 (St. Martin's).
Terror, 1986 (Berkley).
The Annals of the Heechee, 1987 (Ballantine/Del Rey).
Chernobyl, 1987 (Bantam).
Narabedla Ltd., 1988 (Ballantine/Del Rey, 1989).
Land's End, with Jack Williamson, 1988 (TOR).
Homegoing, 1989 (Ballantine/Del Rey).
Outnumbering the Dead, 1990 (St. Martin's, 1992).
The World at the End of Time, 1990 (Ballantine/Del Rey, 1991).
The Singers of Time, with Jack Williamson, 1991 (Bantam).
Stopping at Slowyear, 1991 (Bantam, 1992).
Mining the Oort, 1992 (Ballantine/Del Rey, 1993).
The Voices of Heaven, 1994 (TOR, 1995).
Mars Plus, with Thomas T. Thomas, 1994 (Baen, 1995).
The Other End of Time, 1996 (TOR, 1997).
The Siege of Eternity, 1997 (TOR, 1998).
O Pioneer! 1998 (TOR, 1999).
The Far Shore of Time, 1999 (TOR, 2000).
The Boy Who Would Live Forever, 2004 (TOR, 2005).
The Last Theorem, with Arthur C. Clarke, 2008 (Ballantine/Del Rey).
All the Lives He Led, 2011 (TOR).

STORY COLLECTIONS

Alternating Currents, 1956 (Ballantine, 1969).
The Case against Tomorrow, 1957 (Ballantine, 1965).
Tomorrow Times Seven, 1959 (Ballantine, 1969).
The Man Who Ate the World, 1960 (Ballantine).
Turn Left at Thursday, 1961 (Ballantine).
The Wonder Effect, with C. M. Kornbluth, 1962 (Ballantine, 1969).
The Abominable Earthman, 1963 (Ballantine).
Digits and Dastards, 1966 (Ballantine).
Day Million, 1970 (Pan, 1973).
The Gold at the Starbow's End, 1972 (Ballantine).
The Best of Frederik Pohl, 1975 (Doubleday).
The Early Pohl, 1976 (Doubleday).
In the Problem Pit, 1976 (Bantam).
Critical Mass, with C. M. Kornbluth, 1977 (Bantam).
Before the Universe, with C. M. Kornbluth, 1980 (Bantam).
Planets Three, 1982 (Berkley).
Midas World, 1983 (TOR).
Pohlstars, 1984 (Ballantine/Del Rey).

Our Best: The Best of Frederik Pohl and C. M. Kornbluth, 1987 (Baen).
The Day the Martians Came, 1988 (St. Martin's, 1989).
The Gateway Trip, 1990 (Ballantine/Del Rey, 1992).
Platinum Pohl, 2005 (Orb).

NONFICTION

Tiberius, as by Ernst Mason, 1960 (Ballantine).
Practical Politics, 1971 (Ballantine).
The Way the Future Was, 1978 (Bantam/Del Rey, 1979).
Science Fiction: Studies in Film, 1981, with Frederik Pohl IV (Ace).
Our Angry Earth, with Isaac Asimov, 1991 (TOR, 1993).
Chasing Science, 2000 (TOR).
The Way the Future Blogs, 2009– (www.thewaythefutureblogs.com).

SELECTED SHORT STORIES

Pohl wrote nearly two hundred short stories. I have included only stories discussed in the text, along with the collections they appeared in. In cases of multiple listings, in-text page citations refer to the first collection listed. For a full listing of Pohl's bibliography, I point the reader to the monumental Internet Science Fiction Database (isfdb.org). Stories are listed by publication date.

"Elegy to a Dead Planet: Luna," poem, 1937 (in *The Early Pohl*).
"The Dweller in the Ice," 1941 (in *The Early Pohl*).
"Best Friend," with C. M. Kornbluth, 1941 (in *Before the Universe*, *The Wonder Effect*).
"It's a Young World," 1941 (in *The Early Pohl*, *Day Million*).
"Earth, Farewell!" 1943 (in *The Early Pohl*).
"Donovan Had a Dream," 1947 (in *Planets Three*).
"Let the Ants Try," 1949 (in *Alternating Currents*, *In the Problem Pit*, *Platinum Pohl*).
"A Big Man with the Girls," with Judith Merril, uncollected, 1953; *Future*, March 1953.
"The Midas Plague," 1954 (in *The Case against Tomorrow*, *The Best of Frederik Pohl*, *Midas World*).
"The Tunnel under the World," 1955 (in *Alternating Currents*, *The Best of Frederik Pohl*).
"Target One," 1955 (in *Alternating Currents*).
"Rafferty's Reasons," 1955 (in *Alternating Currents*, *In the Problem Pit*).
"Happy Birthday, Dear Jesus," 1956 (in *Alternating Currents*, *The Best of Frederik Pohl*).
"The Census Takers," 1956 (in *The Case against Tomorrow*, *The Best of Frederik Pohl*).
"The Day of the Boomer Dukes," 1956 (in *Tomorrow Times Seven*).
"The Man Who Ate the World," 1956 (in *The Man Who Ate the World*, *In the Problem Pit*, *Midas World*).
"My Lady Greensleeves," 1957 (in *The Case against Tomorrow*, *Platinum Pohl*).
"Mars By Moonlight," 1958 (in *Turn Left at Thursday*).
"The Knights of Arthur," 1958 (in *Tomorrow Times Seven*, *Platinum Pohl*).

"The Wizards of Pung's Corners," 1958 (in *The Man Who Ate the World*).

"The Waging of the Peace," 1959 (in *The Man Who Ate the World*).

"Whatever Counts," 1959 (in *The Abominable Earthman*).

"The Day the Icicle Works Closed," 1960 (in *The Man Who Ate the World, The Best of Frederik Pohl, Platinum Pohl*).

"The Quaker Cannon," with C. M. Kornbluth, 1961 (in *Critical Mass, The Wonder Effect, Our Best*).

"The Abominable Earthman," 1961 (in *The Abominable Earthman*).

"The World of Myrion Flowers," with C. M. Kornbluth, 1961 (in *Critical Mass, The Wonder Effect, Our Best*).

"The Deadly Mission of Phineas Snodgrass," 1962 (in *Day Million, In the Problem Pit*).

"The Children of Night," 1964 (in *Digits and Dastards, The Best of Frederik Pohl*).

"Father of the Stars," 1964 (in *Digits and Dastards, The Best of Frederik Pohl*).

"Under Two Moons," 1965 (in *Day Million*).

"Day Million," 1966 (in *Day Million, The Best of Frederik Pohl, Platinum Pohl*).

"Earth Eighteen," 1966 (in *Digits and Dastards*).

"The Day after the Day the Martians Came," 1967 (in *Day Million, The Best of Frederik Pohl, The Day the Martians Came, Platinum Pohl, Dangerous Visions* [edited by Harlan Ellison]).

"The Gold at the Starbow's End," 1972 (in *The Gold at the Starbow's End, Platinum Pohl*).

"The Merchants of Venus," 1972 (in *The Gateway Trip, The Gold at the Starbow's End, Platinum Pohl*).

"Shaffery among the Immortals," 1972 (in *The Gold at the Starbow's End, Platinum Pohl*).

"The Meeting," with C. M. Kornbluth, 1972 (in *Critical Mass, Our Best, Platinum Pohl*).

"In the Problem Pit," 1973 (in *In the Problem Pit*).

"We Purchased People," 1974 (in *Pohlstars*).

"Spending a Day at the Lottery Fair," 1983 (in *Pohlstars, Platinum Pohl*).

"Second Coming," 1983 (in *Pohlstars*).

"Sitting around the Pool, Soaking up the Rays," 1984 (in *Tales from the Planet Earth*).

"Fermi and Frost," 1985 (in *Platinum Pohl*).

"A Visit to Belindia," 1994 (in *Future Quartet*, [edited by Charles Sheffield])

"The Mayor of Mare Tranq," 1996 (in *Platinum Pohl, The Williamson Effect* [edited by Roger Zelazny]).

"The Golden Years of *Astounding*," 1997 (in *Alternate Skiffy* [edited by Mike Resnick and Patrick Nielsen Hayden]).

SELECTED ESSAYS

The following list includes only essays and editorials cited in the text. Again, I point the interested reader to the Internet Science Fiction Database (isfdb .org) for a full listing of Pohl's essays.

"The Art and Agony of Collaboration," *Preferred Risk*, 179–83.

"The Day after Tomorrow," *Galaxy*, October 1965, 4–7.

"Editor's Note," *Star 1*, 1–2

"Frederik Pohl," *Contemporary Authors* 188 (Farmington Hills, Mich.: Gale, 2001), 333–55.

"Golden Ages Gone Away," *In the Problem Pit and Other Stories*, 95–105.

"Honor for Prophets," *Galaxy*, February 1963, 4–6.

"How to Count on Your Fingers," *Digits and Dastards*, 162–78.

"The Ideas in Science Fiction," filmed lecture, *The Literature of Science Fiction*, produced and directed by James Gunn, 1975 (Lawrence, Kan.: Digital Media Zone, 2002 [DVD]).

"Introduction," *Day Million*, 7–9.

"Jack," *In Memory of Wonder's Child: Jack Williamson* (Royal Oak, Mich.: Haffner, 2007), 15–17.

"On Binary Digits and Human Habits," *Digits and Dastards*, 179–92.

"On My Way Back to the Future." *Locus*, January 2009, 6–7, 32–35, 54.

"On Velocity Exercises," in *Those Who Can: A Science Fiction Reader*, edited by Robin Scott Wilson (New York: Mentor, 1972).

"The Politics of Prophecy," *Political Science Fiction*, edited by. Donald M. Hassler and Clyde Wilcox (Columbia: University of South Carolina Press, 1997), 7–17.

"Power Play," *Omni*, April 1979, 68–77.

"Ragged Claws," in *Hell's Cartographers* (New York: Harper and Row, 1975), 144–72.

"The Science Fiction Professional," in *The Craft of Science Fiction*, edited by Reginald Bretnor (New York: Harper and Row, 1976).

"SF: The Game-Playing Literature," *In the Problem Pit and Other Stories*, 190–93.

"A Short Term Solution." *Galaxy*, April 1975, 9–17.

"The Story of the Space Merchants," in *The Space Merchants* (New York: St. Martin's, 2011).

"The Study of Science Fiction: A Modest Proposal," *Science Fiction Studies*, March 1997, 11–16.

"A Tribute to Gunn," *Lone Star Con 3*, 71st World Science Fiction Convention Program, San Antonio, 2013, 10.

"What Science Fiction Is," *If*, March 1968, 4.

"Wiped Out," *If*, July 1967, 4–5.

SELECTED ANTHOLOGIES EDITED BY POHL

Tomorrow, the Stars, as by Robert A. Heinlein, ghost edited by Pohl and Judith Merril, 1952 (Signet).

Beyond the End of Time, 1952 (Doubleday).

Star Science Fiction, vols. 1–6, 1953–1959 (Ballantine).

Shadow of Tomorrow, 1953 (Doubleday).

Assignment in Tomorrow, 1954 (Doubleday).

Star Short Novels, 1954 (Ballantine).

The Expert Dreamers, 1962 (Doubleday).

Nightmare Age, 1970 (Ballantine).

Science Fiction of the Forties, with Martin H. Greenberg and Joseph Olander, 1978 (Avon).

Galaxy: Thirty Years of Innovative Science Fiction, 1980 (Wideview).

Yesterday's Tomorrows, 1982 (Berkley).

Tales from the Planet Earth, with Elizabeth Anne Hull, 1986 (St. Martin's).

Worlds of If: A Retrospective Anthology, 1986 (Bluejay).

The SWFA Grand Masters, vols. 1–3, 1999–2001 (TOR).

MAGAZINE EDITORIAL POSTS

Astonishing Stories, February 1940–September 1941.
Super Science Stories, March 1940–August 1941.
Star Science Fiction Magazine, one issue, 1958.
Galaxy, December 1961–May 1969.
If, January 1962–May 1969.
Worlds of Tomorrow, April 1963–May 1967.
International Science Fiction, two issues, 1967–68.

INTRODUCTION: ALL THE LIVES HE LED

1. Aldiss, "Science Fiction's Mother Figure," 52–86.
2. Pohl, "A Tribute to Gunn," 10.
3. Hull, "Frederik Pohl," 98.
4. McKitterick, "Frederik Pohl: Mr. Science Fiction (A Love Story)," 5.
5. Ibid., 5.
6. Budrys, "Memoir," 101.
7. Aldiss, *Trillion Year Spree*, 25–53.
8. Asimov, *I. Asimov*, 63.
9. Aldiss, *Trillion Year Spree*, 240.
10. Asimov, "The History of Science Fiction after 1938."
11. Del Rey, *World of Science Fiction*, 79.
12. Gunderloy and Janice, *The World of Zines*, 35.
13. Pohl, *Yesterday's Tomorrows*, xiv.
14. Ibid.
15. Dozois, "Appreciation," 128.
16. Gunn, Letter to Pohl, July 27, 1953.
17. Pohl, "Study of Science Fiction," 11.
18. Mendlesohn, "Introduction: Reading Science Fiction," 1–2.
19. Pohl, "Power Play," 69.
20. Amis, *New Maps of Hell*, 118–33.
21. Pohl, "A Short Term Solution," 10.
22. Pohl, Introduction to *Day Million*, 7–8.
23. Pohl, "The Ideas in Science Fiction."
24. Pohl, "SF: The Game Playing Literature," 190.
25. Pohl, "The Ideas in Science Fiction."
26. Pohl, "Honor for Prophets," 6.
27. Pohl, "The Day After Tomorrow," 6.
28. Platt, *Dream Makers*, 65.
29. Pohl, "What Science Fiction Is," 4.
30. Pohl, "Wiped Out," 5.
31. Platt, *Dream Makers*, 65.

1. Pohl, *The Way the Future Was*, 1.
2. Pohl, "Frederik Pohl," *Contemporary Authors*, 341.
3. Pohl, "Ragged Claws," 167.
4. Pohl, "Frederik Pohl," 340.
5. Pohl, "Ragged Claws," 145.
6. Hartwell, *Age of Wonders*, 13.
7. Pohl, *The Way the Future Was*, 8.
8. Pohl, "Frederik Pohl," 340.
9. Pohl, "Ragged Claws," 166.
10. Pohl, *The Way the Future Was*, 5.
11. Pohl, "Ragged Claws," 147.
12. Pohl, "Editor's Note," *Star 1*, 1.
13. Pohl, "On My Way Back to the Future," 34.
14. Pohl, *Science Fiction: Studies in Film*, 13.
15. Ibid., 57.
16. Pohl, *The Way the Future Was*, 4.
17. Ibid., 1.
18. Pohl, "Frederik Pohl," 342.
19. Pohl, *The Way the Future Was*, 21.
20. Pohl, *Early Pohl*, 2. See also *The Way the Future Was*, 27.
21. Moskowitz, *Immortal Storm*, 32–33.
22. Pohl, *The Way the Future Was*, 17–18.
23. Ibid., 29.
24. Pohl, *Early Pohl*, 3.
25. Pohl, *Yesterday's Tomorrows*, 3.
26. Ebert, "How Propeller-Heads . . .," 13.
27. Ibid., 17.
28. Pohl, *The Way the Future Was*, 35.
29. Pohl, *Early Pohl*, 3.
30. Sykora, letter, April 10, 1937. Wollheim, postcard, April 18, 1937. Madle, letter, May, 21, 1937.
31. Pohl, *The Way the Future Was*, 67.
32. Asimov, *In Memory Yet Green*, 212.
33. Knight, *Futurians*, 15.
34. Pohl, *The Way the Future Was*, 60; Pohl, "Frederik Pohl," 341.
35. Pohl, *Early Pohl*, 69–70; Pohl, "Frederik Pohl," 341.
36. Pohl, *The Way the Future Was*, 112.
37. Pohl, "The Politics of Prophecy," 10.
38. Knight, *Futurians*, 136.
39. Merril, *Better to Have Loved*, 43.
40. Pohl, *The Way the Future Was*, 54.
41. Ibid., 88. Also see Moskowitz, *Immortal Storm*.
42. Moskowitz, *Immortal Storm*, 214.
43. Harrison, "Knowing Fred," 280.

44. Pohl, *The Way the Future Was*, 39; Pohl, *Early Pohl*, 8.

45. Asimov, *I. Asimov*, 196–207.

46. Pohl, *The Way the Future Was*, 41.

47. Pohl, "Ragged Claws," 154.

48. Eller, *Becoming Ray Bradbury*, 42.

49. Pohl, *The Way the Future Was*, 78.

50. Ibid., 75.

51. Ibid., 98.

52. Ibid., 103.

53. Eller, *Becoming Ray Bradbury*, 44.

54. Pohl, *Yesterday's Tomorrows*, 9.

55. Pohl and Kornbluth, *Our Best*, 139–41.

56. Knight, *Futurians*, 48; Rich, *C. M. Kornbluth*, 63–64.

57. Knight, *Futurians*, 72.

58. Slusser, *Gregory Benford*, 174.

59. Knight, *Futurians*, 45.

60. Baumgardt, receipt, July 25, 1939.

61. Pohl, *The Way the Future Was*, 112–13.

62. Ibid., 91.

63. Knight, *Futurians*, 99.

64. Ibid., 110.

65. Pohl, letter, July 27, 1941.

66. Knight, *Futurians*, 120.

67. Pohl, letter, October 16, 1941.

68. Wollheim, *Universe Makers*, 67.

69. Pohl, *The Way the Future Was*, 188.

70. Pohl, *Early Pohl*, 72.

71. Ibid., 85.

72. Pohl, *The Way the Future Was*, 127; Pohl, *The Way the Future Blogs*, August 18, 2011.

73. Pohl, *The Way the Future Blogs*, August 6, 2011.

74. Pohl, *Early Pohl*, 39–40.

75. Nicholls, "Conceptual Breakthrough," 254–57.

76. Pohl, *Early Pohl*, 81.

77. Asimov, *In Memory Yet Green*, 359. Patterson, *Robert A. Heinlein*, 310–11.

78. Pohl, *The Way the Future Was*, 129.

79. Pohl, *Early Pohl*, 129–30.

80. Ibid., 131–32.

81. Pohl, *The Way the Future Was*, 132. Williamson, *Wonder's Child*, 138–42.

82. Pohl, *Early Pohl*, 170–72.

83. Pohl, *The Way the Future Blogs*, May 20, 2013.

84. Daugherty, *Just One Catch*, 85–91.

85. Pohl, "Story of the Space Merchants," v–vi.

86. See http://www.britannica.com/EBchecked/topic/594862/Tiberius.

87. Pohl, *The Way the Future Was*, 136.

88. Ibid., 141.

89. Ibid., 146.

90. Knight, *Futurians*, 173–74.

91. Pohl, *The Way the Future Was*, 148–49.

92. Ibid., 154.

93. Pohl, *Yesterday's Tomorrows*, 100.

94. Pohl, *The Way the Future Was*, 154.

95. Manlove, *Science Fiction: Ten Explorations*, 40.

96. Merril, *Better to Have Loved*, 94.

97. Pohl, *The Way the Future Was*, 193.

98. Merril, *Better to Have Loved*, 95.

99. Del Rey, *World of Science Fiction*, 144.

100. Malzberg, *Breakfast in the Ruins*, 219–43.

101. Pohl, *The Way the Future Was*, 165–56; Knight, *Futurians*, 186–88.

102. Pohl, *The Way the Future Was*, 170.

103. Asimov, *I. Asimov*, 64.

104. Asimov, *In Memory Yet Green*, 577–78.

105. Williamson, *Wonder's Child*, 178.

106. Ibid., 179.

107. Pohl, *The Way the Future Was*, 178; Knight, *Futurians*, 189.

108. Knight, *Futurians*, 194.

109. Merril, *Better to Have Loved*, 105.

110. Pohl, *The Way the Future Was*, 194.

111. Pohl, letter to James Gunn, June 10, 1952.

112. Pohl, *Yesterday's Tomorrows*, 32.

113. Ketterer, *Imprisoned in a Tesseract*, 85–87.

114. McAleer, *Odyssey*, 94–95.

115. Harrison, "Knowing Fred," 280.

116. Pohl, letter to Jack Williamson, May 22, 1952.

117. Gunn, letter to Pohl, undated.

118. Pohl, letter to Gunn, March 3, 1952; Pohl, letter to Gunn, March 4, 1952; Gunn, letter to Pohl, March 8, 1952; Pohl, letter to Gunn, March 12, 1952.

119. Gunn, *My Unlikely Life*.

120. Pohl, Letter to Gunn, November 7, 1952.

121. Pohl, Letter to Gunn, July 21, 1953.

122. Pohl, *Yesterday's Tomorrows*, 98–99.

123. Heinlein, *Tomorrow, the Stars*, x.

CHAPTER 2. THE GALAXY YEARS, 1952–1969

1. Pohl, "Ragged Claws," 162.

2. Gold, "Random Notes," 3.

3. Pohl, *The Way the Future Was*, 187.

4. Conklin, review of *Star Science Fiction*, 120.

5. Reinsberg, review of *Star Science Fiction*, 144.

6. Silverberg, "Fred," 260.

7. Delany, "Science Fiction and 'Literature,'" 104.

8. Ibid.

9. Gunn, "Touchstones," 310.
10. Otto, *Green Speculations*, 106–7.
11. Luckhurst, *Science Fiction*, 111.
12. Conklin, review of *Space Merchants*, 114–15.
13. Maclean, review of *Space Merchants*, 26, 36.
14. Pringle, *Science Fiction: 100 Best Novels*, 44.
15. Merril, *Better to Have Loved*, 133, 139; Pohl, *The Way the Future Blogs*, December 12, 2010.
16. Pohl, *The Way the Future Was*, 214.
17. Pohl, "SF: The Game-Playing Literature," 191.
18. Ellison, *Essential Ellison*, 303; Linna, introduction, 6.
19. Pohl, *Science Fiction: Studies in Film*, 177.
20. Debord, *Society of the Spectacle*, 5.
21. Gold, "Breakthrough," 4.
22. Pohl, "Ideas in Science Fiction."
23. Conklin, review of *Gladiator-At-Law*, 110.
24. Frazier, review of *Search the Sky*, 128.
25. Conklin, review of *Search the Sky*, 120.
26. Hassler, "Swift, Pohl, and Kornbluth: Publicists Anatomize Newness," 19–20.
27. Santesson, review of *Undersea City*, 118.
28. Conklin, review of *Undersea Quest*, 93.
29. Pohl, "Jack," 17.
30. Knight, review of *Preferred Risk*, 106–7.
31. Santesson, review of *Preferred Risk*, 110.
32. Gale, review of *Preferred Risk*, 87.
33. Pohl, "Art and Agony of Collaboration," 179.
34. Pohl, introduction to *Critical Mass*, ix.
35. Pohl, *Science Fiction: Studies in Film*, 131.
36. Pohl, introduction to *Critical Mass*, ix.
37. Gale, review of *Slave Ship*, 123.
38. Santesson, review of *Alternating Currents*, 127.
39. Knight, *Futurians*, 204–5.
40. Pohl, *Star 4*, 25.
41. Amis, *New Maps of Hell*, 118–19.
42. Pohl, *Yesterday's Tomorrows*, 209.
43. Solstein, *Campbell's Golden Age of Science Fiction*.
44. Gunn, "Fred and Me," 165.
45. Ellison, "Memoir," 273.
46. Ibid., 289.
47. Pohl, *Pohlstars*, 76.
48. Silverberg, *Other Spaces*, 67–68.
49. Silverberg, "Fred," 261.
50. Page, "Miles J. Breuer," xxxii.
51. Budrys, review of *Reefs of Space*, 158.
52. Miller, review of *Plague of Pythons*, 163.
53. Pohl, *The Way the Future Blogs*, May 26, 2009.

54. Miller, review of *Age of the Pussyfoot*, 166.

55. Brin, "Frederik Pohl—Architect of Worlds," 92.

56. Aldiss, *Twinkling of an Eye*, 282. Pohl, *The Way the Future Was*, 282.

CHAPTER 3. GATEWAYS, 1970–1987

1. Pohl, "Frederik Pohl," 348.

2. Pohl, *The Way the Future Was*, 285.

3. Ibid., 268–69.

4. Platt, *Dream Makers*, 60.

5. Pohl, *The Way the Future Was*, 269–70.

6. Pohl, *Practical Politics*, ix.

7. Hull, *Gateways*, 15.

8. Page, "Evolution and Apocalypse in the Golden Age," 40–42.

9. Pohl, *Yesterday's Tomorrows*, 100.

10. Ibid., 394–95.

11. James, *Science Fiction in the 20th Century*, 176.

12. Bova, "Popular Wisdom," 178.

13. Pohl, *The Way the Future Was*, 266.

14. Del Rey, "Frederik Pohl: Frontiersman," 55–64.

15. Pohl, *Yesterday's Tomorrows*, 411.

16. Pohl, "On Velocity Exercises," 323–28.

17. Pohl, "Science Fiction Professional," 292–312.

18. Gunn, "Teaching Science Fiction," 85.

19. McKitterick, "Frederik Pohl: Mr. Science Fiction (A Love Story)," 5–6.

20. Pohl, "The Ideas in Science Fiction."

21. Willis, "Fred Pohl Appreciation," 184.

22. See http://www.sfcenter.ku.edu/news.htm#94.

23. Pohl, *The Way the Future Blogs*, November 19, 2012.

24. Pohl, "Frederik Pohl," 350.

25. Samuelson, "Critical Mass," 124.

26. Pohl, *The Way the Future Blogs*, March 19, 2013; Hull, *Gateways*, 13.

27. Del Rey, review of *Man Plus*, 173.

28. Wolfe, *Known and the Unknown*, 185.

29. Aldiss, *Trillion Year Spree*, 403.

30. Harris-Fain, *Understanding Contemporary American Science Fiction*, 69.

31. Benford, "Physics through Science Fiction," 216.

32. Robinson, review of *The Way the Future Was*, 173.

33. Budrys, review of *Jem*, 27.

34. Clareson, *Frederik Pohl*, 126.

35. Robinson, review of *Beyond the Blue Event Horizon*, 169–70.

36. Easton, review of *Beyond the Blue Event Horizon*, 166.

37. Brin, "Pole Star," 35.

38. Pohl, *The Way the Future Blogs*, March 13, 2014.

39. Pohl, "Frederik Pohl," 341.

40. Aldiss, *Trillion Year Spree*, 405.

41. Delany, "Science Fiction and 'Literature,'" 104.

42. Easton, review of *Gateway Trip*, 167.

43. Easton, review of *The Years of the City*, 183.

44. Budrys, review of *The Years of the City*, 16.

45. Hull, email to the author, October 21, 2014.

46. Easton, review of *Tales from the Planet Earth*, 165.

CHAPTER 4. THE BOY WHO WOULD LIVE FOREVER, 1988–2013

1. Hull, email to the author, July 4, 2014.

2. Ibid.

3. Harris-Fain, *Understanding American Science Fiction*, 140–41.

4. Asimov, *It's Been a Good Life*, 201.

5. Hull, email to the author, July 5, 2014.

6. Hull, "Frederik Pohl," 99.

7. Pohl, *The Way the Future Blogs*, January 19, 2009.

8. Letson, review of *All the Lives He Led*, 9.

9. Pohl, *The Way the Future Blogs*, January 12, 2009.

10. Hull, *Gateways*, 16.

CONCLUSION

1. Haldeman, "Frederik Pohl," 33.

2. Gunn, "Fred," 34.

3. Hassler, "Pohl Hero," 34.

4. McKitterick, "Mr. Science Fiction," 16.

Aldiss, Brian W. "Science Fiction's Mother Figure." In *The Detached Retina*, 52–86. Syracuse, N.Y.: Syracuse University Press, 1995.

———. *Trillion Year Spree*. New York: Atheneum, 1986.

———. *The Twinkling of an Eye*. New York: St. Martin's, 1998.

Aldiss, Brian W., and Harry Harrison. Eds. *Hell's Cartographers*. New York: Harper and Row, 1975.

Amis, Kingsley. *New Maps of Hell*. New York: Harcourt, Brace, 1960.

Asimov, Isaac. "The History of Science Fiction after 1938." *The Literature of Science Fiction*. Film series. Produced and directed by James Gunn.

———. *I. Asimov*. New York: Doubleday, 1994.

———. *In Memory Yet Green: The Autobiography of Isaac Asimov, 1920–1954*. New York: Doubleday, 1979.

———. *It's Been a Good Life*. Edited by Janet Jeppson Asimov. Amherst, Mass.: Prometheus, 2002.

Benford, Gregory. "Physics through Science Fiction." In *Reading Science Fiction*, edited by James Gunn, Marleen S. Barr, and Matthew Candelaria, 212–18. London: Palgrave, 2009.

Bova, Ben. "The Popular Wisdom." *Analog*, February 1972, 4–7, 176–78.

Brin, David. "Frederik Pohl—Architect of Worlds." In Hull, *Gateways*, 92–93.

———. "Pole Star." *Locus*, October 2013, 34–35.

Budrys, Algis. "Memoir ('The Man who Tasted Ashes')." In *Worlds of If: A Retrospective Anthology*, edited by Frederik Pohl, Martin Harry Greenberg, and Joseph D. Olander, 95–103. New York: Bluejay, 1986.

———. Review of *Jem*. *Fantasy and Science Fiction*, September 1979, 27–28.

———. Review of *The Reefs of Space*. *Galaxy*, February 1965, 158.

———. Review of *The Years of the City*. *Fantasy and Science Fiction*, March 1985, 16–18.

Clareson, Thomas. *Frederik Pohl*. Mercer Island, Wash.: Starmont, 1987.

Conklin, Groff. Review of *Gladiator-At-Law*. *Galaxy*, October 1955, 110.

———. Review of *Search the Sky*. *Galaxy*, June 1954, 120.

———. Review of *The Space Merchants*. *Galaxy*, August 1953, 114–15.

———. Review of *Star Science Fiction*. *Galaxy*, June 1953, 120–21.

———. Review of *Undersea Quest*. *Galaxy*, July 1955, 93.

Daugherty, Tracy. *Just One Catch: A Biography of Joseph Heller*. New York: St. Martin's, 2011.

Debord, Guy. *Society of the Spectacle*. Detroit: Black and Red, 1977.

Delany, Samuel R. "Science Fiction and 'Literature'; or, The Conscience of the King."

In *Speculation on Speculation*, edited by James Gunn and Matthew Candelaria, 95–118. Lanham, Md.: Scarecrow, 2005.

Del Rey, Lester. "Frederik Pohl: Frontiersman." *Fantasy and Science Fiction*, September 1973, 55–64.

———. Review of *Man Plus*. *Analog*, October 1976, 173.

———. *The World of Science Fiction: 1926–1976*. New York: Ballantine, 1979.

Dozois, Gardner. "Appreciation." In Hull, *Gateways*, 128–29.

Easton, Tom. Review of *Beyond the Blue Event Horizon*. *Analog*, September 1980. 165–66.

———. Review of *The Gateway Trip*. *Analog*, September 1991, 167.

———. Review of *Tales from the Planet Earth*. *Analog*, September 1987, 165.

———. Review of *The Years of the City*. *Analog*, April 1985, 182–83.

Ebert, Roger. "How Propeller-Heads, BNFS, Sercon Geeks, Newbies, Recovering Gafiators, and Kids in Basements Invented the World Wide Web, All Except for the Delivery System." *Asimov's Science Fiction*, January 2005, 12–17.

Eller, Jonathan. *Becoming Ray Bradbury*. Urbana: University of Illinois Press, 2011.

Ellison, Harlan. *The Essential Ellison*. Las Vegas: Morpheus, 2001.

———. "Memoir ('I Have No Mouth, and I Must Scream')." *Worlds of If: A Retrospective Anthology*, edited by Frederik Pohl, Martin Harry Greenberg, and Joseph D. Olander, 272–89. New York: Bluejay, 1986.

Frazier, Robert. Review of *Search the Sky*. *Fantastic Universe*, September 1954, 128.

Gale, Floyd C. Review of *Preferred Risk*. *Galaxy*, April 1956, 87.

———. Review of *Slave Ship*. *Galaxy*, October 1957, 123.

Gold, Horace. "Breakthrough." *Galaxy*, June 1954, 4–5.

———. "Random Notes." *Galaxy*, June 1952, 2–3.

Gunderloy, Mike, and Cari Goldberg Janice. *The World of Zines: A Guide to the Independent Magazine Revolution*. London: Penguin, 1992.

Gunn, James. "Fred." *Locus*, October 2013, 34.

———. "Fred and Me." In Hull, *Gateways*, 165–69.

———. "My Unlikely Life." Unpublished memoir.

———. "Teaching Science Fiction." *Science Fiction Studies*, November 1996. Reprinted in *Inside Science Fiction*, by James Gunn (Lanham, Md.: Scarecrow, 2006), 79–88.

———. "Touchstones." In *Speculation on Speculation*, edited by James Gunn and Matthew Candelaria, 301–10. Lanham, Md.: Scarecrow, 2005.

Haldeman, Joe. "Frederik Pohl." *Locus*, October 2013, 33.

Harris-Fain, Darren. *Understanding Contemporary American Science Fiction: The Age of Maturity, 1970–2000*. Columbia: University of South Carolina Press, 2005.

Harrison, Harry. "Knowing Fred." In Hull, *Gateways*, 280–84.

Hartwell, David G. *Age of Wonders: Exploring the World of Science Fiction*. New York: Tor, 1996.

Hassler, Donald M. "Pohl Hero." *Locus*, October 2013, 34.

———. "Swift, Pohl, and Kornbluth: Publicists Anatomize Newness." In *Political Science Fiction*, edited by Donald M. Hassler and Clyde Wilcox, 18–25. Columbia: University of South Carolina Press, 1997.

Heinlein, Robert A., ed. *Tomorrow, the Stars*. New York: Doubleday, 1952.

Hull, Elizabeth Anne. "Frederik Pohl." In *The SFWA Grand Masters*, 3:97–100. New York: Tor, 2001.

————, ed. *Gateways*. New York: Tor, 2010.

James, Edward. *Science Fiction in the 20th Century*. Oxford: Oxford University Press, 1994.

Ketterer, David. *Imprisoned in a Tesseract: The Life and Work of James Blish*. Kent, Ohio: Kent State University Press, 1987.

Knight, Damon. *The Futurians*. New York: Day, 1977.

————. Review of *Preferred Risk*. *Original Science Fiction Stories*, July 1956, 106–7.

Letson, Russell. Review of *All the Lives He Led*. *Locus*, April 2011, 46.

Linna, Miriam. Introduction to *Raw Rumbles: The Hal Ellson Omnibus*, 5–8. San Francisco: Rudos and Rubes, 2008.

Luckhurst, Roger. *Science Fiction*. Cambridge: Polity, 2005.

MacLean, Katherine. Review of *The Space Merchants*. *Dynamic*, January 1954, 26, 36.

Malzberg, Barry N. *Breakfast in the Ruins*. New York: Baen, 2007.

Manlove, C. N. *Science Fiction: Ten Explorations*. London: Macmillan, 1986.

McAleer, Neil. *Odyssey: The Authorized Biography of Arthur C. Clarke*. London: Gollancz, 1992.

McKitterick, Christopher. "Frederik Pohl: Mr. Science Fiction (A Love Story)." *Foundation* 117 (Spring 2014): 5–17.

Mendlesohn, Farah. "Introduction: Reading Science Fiction." In *The Cambridge Companion to Science Fiction*, 1–14. Cambridge: Cambridge UP, 2003.

Merril, Judith, and Emily Pohl-Weary. *Better to Have Loved: The Life of Judith Merril*. Toronto: Between the Lines, 2002.

Miller, P. Schuyler. Review of *The Age of the Pussyfoot*. *Analog*, July 1969, 166.

————. Review of *A Plague of Pythons*. *Analog*, July 1967, 163.

Moskowitz, Sam. *The Immortal Storm*. Westport, Conn.: Hyperion, 1974.

Murray, Terry A. *Science Fiction Magazine Story Index, 1926–1995*. Jefferson, N.C.: McFarland, 1999.

Nicholls, Peter. "Conceptual Breakthrough." *The Encyclopedia of Science Fiction*, edited by John Clute and Peter Nicholls, 254–57. London: Orbit, 1993.

Otto, Eric C. *Green Speculations: Science Fiction and Transformative Environmentalism*. Columbus: Ohio State University Press, 2012.

Page, Michael R. "Evolution and Apocalypse in the Golden Age." In *Green Planets: Ecology and Science Fiction*, edited by Gerry Canavan and Kim Stanley Robinson, 40–55. Middletown, Conn.: Wesleyan University Press, 2014.

————. "Miles J. Breuer: Science Fiction Pioneer of the Nebraska Plains." In *The Man with the Strange Head and Other Early Science Fiction Stories*, by Miles J. Breuer, edited by Michael R. Page, ix–xxxviii. Lincoln: University of Nebraska Press, 2008.

Patterson, William H., Jr. *Robert A. Heinlein: In Dialogue with His Century, Vol. I—Learning Curve (1907–1948)*. New York: Tor, 2010.

Platt, Charles. *Dream Makers: The Uncommon People Who Write Science Fiction*. New York: Berkley, 1980.

Pringle, David. *Science Fiction: The 100 Best Novels*. New York: Carroll and Graff, 1985.

Reinsberg, Mark. Review of *Star Science Fiction Stories*. *Imagination*, September 1953, 144.

Resnick, Mike, and Patrick Nielsen Hayden, eds. *Alternate Skiffy*. Berkeley Heights, N.J.: Wildside, 1996.

Rich, Mark. *C. M. Kornbluth: The Life and Works of a Science Fiction Visionary*. Jefferson, N.C.: McFarland, 2010.

Robinson, Spider. Review of *Beyond the Blue Event Horizon*. *Analog*, May 1980, 169–70.

———. Review of *The Way the Future Was*. *Analog*, December 1978,. 172–73.

Samuelson, David N. "Critical Mass: The Science Fiction of Frederik Pohl." In *Voices for the Future Volume Three*, edited by Thomas Clareson and Thomas Wymer, 106–27. Bowling Green, Ohio: Bowling Green University Press, 1984.

Santesson, Hans Stefan. Review of *Alternating Currents*. *Fantastic Universe*, June 1956, 127.

———. Review of *Preferred Risk*. *Fantastic Universe*, February 1956, 110.

———. Review of *Undersea City*. *Fantastic Universe*, October 1958, 118.

Silverberg, Robert. "Fred." In Hull, *Gateways*, 260–63.

———. *Other Spaces, Other Times*. New York: Nonstop, 2009.

Slusser, George. *Gregory Benford*. Urbana: University of Illinois Press, 2014.

Solstein, Eric. *John W. Campbell's Golden Age of Science Fiction*. Documentary. Digital Media Zone, 2002. DVD.

Sykora, William. Letter to Donald Wollheim, April 10, 1937. Donald A. Wollheim Archive, Kenneth Spencer Research Library, University of Kansas.

Warner, Harry, Jr. *All Our Yesterdays*. Chicago: Advent, 1969.

Williamson, Jack. *Wonder's Child: My Life in Science Fiction*. Dallas: BenBella, 2005.

Willis, Connie. "Fred Pohl Appreciation." In Hull, *Gateways*, 181–82.

Wolfe, Gary K. *The Known and the Unknown: The Iconography of Science Fiction*. Kent, Ohio: Kent State University Press, 1979.

Wollheim, Donald A. *The Universe Makers*. New York: Harper and Row, 1971.

LETTERS CITED IN TEXT

Baumgardt, Doris. Receipt to Donald A. Wollheim, July 25, 1939. Donald A. Wollheim Archive, Kenneth Spencer Research Library, University of Kansas.

Gunn, James. Letter to Frederik Pohl. Undated (c. February 1952). James Gunn Archive, Kenneth Spencer Research Library, University of Kansas.

———. Letter to Frederik Pohl. March 8, 1952. James Gunn Archive, Kenneth Spencer Research Library, University of Kansas.

———. Letter to Frederik Pohl. July 27, 1953. James Gunn Archive, Kenneth Spencer Research Library, University of Kansas.

Madle, Robert. Letter to Donald Wollheim, May 21, 1937. Donald A. Wollheim Archive. Kenneth Spencer Research Library, University of Kansas.

Pohl, Frederik. Letter to James Gunn, March 3, 1952. James Gunn Archive, Kenneth Spencer Research Library, University of Kansas.

———. Letter to James Gunn, March 4, 1952. James Gunn Archive, Kenneth Spencer Research Library, University of Kansas.

———. Letter to James Gunn, March 12, 1952. James Gunn Archive, Kenneth Spencer Research Library, University of Kansas.

———. Letter to James Gunn, June 10, 1952. James Gunn Archive, Kenneth Spencer Research Library, University of Kansas.

———. Letter to James Gunn, November 7, 1952. James Gunn Archive, Kenneth Spencer Research Library, University of Kansas.

———. Letter to James Gunn, July 21, 1953. James Gunn Archive, Kenneth Spencer Research Library, University of Kansas.

———. Letter to Jack Williamson, May 9, 1952. Jack Williamson Science Fiction Library Archive, Eastern New Mexico University.

———. Letter to Donald A. Wollheim, July 27, 1941. Donald A. Wollheim Archive, Kenneth Spencer Research Library, University of Kansas.

———. Letter to Donald A. Wollheim, October 16, 1941. Donald A. Wollheim Archive, Kenneth Spencer Research Library, University of Kansas.

Wollheim, Donald A. Postcard to Members of the International Scientific Association, April 18, 1937. Donald A. Wollheim Archive. Kenneth Spencer Research Library, University of Kansas.

Cassavettes, John, 74
cataclysm, 203–4; in *All the Lives He Led*,
   191–95; in *Chernobyl* 154–56; in *Coming
   of the Quantum Cats*, 152; in *Drunkard's
   Walk*, 87; in "Fermi and Frost," 149–50;
   in "Gold at the Starbow's End," 109; in
   Jem, 124–29; in *Land's End*, 159; in *Man
   Plus*, 118–20; in *Space Merchants*, 48, 50; in
   "Wizard's of Pung's Corners," 73–74; in
   Wolfbane, 78–83. *See also* atomic bomb;
   climate change; ecological crisis
Catch-22 (Heller), 34
Cather, Willa, 178–79
Chandler, A. Bertram, 154
China, 68, 85, 116, 152; in *Black Star Rising*,
   146–48; in *Jem*, 125–28
Childhood's End (Clarke), 43, 49, 190
Citizen's Advisory Council, 148
City (Simak), 32
City at the World's End, The (Hamilton), 163
civil rights, 75, 85
Clareson, Thomas, 124
Clarion Writers' Workshop, 114–15
Clark, G. G., 17, 19
Clarke, Arthur C., 1, 3, 136, 141; *Against the
   Fall of Night*, 30, 93; *Childhood's End*, 43, 49,
   190; "Deep Range," 67; *Fountains of Para-
   dise*, 189; *Last Theorem*, 2, 7, 186–90, 191,
   210; "Nine Billion Names of God," 49
Clavell, James, 191
Clement, Hal, 43
climate change, 8, 58, 156; in *Homegoing*,
   159–63; *Our Angry Earth*, 169–70; Pohl's
   thoughts on, 203–4
Cline, Ernest, 121
Clockwork Orange (Burgess), 62
Clute, John, 123
Coblentz, Stanton, 15
Cold War, 7, 47, 69, 79, 87, 106, 109, 163, 175,
   178, 181; in *Chernobyl*, 154–56; Citizens'
   Advisory Council, 148; in *Cool War*,
   131–33; in *Jem*, 124–29; in *Man Plus*, 117–20;

in *Plague of Pythons*, 94–96; in *Preferred
   Risk*, 71–73; in "Quaker Cannon," 85–86;
   in *Slave Ship*, 75–76; in *Terror*, 153–54
Collier's, 42
Collins, Suzanne, 63
Computer Conspiracy (Reynolds), 89
computers, 61, 88, 91, 121, 167, 202; in *Age
   of the Pussyfoot*, 97–100; in *Annals of the
   Heechee* and *Heechee Rendezvous*, 139–41; in
   Beyond the Blue Event Horizon, 130–31; in
   Last Theorem, 188–89; in *Man Plus*, 119–20;
   in *O Pioneer!*, 179; in *Slave Ship*, 75–76
Conceptual Breakthrough, 30
Condon, Richard, 87
Conjure Wife (Leiber), 42
Conklin, Groff, 46, 49, 57, 65, 67, 68, 71
Conrad, Joseph, 179
consumerism, 6, 37, 48, 69–70, 74, 76–78, 84,
   137, 149, 159; in *Gladiator-At-Law*, 60–65;
   in "Happy Birthday, Dear Jesus," 77;
   in "Midas Plague," 59–60; in *Search the
   Sky*, 66–67; in *Space Merchants*, 48–58; in
   "Tunnel Under the World," 69–70; Kingsley Amis's remarks on, 86–87
corporations, corporatism, 48, 74, 75, 77;
   in *Gateway*, 121–23; in *Gladiator-At-Law*,
   61–65; in *Merchants' War*, 137–38; in *Mining the Oort*, 173–75; in *O Pioneer!*, 180–81;
   in *Preferred Risk* 71–73; in *Search the Sky*
   66–67; in *Space Merchants*, 50–58; Pohl's
   speaking at, 105–6
Cosmic Stories, 24
cosmology, 7, 131, 150, 163, 168–69
Craft of Science Fiction (Bretnor), 115
Creation of Tomorrow (Carter), 123
"Criminal in Utopia" (Reynolds), 89
"Cross of Centuries" (Kuttner), 84
cryonics, cryogenics, 131, 139, 206; in *Age of
   the Pussyfoot*, 96–100; in *Preferred Risk*,
   71–73; in *Voices of Heaven*, 177; in *World
   at the End of Time*, 163–66; in *Years of the
   City*, 145–46

Fermi Paradox, 136, 158, 168

Fearn, John Russell, 24

Federici, Carlos, 154

Female Man, The (Russ), 3, 112–13

Fermat's Last Theorem, 187–89

"First Contact" (Leinster), 83

First Men in the Moon, The (Wells), 160

Footfall (Niven and Pournelle), 160, 162–63

Forbidden Planet (film), 74

Forever Peace (Haldeman), 120

Forever War (Haldeman), 108, 203

"For I Am a Jealous People" (Del Rey), 67

Forster, E. M., 32

"Foster, You're Dead" (Dick), 67

Frazier, Robert, 67

Foundation: International Review of Science Fiction, 198

Foundation series (Asimov), 65, 122, 137

Fountains of Paradise (Clarke), 189

Frankenstein (film), 15

Frankenstein (Shelley), 2

Frazier, Robert, 67

Freas, Frank Kelly, 141

Fromm, Erich, 49

Future, 24

Future Quartet: Earth in the Year 2042, 97

Futurians, 4, 19–27, 36, 38, 59, 86, 123, 169

Futurians, The (Knight), 19, 123

Gaiman, Neil, 195

galactic civilizations, 113–14, 123–31, 138–41, 158

Galaxy, 6, 41–42, 45, 46, 48, 49, 55, 57, 58, 59, 65, 67, 69–71, 75–76, 78, 107, 115, 120, 124; Pohl's editorship of, 5, 9, 19, 32, 83, 87–83, 101–3, 105, 113, 184, 208

Gale, Floyd C., 71, 75

Gallun, Raymond Z., 18, 24

Gateways (Hull), 195

G-8 and His Battle Aces, 27, 33, 74

gender issues, 34–35, 66, 101–2, 188, 194

Gernsback, Hugo, 1, 13, 17–19

Gibson, William, 117, 120, 131, 139, 179

Gold, Horace L., 19, 41–42, 45, 48, 49, 55, 58, 65, 70, 83

Golden Spike (Ellson), 62

Great Silence. *See* Fermi Paradox

Greenberg, Martin H., 153

Greene, Graham, 75

Gribbin, John, 133, 152–53

Gunn Center for the Study of Science Fiction, 2, 115

Gunn, James, 2, 5, 8, 11, 52, 97, 114, 195, 197, 200, 203; *Alternate Worlds*, 115,123; as Pohl's client, 3, 43–45; "Immortals," 84; *Listeners*, 89; *Literature of Science Fiction* film series, 65, 116; writing and teaching workshops, 3, 6, 115–16, 142, 167, 179, 191

Gunner Cade (Kornbluth and Merril), 42

"Guardian Angel" (Clarke), 43

Gulliver's Travels (Swift), 66

Haldeman, Joe, 108, 120, 195, 197, 203

Hamilton, Edmond, 39, 163

Hamling, William, 89

hard science fiction, 23, 109, 118–20, 122

Harris-Fain, Darren, 120, 163

Harrison, Harry, 22, 43, 56, 89, 91, 103, 115, 116, 154, 195

Hartwell, David, 14

Harvest of Stars (Anderson), 163

Hassler, Donald, 67, 197

Hawking, Stephen, 150, 152–53, 166

Hawley, Cameron, 62

Heart of Darkness (Conrad), 179

"Heavy Planet" (Rothman), 23

Heinlein, Robert A., 1, 3, 5, 24, 27, 30, 33, 91, 117, 136, 148, 156, 186, 191, 194; *Farnham's Freehold*, 88; "Life-Line," 23; *Moon is a Harsh Mistress*, 88, 175; *Podkayne of Mars*, 88, 173; *Puppet Masters*, 48; *Space Cadet*, 68, 173, 174; *Starship Troopers*, 203; *Tomorrow, the Stars* (ed.), 46

Tranq," 169; "Meeting" (w/Kornbluth), 110, 145; "Merchants of Venus," 108, 110–11, 118, 120, 141–42; "Midas Plague," 6, 8, 58–60, 61, 67, 69, 76, 77, 79, 86, 120, 137, 142; "Middle of Nowhere," 70; "My Lady Greensleeves," 78, 144; "Pythias," 70; "Quaker Cannon" (w/Kornbluth), 85–86; "Rafferty's Reasons," 78; "Red Moon of Danger," 38; "Richest Man in Levittown," 78; "Sad Solarian Screenwriter Sam," 110; "Second Coming," 149; "Shaffery among the Immortals," 110; "Sitting by the Pool, Soaking up the Rays," 154; "Small Lords," 7; "Snowmen," 34; "Spending the Day at the Lottery Fair," 8, 129, 148, 173; "Target One," 7, 70, 78; "Trouble in Time" (w/Kornbluth), 31; "Tunnel under the World," 7, 8, 69, 77, 86, 139; "Under Two Moons," 92; "Visit to Belindia," 97; "Waging of the Peace," 16, 84; "Wapshot's Demon," 76; "We Purchased People," 31, 84, 154; "Whatever Counts," 7, 83–84, 86; "What to Do until the Analyst Comes," 78; "With Redfern on Capella XII," 78; "Wizards of Pung's Corners," 8, 73, 78, 84; "World of Myrion Flowers" (w/Kornbluth), 85

Pohl, Frederik (Rick) IV, 58, 135

Pohl, Kathy, 110

"Pohl Hero" (Hassler), 197

Pohl-Weary, Emily, 39

Poitier, Sidney, 74

politics, 7, 20, 34, 38, 47, 79, 89, 93, 109, 162, 170; in All the Lives He Led 191–95; in Chrenobyl, 154–56; in Coming of the Quantum Cats, 150–53; in Cool War, 131–33; in Jem, 124–29; in Last Theorem, 186–90; in Mining the Oort, 174–75; in O Pioneer!, 178–81; Practical Politics, 106–7, 108; in Presidential Year, 74–75; in Slave Ship, 75–76; in Syzygy, 134–35; in Voices of Heaven, 176–78; in Years of the City, 143–48

Pompeii, 34, 72, 133, 191–95

Popular Publications, 23–24, 26–27, 33, 36

Popular Science, 36–37, 40, 184

Population Bomb (Ehrlich), 107

Porter, Gene Stratton, 209

posthumans, 101–2, 117–20, 129, 139

Pournelle, Jerry, 148, 160, 162, 174, 210

Pringle, David, 57

Prospect of Immortality, The (Ettinger), 96

Proust, Marcel, 14

psychology, 83, 99, 109, 112, 119

psychotherapy, 76–77, 112, 119, 120–21, 135, 176–78

public relations. See advertising

Puppet Masters, The (Heinlein) 48

Quinn, Daniel, 83

Rabkin, Eric, 88, 123

Random House, 117

Ready Player One (Cline), 121

Reagan, Nancy, 152

Reagan, Ronald, 7, 127, 148, 150–53, 156

Red Bank, N.J., 42–43, 46, 73, 106, 131

Red Mars (Robinson), 173

Reinsberg, Mark, 49

Reisman, David, 49

religion, religious fundamentalism, 66, 149–54, 156–57, 165–66, 176–78, 182, 193

"'Repent Harlequin,' Said the Ticktockman" (Ellison), 89

Retief series (Laumer), 89, 178–79

"Revolt of the Pedestrians" (Keller), 32

Reynolds, Mack, 89, 207–208

Riverworld series (Farmer), 89, 182

"Robbie" (aka "Strange Playfellow") (Asimov), 24

Roberts, Jane, 80

Robinson, Frank M., 43, 195

Robinson, Kim Stanley, 173

Robinson, Spider, 123, 129, 154

robots, 31, 36, 59–60, 69, 76–77, 139

MICHAEL R. PAGE is a lecturer in the department of English at the University of Nebraska. He is the author of *The Literary Imagination from Erasmus Darwin to H. G. Wells: Science, Evolution, and Ecology.*

MODERN MASTERS OF SCIENCE FICTION

John Brunner   *Jad Smith*

William Gibson   *Gary Westfahl*

Gregory Benford   *George Slusser*

Greg Egan   *Karen Burnham*

Ray Bradbury   *David Seed*

Lois McMaster Bujold   *Edward James*

Frederik Pohl   *Michael R. Page*

THE UNIVERSITY OF ILLINOIS PRESS

is a founding member of the

Association of American University Presses.

_____

Designed by Kelly Gray

Composed in 10.75/14.5 Dante

with Univers display

by Lisa Connery

at the University of Illinois Press

Manufactured by Cushing-Malloy, Inc.

University of Illinois Press

1325 South Oak Street

Champaign, IL 61820-6903

www.press.uillinois.edu